Myths, Misconceptions, and Invalid Assumptions of Counseling and Psychotherapy

Myths, Misconceptions, and Invalid Assumptions of Counseling and Psychotherapy

Jeffrey A. Kottler
and
Richard S. Balkin

OXFORD
UNIVERSITY PRESS

OXFORD
UNIVERSITY PRESS

Oxford University Press is a department of the University of Oxford. It furthers the University's objective of excellence in research, scholarship, and education by publishing worldwide. Oxford is a registered trade mark of Oxford University Press in the UK and certain other countries.

Published in the United States of America by Oxford University Press
198 Madison Avenue, New York, NY 10016, United States of America.

Library of Congress Cataloging-in-Publication Data
Names: Kottler, Jeffrey A., author. | Balkin, Richard S., author.
Title: Myths, misconceptions, and invalid assumptions of counseling and psychotherapy / Jeffrey A. Kottler, Richard S. Balkin.
Description: New York, NY : Oxford University Press, [2020] |
Includes bibliographical references and index. |
Identifiers: LCCN 2019048946 (print) | LCCN 2019048947 (ebook) |
ISBN 9780190090692 (hardback) | ISBN 9780190090715 (epub) |

1 3 5 7 9 8 6 4 2

Printed by Sheridan Books, Inc., United States of America

CONTENTS

Introduction

"So," the client pressed, "tell me again how this therapy stuff is supposed to work."

"Um, what do you mean?" the therapist answered, stalling for time.

"Just what I said. I don't really get this. I mean I'm here and all. And I do want help. But I don't really understand how this is going to make much of a difference. I've had many of these problems my whole life so I don't see what you can do to make them go away, unless you've got some drugs or something."

"Drugs could be an option at some point, but usually most people feel better by talking through their difficulties."

"So, then, what? I tell you my problems, and then do you *what* exactly?"

"We've gone over this a bit already," the therapist answered, folding his arms and leaning back. "I've told you that first we have to collect some basic information about . . ."

"You mean *you* have to collect the information. I'm already well aware of what happened. *Too* aware if you ask me."

"Sure, it's important that I learn more about what happened, why you're having such difficulty right now. And we also have to get into your background and discover some of the possible causes that might be making this situation so much worse for you right now."

"Yeah, yeah. I get all that. But my question is how does therapy even help me? I know we talk and stuff. I've seen movies and television shows. You sit there and listen and say a few things and maybe even tell me some things I don't know. But all this stuff you told me about these different approaches, how some require me to think differently, and some want me

Myths, Misconceptions, and Invalid Assumptions of Counseling and Psychotherapy. Jeffrey A. Kottler and Richard S. Balkin, Oxford University Press (2020). © Oxford University Press.
DOI: 10.1093/oso/9780190090692.001.0001

to talk about feelings, and some require homework I'm supposed to do. I hope you realize how crazy this all sounds."

A FEW ESSENTIAL QUESTIONS

In some sense, it *does* seem a little strange when we hear ourselves explaining how therapy works with such authority and confidence, especially when we are sometimes quite uncertain about the whole enterprise. We do have confidence and trust in our ability to help people with most of the difficulties they bring to us. There is overwhelming evidence that the vast majority of clients are significantly improved as a result of our treatments. Advances in the models, methods, and strategies during the last few decades have allowed us to work more swiftly and efficiently, to reach a much more economically and culturally diverse population. The evidence supporting some of our chosen interventions has increased to the extent that we can now predict with greater certainty which individuals, presenting specific symptoms in particular circumstances, will respond best to what we do—and how we do it. The earliest theorists would hardly recognize the improved precision and effectiveness by which we could assist people with issues and disorders that would have been unimaginable previously. We have reason to feel proud of our achievements and successes.

But here's the question we wish to address: Do we *really* know and understand as much as we pretend to? Is the foundation upon which we stand actually as stable and certain as we think, or at least claim to believe? Are the major assumptions and "truths" that we take for granted and accept as foundational principles really supported by solid data? And how might these assumptions, beliefs, and constructs we hold so sacred perhaps compromise and limit increased creativity and innovation? These are some of the uncomfortable and provocative questions that we wish to raise, and perhaps challenge, so that we might consider alternative conceptions that might further increase our effectiveness and improve our knowledge base grounded with solid evidence.

NARROW WINDOWS OF PERCEPTION

Myths and misconceptions rule our lives in so many ways. There are cries of "fake news" that supposedly distort reality and present "facts" that are actually exaggerated beliefs or downright lies. Social media, even reputable sources of journalism, usually highlight acts of violence, report crimes, and profile conflicts, skirmishes, and wars around the world. They feature stories of abuse, neglect, and injustices, leading to the distinct impression that the world has lapsed into a depressing, terrible state of affairs. We don't mean to minimize poverty, child abuse, violent crime, school shootings, oppression of women, minorities, refugees, and immigrants, which are significant problems, but there is a prevailing myth that our existence is in far worse shape than ever before. It is commonplace for every generation to mourn the "good 'ol days" when things were so much better. We talk about the past as so much better than whatever we have managed to achieve in the present, perpetuating the myth that all progress improves the quality of life. And yet, some of us are wistful about the days when almost all conversations took place face to face, uninterrupted by the intrusions of mobile devices.

The agricultural revolution that took place over 5,000 years ago supposedly freed our species from the uncertainty of life as a forager and wanderer. No longer would we have to relocate every few weeks to find new sources of food. And yet once we became dependent on farming and herding, there were all kinds of undesirable consequences (Harari, 2015). Our diets became drastically restricted to just a few grains, vegetables, and sources of protein instead of the varied, more nutritious options while on the road. In addition, we had no immunity to the diseases that animals spread, leading to epidemics of cholera, smallpox, and encephalitis, among others. Just as dispiriting, the 20-hour or so "work week" of the typical scavenger now exceeded 50 hour or longer for shepherds and farmers. Life may appeared more convenient and comfortable, but at considerable cost in other areas. Certainly we can relate to this phenomenon in the sense that new technologies have made it possible, if not obligatory, that we remain accessible at all times to anyone who wants to reach us.

Steven Pinker (2018) rattles off an impressive list of all the reasons why the world has never been better, carefully supported with data. Once upon a time, just a few generations ago, life expectancy was about 50 years of age, 90% of the world lived in poverty and dealt with regular famines. Some of the worst diseases like cholera, polio, small pox, and malaria that have plagued our species have been mostly eradicated. During the last century alone, we are 96% less likely to die in a car crash and 99% less likely to perish in a plane crash. Droughts, floods, wildfires, storms, earthquakes, and wars have resulted in significantly fewer casualties and deaths. Literacy has improved at a staggering rate, and close to 90% of nations in the world report that their level of happiness and well-being have significantly improved in the last several decades. In almost every domain of daily life, time devoted to chores, as well as dangers and annoyances, have been reduced to levels that were unimaginable previously. And yet with that said, there is the continued perception by many people that the world is going down the tubes.

In a similar vein, as much as psychotherapy, counseling, and mental health treatments have taken hits as less scientific and less effective than other medical and health specialties, we are still remarkably successful, even efficient, in our work, with overwhelming evidence to support what we do. There may be considerable debate about exactly what we do, and how we should do it, but the results are nevertheless usually quite satisfactory. Rather than being defensive, we should feel greater pride for the state of our profession.

In this book, we raise the often neglected, forbidden, and sometimes secret doubts and uncertainties related to the wonderful—and sometimes—mysterious work we do. While it may appear, at first, as if this is a discouraging set of topics to pursue, possibly denigrating the very validity of our profession, we actually hope the opposite is true—that such an open and honest dialogue will lead to even greater accuracy and self-acceptance.

As you might imagine, some of the reviewers who initially examined the proposal for this book were somewhat perplexed—they were a bit intrigued, but also skeptical. One reviewer, who pleaded that he didn't have time to do a thorough evaluation, acknowledged that the book was indeed quite provocative. "I would disagree with about half of what they say," he admitted, but then continued, "but I'd fervently support the other half!" We consider this high praise and exactly the sort of reactions we hope to trigger, leading to dialogue, debate, critical thinking, and more polished research to address some of the questions that we raise.

There were also reviewers and critics who questioned whether exploring our doubts and uncertainties related to our profession was indeed a useful and constructive enterprise. Would it not undermine the legitimacy of our work and lead to increased skepticism if we uncover and bring into greater focus precisely those things about which we feel most unsure? After all, so much of our effectiveness is driven by a certain amount of faith and passionate confidence. Why spend valuable time and resources questioning some of our most basic principles and practices that form the foundation of what we do? And yet, throughout history, it is precisely this reluctance to challenge the status quo that led to stagnation, if not ongoing ignorance.

Even on the most basic level do any of us really know and understand the "truth" about ourselves, much less anyone else? It is commonplace that people misidentify what they are truly feeling at any point in time. During those moments when they do assign a label to an emotional sensation it often results in reducing their whole being to that simplistic condition: "I feel depressed," so that means "I *am* depressed." The more complex and comprehensive reality is that we do not actually *become* our feelings, and they do not solely hold our truth. It is usually worth exploring more deeply, both in therapy and in daily life, how the relentless pursuit of so-called happiness, or even the now more popular term, "well-being," leads to on-going frustration, dissatisfaction, and perhaps misery. Likewise, many biases, prejudices, and beliefs within our culture remain supported and unchallenged because people refuse to consider their assumptions and "knowledge" are obsolete or lack empirical evidence.

For decades African Americans and other oppressed minorities were seen (and are still seen by some) as inferior because of a perceived lack of advancement compared to the majority population. "After all," they may argue, "these people have been freed from slavery so long ago and yet they still live in poverty and are disproportionately involved in crime." Such entrenched beliefs continue because of a failure to examine the larger context of discriminatory laws and cultural system that maintains control by the privileged elite. As an example, consider the case of Clennon King, a "Negro" who, in 1958, attempted to begin studies at the University of Mississippi. After applying to the all-White university, a judge forcibly committed him to a mental institution because, of course, you'd have to be insane to think a Black person could attend this august institution. This may now seem like a rather far-fetched instance of unsupported myths and misconceptions but consider that this was indeed the prevailing belief in the American South during this era.

So, dear readers, we beg your indulgence and ask you to keep an open mind as you consider some of the issues we raise. Our intention is not to sow increased doubt and uncertainty that could undermine continued effectiveness. There has been overwhelming and consistent solid evidence for decades that the vast majority of times (80%–90%) clients leave therapy sessions significantly improved and satisfied with their experiences. During those times when they don't report complete "cures" of their symptoms, they still report feeling grateful for what they learned. We'd like to suggest, similarly, that even if you don't agree with some of the issues we've explored or some of the conclusions we've reached, we hope you find the process of critical examination to be useful, if not enlightening. After all, it is only when we question why we do things a certain way that we are led to consider more effective alternatives.

In this volume, we have selected several dozen issues in our field, many of which are considered generally accepted principles or operating assumptions. We put them under close scrutiny to examine them more carefully. Throughout this discussion, we've considered a wide variety of subjects, ranging from those that relate to our espoused beliefs, theoretical models, favored techniques and interventions to accreditation and licensing requirements. We have also addressed some of the sanctioned statements about the nature and meaning of empirically supported and evidence based treatments. We even question what we can truly "know" for sure and how we can be certain these things are true.

We welcome you to join us on this exciting, stimulating, and at times disorienting and confusing journey. Our hope is that by reflecting on these issues it will encourage you to become more reflective—and critical—in considering your own professional practices.

Jeffrey A. Kottler
Houston, Texas
Richard S. Balkin
Oxford, Mississippi

CHAPTER 1

⌒⌒⌒

What We Know, What We Think We Know, and What We Really Don't Know Much at All

There are questions that science has been grappling with for centuries, mysteries that have been studied and investigated by the brightest minds of their generation. How was the universe created? How did life originate? What is dark matter and, if it really exists, then why can't we see it? Does intelligent life exist anywhere else in the universe? Does existence have any special meaning or purpose? How do we measure evidence or determine statistical significance?

The perplexing mysteries that might interest us most are often related to certain common human behaviors that seem, at first, to be inexplicable. After centuries of studies, anthropologists, geneticists, ecologists, and geographers have yet to figure out why the first *Homosapiens* ever migrated from their original homeland in Ethiopia. Was it volcanic eruptions and subsequent climate change, overpopulation, diminished resources, or pure wanderlust that led people to leave their familiar surroundings? Our knowledge of the most basic things about our world is hardly a tidy list of facts, argues Harcourt (2015): "Science is a groping toward understanding" (p. 13). It is an ongoing process of testing our ideas with no real hope of ever arriving at certainty about hardly anything, especially if it involves why people act the ways they do.

Why does altruism exist in which people give away things to, or even risk their lives for perfect strangers who have no direct genetic linkage? If

Myths, Misconceptions, and Invalid Assumptions of Counseling and Psychotherapy. Jeffrey A. Kottler and Richard S. Balkin, Oxford University Press (2020). © Oxford University Press.
DOI: 10.1093/oso/9780190090692.001.0001

the purpose of all life is procreation, then how do we explain the enduring prevalence of homosexuality? Why do people laugh or cry? What are the functions of dreams?

We can offer theories that may partially account for such peculiar responses such as why water leaks out of the eyes during emotional arousal. There are theories that weeping represents a leeching of excess emotional hormones or that it's a form of communication as a literal cry for help or surrender, that it authenticates the meaning of messages, or that it can be a tool for manipulation. Or take yawning for instance. There are certainly no shortage of theories to explain this strange behavior in which people stretch their mouths and inhale a deep breath. It has been commonly noticed that it takes place during changes in a state of alertness (fatigue, waking, boredom), whether internally or in the environment. Yawning has not only been frequently observed in dogs and cats but also occurs in human fetuses as well as fish and snakes, among other animals.

It has been assumed that the purpose of yawning is to increase the flow of oxygen to the brain, and, indeed, another theory associates yawning with providing a thermoregulatory effect to cool the blood (Koren, 2013). But what about the contagious effects of the behavior, of which little is understood? Why is it that when someone yawns in a room, it affects others? Even *reading* the word, *yawn* sometimes makes some people yawn! Once again, a common explanation that is *not* supported by research is that it somehow reflects empathic responses (Bartholomew & Cirulli, 2014). Studies on this subject, among which there have been very few, usually end with a statement similar to the following: "There is much we don't know or understand until additional research is undertaken."

THE MYSTERIOUS AND UNKNOWN IN COUNSELING AND PSYCHOTHERAPY

There are so many other mysteries that we pretend to understand to a far greater extent than is actually warranted. This is certainly the case in the physical world in which phenomena like black holes, parallel universes, quantum waves, naked singularities, and string theory confound scientists. Given the relative imprecision and unpredictability of human behavior— much less the uncertainty implicit in therapeutic and change endeavors— the amount that we *don't* know far exceeds that which we understand with reasonable confidence. Even those things we believe we know for certain are just transitory theories that may soon be discredited. For example, consider the "truths" that operated among experts during the time of John

Watson, one of the most prominent social science researchers of all time. Watson, you may recall, was the founder of behaviorism and one of the first child-care experts on the scene. Based on his research, he advised parents to never hug or kiss their children, warning that doing so would cause them to grow up to be needy, dependent, insecure, self-involved, and spoiled (Halley, 2007). This was considered to be the greatest wisdom of the times, and yet it was based on ignorance, myths, and misconceptions that would soon be replaced by new and different ideas that were also flawed in many ways. Everything we know—or think we know—is similarly limited until such time that new and more extensive data are collected and analyzed.

Let's make a list of some things we know, think we know, and probably don't know much about at all. You are welcome to quibble with our selections and the categories we place them in, but the point of this exercise is intended to get you thinking from the outset about the parameters of our understanding. This is a process that is likely to be both disorienting and hopefully in some ways validating and empowering.

A FEW THINGS WE KNOW FOR (ALMOST) CERTAIN

Let's begin with some relative certainties that underpin the whole foundation of our profession. Without these basic assumptions, we could never even show up for work, must less help anyone.

Change Is Possible for Long-Standing Dysfunctional Behavior

Habits, entrenched patterns, chronic self-defeating responses, and even emotional disorders and mental illnesses are amenable to adjustment or "cure" under certain conditions and circumstances, often described as the "core conditions." There are more than a zillion anecdotal cases of people describing their seeming miraculous transformations, which often resulted from incidental experiences of everyday life such as a conversation or reading a story. In *Confessions*, St. Augustine wrote about his despair, loneliness, and spiritual emptiness. He was miserable and desperate to change the trajectory of his life. He felt helpless to make the changes he so desperately craved, those that would guide him to a new identity. Yet every time he tried to give up his bad habits, he inevitably relapsed, feeling even more hopeless and discouraged.

Then, one day Augustine was reclining under a fig tree, with an unopen Bible resting on his lap, when he heard a child singing a haunting tune. He listened closely to the lyrics and heard the chorus, something about "Take it and read." He stared down at the book on his lap and felt like a message from God had been delivered to him. He opened the Bible to a random page and suddenly felt as if all his doubts and troubles vanished in an instant. He traced this moment to his religious conversion and a completely new dedication in his life. Whether this single event was truly all it took for him to change his life is hardly the point but rather that experiences like this are commonly reported as a result of trauma, travel, transitions, and, yes, therapeutic conversations.

Psychotherapy Works Pretty Well Most of the Time

How do we know this? In a classic journal article, Eysenck (1952) concluded from a survey of literature that psychoanalysis (as it was practiced at the time) was not conducive to treating psychological distress. Although Eysenck was rejected and shunned from clinical communities, he became a staunch advocate for alternative, far more active approaches to psychotherapy. As a result of the controversy that followed, the profession became less reliant on literature reviews and more reliant on clinical trials that scrupulously studied and measured outcomes. This has now become standard procedure in which numerous funding agencies support massive research projects to investigate what works best with particular people and their presenting problems (Arnow, King, & Wagner, 2019; Blanco, Rafful, & Olfson, 2013).

When over three decades ago, *Consumer Reports*, a nonprofit organization, surveyed their thousands of readers about their experiences in therapy they found that 90% reported mostly positive, helpful experiences. This report finally provided data to support the optimism of mental health professionals. Since that time, hundreds of additional studies have clearly established the benefits and limitations of particular models, techniques, or access to services. It would appear, for example, that abbreviated forms of therapy appear to be especially effective in attaining desired goals and meeting client expectations (Proctor & Hargate, 2013; Schmit, Balkin, Hunnicutt Hollenbaugh, & Oliver, 2018). It has even been surprising to learn that attending a single session can be helpful for some people in terms of reducing their distress and increasing their coping abilities (Harper-Jacques & Foucault, 2014). We may debate and dispute which therapies work better than others, in what circumstances, with which clients, presenting which complaints, but the overwhelming evidence is that the vast majority of people feel better afterward and say they got their money's worth (Castonguay & Beutler, 2006; Proctor & Hargate, 2013; Timulak & Keogh, 2017).

We Have a Good Idea of the Optimal Conditions Under Which Therapy Is Generally Helpful and Leads to Best Outcomes

Freud started us out by suggesting that talking to someone in a private, secluded setting, or mostly letting *them* talk about their problems, would help them to come to terms with unresolved issues in the past. Whether much of his original ideas have been supported or not (mostly not), that certainly got us thinking about the best way to structure a helping relationship.

When Carl Rogers tried to empirically investigate exactly which relational factors might be best in a therapeutic encounter, he identified several key features that are still part of our lore today. While some of his favored elements such as authenticity and genuineness sounded admirable, they may not have stood the test of time compared to other features that have been empirically supported (Duncan, 2014; Kottler & Balkin, 2017; Lambert, 2013; Wampold, 2001). For example, about 40 years ago, Bordin (1979) conceptualized how to measure the working alliance, evaluating the extent to which clients and therapists collaborate well together on consensual goals. Since that time, researchers such as Lambert (2013) and Duncan (2014) have expanded on the concept of *working alliance*, highlighting the additional importance of hopefulness as a key factor. Duncan, as well as Schuckard, Miller, and Hubble (2017), also found that soliciting and responding to client feedback is absolutely crucial to making needed adjustments to better satisfy the unique needs of each individual, rather than pursuing "one size fits all" approaches.

WHAT WE PASSIONATELY BELIEVE MAY (OR MUST) BE TRUE, BUT ISN'T NECESSARILY SUPPORTED WITH DEFINITIVE EVIDENCE

In addition to those things that we think we know for sure, there are also beliefs, assumptions, and ideas we hold that don't necessarily have the kind of support that we pretend they do. Consider common teaching practices that are used almost universally and yet have little or no evidence that they are effective. One review (Duke, 2016) mentioned several examples that are all too familiar, such as weekly spelling tests, homework, offering prizes for reading, looking up vocabulary lists, and taking away recess as a punishment. However, no compelling evidence suggests that *any* of these practices work well, but that doesn't seem to have much impact on educational practices. Likewise, within the field of therapy, there are certain standard practices we will explore that have little or no evidence to support them. It is not dissimilar to some of the more common beliefs in the wider world that people insist are factual, such as the belief that lightning never strikes the same place twice. Actually, quite the opposite is true: The Empire State Building in New York gets hit about 100 times every year.

It is perhaps not surprising that the same human tendency to prefer familiar and comfortable practices, remaining oblivious (or in denial) that they are not based in solid evidence, would also exist in our professional practices. There are notions we remain committed to that are—to be kind—not exactly irrefutable truths but rather common beliefs and practices we just take for granted. Let's take a look at a few.

One Favored Theoretical Approach Is Better Than All the Rest

There are devoted followers of various approaches to therapy, often stating unequivocally and (over)confidently that their chosen model is overwhelmingly superior to all other options on the market. There have been ferocious conflicts over the years about which model is superior to all the rest. Many of the theorists themselves were some of the most passionate advocates for their ideas.

We will discuss the French psychoanalyst Jacques Lacan in a later chapter related to his practice of variable-length sessions, but for now we mention him as a lightning rod for those colleagues who didn't share his ideas. He was both celebrated and despised, called a genius and a fraud, but he seemed to thrive in the role of a "bad boy" who demeaned any theory that didn't jive with his own. Given that his writing and seminars were often described as incomprehensible and incoherent, he had the ready argument that nobody really understood his ideas—which is probably true. He was hardly the only fierce advocate for pet ideas that were believed to be the only path to salvation as this is still rather commonplace today.

We Can Accurately and Reliably Determine That We Really Helped Someone and That the Changes Endured Over Time

Let's be honest: Although we are supposed to do follow-ups to make sure that progress continued over time, we rarely have time for that sort of thing. And even when we check in on clients on a regular basis, their self-reports may not be very thorough or accurate. This brings up the issue of whether clients even know how they are really feeling, much less the source of these reactions. After all, their confusion, uncertainty, and lack of clarity are what brought them into therapy in the first place.

The focus on seeking client feedback and assessing it formally is still rather novel, taking hold only in the last decade with brief, informative measures on working alliance and well-being developed for general use. Yet often we insist that we can reliably tell when therapy is working and when it is failing, even though there isn't much evidence to support this claim (Wampold & Imel, 2015).

Another reality is that it is difficult to really tell that we helped someone and that positive changes have been maintained over time. Client follow-up in our field is pitiful, despite the admonishments that it is an important part of our job. The truth is that we are so busy and overwhelmed that many practitioners plead they just don't have the time and resources to check on the current status of clients from months or years ago. We often assume instead that if clients really need us for some reason, it is their responsibility to let us know.

Another challenge in this follow-up endeavor is that it is not a simple matter to determine what qualifies as a "positive outcome." Take substance abuse as an example. It may seem obvious and logical that success would be assessed according to whether the client maintains sobriety. According to that criterion, if someone remains clean and sober for six months after treatment, with no relapses, this would mean success. But this specific, limited measure doesn't take into account all the other potential benefits and issues that may have been addressed, including mood disruption, stress management, and interpersonal relationships (Balkin & Juhnke, 2018).

This raises the question: How do we really ever know the true impact of our interventions, especially when the effects might not ever become evident until weeks, months, or even years later?

When We Are Reasonably Sure That the Outcome Was Successful and Will Endure, We Know What We Did That Was Most Impactful

Change is a mysterious process. It doesn't usually proceed in a linear manner even though such simplified descriptions are convenient when describing cases. Imagine, for example, you are working with an adolescent who had been displaying a number of behavioral problems at school and home. You figure that the best way to determine if therapy is helpful is directly related to the child's coping strategies. You assume that the better he is at coping with his stressors, the fewer problems he would exhibit. And yet when a sample of 120 adolescents admitted to a psychiatric hospital for severe behavioral difficulties was studied, it was discovered that even as the adolescents' coping skills improved, they continued to display increasing problems getting along with others (Balkin, Richey Gosnell, Holmgren, & Osborne, 2017).

Why might this be the case you would justifiably wonder? Well, it depends on *which* coping strategies were employed given they are all hardly the same in their appropriateness for a given child and situation. Just because the adolescent remembered to use mindfulness, exercise, self-talk, or seek support as coping strategies doesn't mean these strategies would necessarily work in every situation.

Another more global example is related to the widespread assumption that if we enjoy a good relationship with clients, they will necessarily accomplish more in their sessions. Although this may generally be true, there is also what is known as a "baseline effect." While it is certainly the case that clients do better when there is a strong working alliance, the opposite is not necessarily always evident. In fact, rather than becoming worse when the relationship is weak, clients instead simply don't make as much progress; they simply stagnate (Balkin & Schmit, 2018). Obviously, this is one of those areas that requires a lot more investigation.

It is also difficult to determine for certain the ultimate results of our interventions because some things we say and do don't have an immediate impact; rather, they have a delayed effect that is evident much later. Sometimes clients report it was months or even years afterward that some idea finally struck them in a way that they'd never noticed previously. Likewise, other clients initially report significant and spectacular progress, but they neglect to tell us that the results didn't last very long.

The relapse rate for certain presenting problems like substance abuse, impulse disorders, and eating disorders is quite high, not to mention the relatively intractable dysfunctional patterns we see in certain personality disorders. In the case of bipolar disorder, the vast majority of clients eventually relapse at some time, leading us to not only expect such regressions but also to help clients prepare for them.

Our Clients Agree With Us About What Was Most Helpful to Them During Sessions

Usually we insist that the client being helped was due to our interventions, techniques, or favored strategies. Or we believe it was because we accurately diagnosed the problems. Or we think it's because we are so smart, wise, experienced, and so skilled in the timing of our interventions. And maybe these things really are the engines of change. Perhaps we really do know better, as a function of our extraordinary acumen, scientific training, measurement instruments, and experienced observations.

As we've previously mentioned, some researchers including Hans Strupp, Michael Lambert, Bruce Wampold, Scott Miller, Barry Duncan, John Norcross, Timothy Carey, and David Burns, among others, have been advocating the critical importance of conducting systematic assessments of outcomes by soliciting feedback from clients. It is almost universally assumed that clients are not just our customers, but experts on their own experience, most intimately informed about what has worked best for them in the past and what has failed miserably.

However (and you know this was coming), clients often report something much, much different than what we might believe made the most difference. When clients are asked what helped them the most in their sessions, what they found most useful, and what was most instrumental in producing their desired outcomes, they almost never mention the things that therapists say are most important. Instead, they talk about feeling heard and understood by their therapist (Binder, Holgersen, & Nielsen, 2009; Frankel & Levitt, 2009; Hodgetts & Wright, 2007; Lambert & Shimokawa, 2011; Schmit, Balkin, Hunnicutt Hollenbaugh, & Oliver, 2018).

Just to clarify, we are *not* saying that clients were actually clearly understood, just that this was their perception. Although they reported a strong connection in the relationship, one that felt safe and free of shame-inducing criticism, this was only *their* belief and experience. It is also significant that they talked a lot about feeling a renewed sense of hope as a result of their conversations, another somewhat universal feature of all approaches.

One point of agreement with their therapist was that they gained a new and different perspective on their situation, one that was far more empowering. They likely used language that was different than their therapist in describing this phenomenon, but that's not all that surprising considering the variety of ways that practitioners themselves conceptualize this process. In fact, almost every therapeutic system has a different term for this, whether called "disputing irrational beliefs," "reframing," "deconstruction," "unique outcomes," "meaning-making," or "challenging cultural scripts."

One point worth mentioning again: Clients don't often know or understand what is, or was, going on in their sessions. It's not uncommon when they attend therapy that they have trouble describing the "real" problem. In some cases, it takes months to discover what may actually be going on—if that is even possible to ever determine definitively. After all, clients exaggerate, distort, minimize, hide, deceive, and even outright lie. They frequently change their minds. Usually they do not even know for sure what happened, must less why.

We Know What Makes a Truly Exceptional Therapist and How to Determine Who These Professionals Are

There is no universally accepted means by which to determine excellence as a therapist, any more than that is the case with respect to other professions (Kottler, 2017). Do we rely on self-reports or single measures of supposedly successful outcomes? Or what about fame and notoriety or reputation in the community? Certainly those in great demand or with a full practice must be better than their peers? Or well-known theorists and authors in the field? Surely they must be exceptional to have attained such wisdom and status. Check out the citation appearing in this paragraph—Kottler just cited himself on this subject. Doesn't that count for something?

The short answer? No. The longer, more detailed answer? Let's just say it's complicated.

There are many possible reasons why someone might be well known in the field or supposedly has a great reputation. Maybe they are great self-promoters or entrepreneurs. Maybe they are good talkers, but not necessarily good clinicians. Just because lots of people like their services doesn't mean it's all that great. Hawaiian or Spirit Airlines consistently have the worst passenger satisfaction but they still have packed flights. So it is with some therapists who have long waiting list but may really suck in their actual ability.

Bottom line? We do have a general idea about what makes a therapist better than the rest (Duncan, 2014; Kottler & Carlson, 2014; S. D. Miller & Hubble, 2011; Norcross & Lambert, 2011, 2014; Prochaska & Norcross, 2014). Such professionals have high integrity and standards for themselves, and their outcomes consistently exceed those of their peers. Moreover, it is not the method that a therapist uses per se but rather the extent to which the therapeutic relationship is tied to the chosen method (Norcross & Lambert, 2014).

We Know Who Difficult Clients Are and What Makes Them That Way

We have lots of names for these individuals—resistant, defiant, hateful, obstructive, toxic, belligerent, dependent, narcissistic, borderline, and so on. We even think we agree about which clients are the most challenging to work with in therapy. But for every practitioner who complains about the frustrations of seeing an angry, defiant adolescent, there are others who actually prefer this population. Likewise, there are therapists who prefer and choose to specialize in working with dual-diagnosed, drug-addicted psychotic patients, impulse disorders, borderline, or narcissistic individuals.

In other words, there really isn't as much consensus as we pretend about who difficult clients are and what they do that is most annoying (Kottler, 1992). Some therapists just hate working with overly compliant, polite YAVIS (youthful, attractive, verbal, intelligent, and successful) clients, finding them boring and a waste of time. The same can be said for the opposite—that is, therapists who struggle most with clients who are "not like them," meaning from backgrounds that are difficult for them to comprehend and value systems that are most at odds with their own. Personally, we might find it most difficult to work with a rigid, conservative, racist, homophobic, entitled, privileged individual, someone who is certain about everything. Yet we know other colleagues who would love to get their hands on such a "gem" to engage with.

WHAT WE REALLY DON'T UNDERSTAND MUCH AT ALL

This last category may be the one we mostly avoid but is the most useful for our further investigations to advance our knowledge and improve our effectiveness. We might stir up a certain amount of defensiveness and passionate debates about these issues, but we urge you to at least consider the tentative nature of what we think we know and understand.

What Causes Emotional Disorders and Mental Illness

A patient with abdominal pain seeks the services of a physician to determine the cause of the discomfort. After first determining whether the pain is acute or chronic, the doctor will then conduct a physical examination inspecting, tapping, listening, and palpitating the affected area. Then a number of lab tests will be ordered for blood count, liver enzymes, stool, and urine—possibly even a pregnancy test to rule out another possibility. Next computed tomography or magnetic resonance scans would be conducted, followed by ultrasound, colonoscopy, or other exams. With the results of each diagnostic method, the doctor can narrow the causes from simple indigestion to something more serious and definitive, whether gastritis, acid reflex, irritable bowel syndrome, peptic ulcers, or Chron's disease. Then, after they are eliminated, more rare conditions would be considered like appendicitis, parasitic infection, hepatitis, or cancer. In each case, the suffering can usually be definitively attributed to a specific cause, which suggests a particular evidence-based treatment, complete with specific data on outcomes related to each medical choice. Now, compare this process of identifying causes of physical illness to what we are faced with when someone says to us, "I just don't feel right," "I'm really upset and I don't know why," or "I've always been this way. I just don't know what's wrong with me."

There have been arguments, and there will likely always be such debates, about the primary underlying reason(s) of why people who are exposed to similar (if not identical) stressors or trauma respond and metabolize the experiences in such different ways. Some become crippled for life. Some go through a period of temporary destabilization and difficulty and then put the events behind them and move on. And some others manage to experience incredible growth and personal transformations as a result of the challenges they faced (Grad & Zeligman, 2017; Renden, 2015), although empirical research is somewhat lacking to support this popular idea (Infrura & Jayawickreme, 2019).

We have various theories to account for the different response differences among our clients. Some point to genetic predisposition factors, whether biochemical/neurological conditions, inherited traits, or personality configurations. Others emphasize environmental influences in early childhood, accumulative experiences, developed hardiness, and resilience. There are also situational/contextual factors to consider such as fatigue, mood, pain tolerance, previous stressors, social setting, sense of helplessness, and emotional stability. People also respond to different kinds of threat, trauma, or crisis depending on its type (physical threat, bullying, shame-inducing, life threatening, etc.) intensity, duration, and personal interpretation of meaning.

The whole function of emotions has been a mystery throughout the ages. Damasio (2018) proposed that, at the most basic level, they are simply mental expressions of homeostasis, meaning that they evolved as a way to motivate us to some action to restore a sense of balance. According to Damasio, homeostasis can best be described as something more than just maintaining stability but rather as the "coordinated processes required to execute life's unthought and unwilled desire to persist and advance into the future, through thick and thin" (p. 34).

Emotional responses are self-regulatory processes that signal that something is curious, upsetting, or exciting. Although neuroscientists would like us to know that feelings are really just biochemical reactions to sensory input, their particular manifestations are still somewhat puzzling. These internal reactions are triggered in the limbic system as an irresistible drive to discover or explore something of interest; compensate for some loss; cope with stress, fear, or anxiety; ignite passion or joy; and so on. Yet whereas nature "invented" feelings to help compensate for changes in the environment and help humans (and other mammals) deal with their circumstances through adaptations, therapists are quite well aware that these responses are not uniform.

With this acknowledged, we might pretend to understand why someone is crippled by depression or anxiety, blaming their genes, childhood, self-talk, family dynamics, relationship conflict, job pressure, or whatever, but there are likely multiple factors at work, some of which will remain hidden or disguised.

When we announce to a client, "*This* is your problem" or "You are clearly suffering from _____ (fill in the blank)," the level of confidence in this proclamation is something less than absolute. Most commonly, it's a rough guess based on very limited and skewed information available.

We Understand Why People Ultimately Change as a Result of What We Do or Say

We include this assumption a second time here because it fits in the "relatively clueless" category as often as it does in the previously described "rough idea" category. Novelists write about this mysterious process of personal transformation all the time. "No one can tell what goes on in between the person you were and the person you become," wrote Stephen King (1990). "No one can chart that blue and lonely section of hell. There are no maps of the change. You just come out the other side. Or you don't" (p. 25).

How do we really come to a definitive explanation for why anyone really does *anything*? Motives are so often hidden or disguised. There are unconscious forces at work. The complexity of human behavior is limitless, and it is very unlikely that it will ever be completely mapped and sequenced as will the molecular markers of human genomes.

Physicist Stephan Hawking once observed, "While physics and mathematics may tell us how the universe began, they are not much use in predicting human behavior because there are far too many equations to solve."

WE WILL NEVER, *EVER* KNOW ENOUGH OR BE GOOD ENOUGH

In this introductory chapter exploring the themes of illusions, delusions, and misperceptions, our last point is both disorienting and somewhat obvious: Despite all our training, preparation, supervision, study, and experience, we will *never* feel like we know enough or are good enough to do the best job our clients deserve. We are expected to project an aura of perfect confidence and expertise to others; in one sense, it is part of our cure. After all, according to Jerome Frank (1963), we are essentially faith healers. We motivate and inspire clients by influencing and persuading them that change is possible, especially if they are willing to surrender habits that are not in their best interest.

The placebo effect fuels and accelerates so much of what we do, capitalizing on our clients' beliefs that change is indeed possible and that therapy is the optimal vehicle by which to do so (Blease & Kirsch, 2016; Colloca, 2018; Fish, 1973; Kirsch, 2005; Rosenthal & Frank, 1956). There are even some researchers who wonder if psychotherapy is basically synonymous and indistinguishable from a placebo, that they share far more in common than just a first letter (Gaab, Locher, & Blease, 2018). Certainly we capitalize on clients' optimistic beliefs to empower our incantations, rituals, and interventions. We are no longer surprised when the most modest suggestions produce profound hypnotic effects. But that isn't to say we truly understand what happened and why or that we always have a clear, defensible rationale for what we do.

For many of us, it has rarely felt safe to admit that the extent of our doubts, uncertainties, and questions about what we are doing—or *not* doing. This introduction has been an overview of some of the issues we wish to cover and to dig more deeply into those areas for which we feel most and least reassured about. There is little doubt that we actually know and understand quite a lot related to human behavior and change processes, especially when we look at the major advances in the past few decades. Consider that, just a generation ago, psychotherapy was basically limited to lying on a couch and free associating. Several decades ago we were limited to just a handful of therapeutic approaches. Nowadays, there are dozens of options, many optimized for specific disorders and problems and brimming with supporting evidence for their effectiveness.

It is certainly true that changes that take place in therapy—or for that matter, in everyday life—still remain a mystery in some respects. If we are honest, we have to admit that there are times during sessions when we have little idea about what to do or how to proceed, much less convince ourselves and our clients we truly understand what is going on and why. And yet it is remarkable how little that seems to matter in terms of the positive outcomes we are able to produce with our "modest talking cure." We have created programs, systems, standards of practice, and professional codes that have increased the consistency, reliability, and power of our interventions.

In the chapters that follow we describe and challenge some of these popular beliefs and practices that may persist, not because they are actually supported with solid evidence, but rather because we have failed to consider other alternatives. Our goal is no less than to take things to another level, one in which we are freed from the traditions, conventions, mindless habits, and unchallenged assumptions that continue to stifle further innovation and increased effectiveness.

CHAPTER 2

ɔⱴɔ

How Myths and Misconceptions
Have Shaped Our World

By our nature, human beings are storytellers. Our brains have evolved over time to organize our knowledge, understanding, and collective memories in the form of stories. We can even conceptualize that one of our main roles as therapists is to hold and honor the stories of our clients, as well as to offer alternative stories that are more useful to them (Kottler, 2015a). The stories clients bring to us are sad, tragic, frustrating affairs in which they are portrayed as victims of circumstances beyond their own control. We listen carefully to the themes embedded in the narratives and then suggest alternative versions of the events in which they become not only survivors of adversity but heroines/heroes of the tale.

Within the larger culture as well, there are collective stories and mythical accounts and legends that unite us as a people, explaining mysterious things about the world around us. Sometimes these myths are based on some semblance of objective reality; other times they are fictitious, distorted stories we tell to create an illusion of understanding. Some of the most prevalent and enduring myths were originally just metaphors to explain phenomena, such as Freud's theory regarding repression and catharsis, Maslow's hierarchy of needs, Skinner's behavioral conditioning, and Durkheim's theory of deviance, all of which endorse the idea that we are victims of internal and external forces outside of our control (Spillane & Martin, 2018).

The whole notion of mental "illness" is a metaphor, just as it has been throughout the ages. When someone was suffering from an emotional

Myths, Misconceptions, and Invalid Assumptions of Counseling and Psychotherapy. Jeffrey Kottler and Richard S. Balkin, Oxford University Press (2020). © Oxford University Press.
DOI: 10.1093/oso/9780190090692.001.0001

affliction, or just displaying what was considered outlandish behavior, they were characterized as having a "sick soul" or "diseased mind." These metaphors take on a cloak of "truth" even as they actually fall into the realm of hyperbole. Over time, beliefs are solidified in a form of mythology that remains impervious to change in light of new evidence or counterarguments. These myths are designed to soothe fears of uncertainty and the unknown.

Joseph Campbell (1949) noted that universal myths exist primarily to serve several functions, most notably to help us understand who we are and where we came from. There are stories that say that Prometheus made humans out of clay or that the first man was created from dust and a woman sprang from his rib. Every culture tells a different story, but one that offers something to hang onto. It is precisely this ability to create and share imagined realities that make it possible for communities to exist since it is by changing myths, telling different stories, that cooperation among people of different backgrounds can occur (Harari, 2015). It is the story (or myth) of the American dream, as one example, that keeps citizens hopeful and optimistic about the possibilities of the future even though the likelihood of anyone in the world actually changing their socioeconomic status is one in a thousand.

What distinguishes a myth from a theory is whether there is reliable, valid, and verifiable evidence to support the beliefs and comprehensive story. Most theories don't, in fact, stand the test of time, even if they continue to exert influence in the shadows. The development of philosophical thought and scientific inquiry helped to apply more systematic rigor to the enterprise of explaining things but still fall short in many ways. We can't, for instance, even be certain what constitutes "reality" with any degree of certainty. The Algonquin Indians of Quebec believed that our waking moments are actually just dreams and the only time we are truly "awake" is when we dream during sleep. Harari (2017) mentions that you can't be certain that you aren't actually a bored teenager living 200 years in the future. You are actually in the middle of a virtual game that simulates the primitive world of the 21st century when people used to read "books" whether in the form of physical objects or digital devices. How do we ever agree on what constitutes so-called reality when we can't even agree on what it is, whether a philosophical position, abstract assumption, molecular structure, neural perception, social construction, phenomenological condition, or state of being.

As we are mostly aware, there is a distinction between so-called objective and subjective reality. The former exists independent in any way from perceptions, beliefs, assumptions, and thoughts. You aren't feeling well and obtain a blood test, which indicates that blood cell count is down, leading to a diagnosis of anemia. Subjective reality, on the other hand, is literally in the eye of the beholder. But there is also a third type of reality—*intersubjective reality*—that depends very much on collective agreement. Money, laws, territorial boundaries, and, for that matter, emotional disorders require consensus on the meaning and value of these entities. Money, whether in the form of paper or virtual currency, is essentially worthless unless everyone agrees on its worth.

FAVORED MYTHS

Despite the honored traditions that scientific and social science disciplines have brought to our profession, as well other healing arts, there have been some pretty wacky notions that have since been discredited. We have since learned that the Earth is, in fact, not flat, nor the center of the universe. Likewise continents are not immovable, but rather constantly drifting and shifting. Medical practitioners who advocated blood-letting have been proven wrong, which was certainly the case for George Washington who was literally bled to death by his doctors for a relatively minor ailment. Going back further in history, Hippocrates, the father of medicine, was certainly a smart guy, but he also believed that the human body was composed of blood (easily recognized) and black and yellow bile (plus phlegm).

The discovery of the double-helix structure of DNA is perhaps one of the most important scientific advances of the last century. Damasio (2018) points out that once this was found to be the essential molecule of life, a cascade of further discoveries followed. Yet since science is based on what is known and understood, it often stands on a wobbly and tenuous foundation. In this case, Francis Crick, one of the Nobel Prize winners for this work, couldn't possibly imagine that a biochemical process so complex and mysterious could possibly occur spontaneously or randomly and so insisted that these first living entities must have been delivered to Earth by an alien spaceship. If this myth seems ridiculous in light of current understanding, consider that other esteemed scientists of the era, like Enrico Fermi, who believed that these aliens still live among us disguised in other forms, perhaps as Hungarians.

Just to keep things in perspective and to emphasize that psychotherapy is certainly not alone in its attachment to ideas and myths that may have little basis in reality, other fields have been led astray for centuries because of entrenched beliefs. For example, physicians used to believe that diseases were caused by miasma, or bad air, rather than bacteria and viruses. And pity poor Ignaz Semmelweis, who was hounded out of the medical profession and ended up insane because he dared to suggest that surgeons were infecting their patients with germs and killing them because they didn't wash their hands and instruments before surgery.

There are a number of influential economic theories that have never been empirically supported, even though they held (and still hold) a dominant influence on current beliefs and behavior. For instance, free market theory serves the rich, privileged, and powerful, but has almost no basis in reality (Madric, 2015). Adam Smith proposed that as long as people are allowed to act in their own self-interest, with minimal government intrusions or interference, goods and services will naturally (magically?) optimize the perfect balance and pricing. Nobel Prizes have been awarded based on these assumptions even though there is no particular evidence that things occur as predicted. In fact, markets free of regulations and control do not perform "as advertised," operating in such a way that those who have the most resources continue to keep and grow them. But it's still a lovely idea that persists because those in power find that it best optimizes *their* economic benefit.

It was just a few decades ago that we believed as facts that (a) dinosaurs died off because of a catastrophic volcanic eruption (it was more likely an asteroid); (b) only nine planets existed in space (there are actually zillions of them); (c) humans simultaneously evolved in multiple locations around the globe (actually only in Ethiopia prior to migration); and (d) humans came into existence after Neanderthals died off (they lived during the same time). Just as every decade technology reinvents itself, rendering devices obsolete, so too do our assumptions, beliefs, and understanding evolve in light of new discoveries.

We suppose that even in using the word *evolve* we should be careful, considering that evolution itself, or at least the notion that natural selection is responsible for the development of our species, is considered a myth by the majority of our kind. Half of all Americans stridently believe that God and divine intervention are responsible for creating our life form, just in the last 10,000 years. (Among those who do believe that evolution occurred over the span of millions of years from lower life forms, only 15% think this happened without God's hand; Swift, 2017.) This means that the theory of evolution itself is considered just a myth by close to half the population. Given that the theory of evolution—supported and confirmed by so many scientists since Darwin's time—is so potentially threatening and objectionable to almost half the population, Harari (2017) wonders why theories of relativity or quantum mechanics aren't more disturbing, considering they are potentially a lot more upsetting in "making a mockery of common sense" (p. 105). One reason for this is because evolutionary explanations negate the idea that human beings are the sole possessors of a soul, consciousness, and tender emotions; they are no more important than any other living creature nor particularly entitled to any special treatment. In other words, myth supersedes science when the stories support our favored beliefs.

PHILOSOPHICAL TRADITIONS

As originally conceived, psychology in general and psychotherapy in particular have been evolutionary offshoots of philosophical traditions. Sigmund Freud was as much a philosopher, archeologist, and literary figure as he was a physician. He was most strongly influenced by German philosophers like Kant, Nietzsche, and Hegel even though he eventually rejected their discipline because he considered it too speculative and imprecise. He strenuously objected to the lack of distinction between mind and consciousness and the number of false conclusions that resulted from the overgeneralization of certain assumptions (Tauber, 2009). He was, at heart, a scientist who, while grateful for what he learned from idealists like Schopenhauer and Hegel and writers like Shakespeare, Goethe, and Dostoyevsky, searched for greater empirical support of his healing method.

William James, considered the founder of the first American department of psychology, was first, and always, a philosopher. Rollo May, Erich Fromm, Irvin Yalom, Victor Frankl, and the existentialist theorists owe clear allegiance to the likes of Heidegger, Kierkegaard, and Sartre. Carl Rogers traces the origin of his humanistic ideas to religious scholars like Paul Tillich and Martin Buber, as well as claiming that reading Kierkegaard helped him "loosen" some of his own thinking about the human condition. Albert Ellis frequently gave credit to the Greek stoic philosopher, Epictetus, for the germination of his seminal ideas on how internal thought processes shape subsequent emotional reactions. He also relied heavily on the works of Socrates, Seneca, and semantic philosophers Wittgenstein and Korzbyski to develop his methods of self-talk.

Even some of Albert Einstein's theories were since debunked. Certainly he was a genius. But he also claimed the universe was static and stationary, an idea that has been proven wrong once the Hubble telescope could track and measure observed shifts. Almost every year, if not each month, we learn that "truths" keep evolving. Eggs are good for you, then bad for you, then good for you if you don't eat the yolks, and then good for you if you eat the whole dang thing. What are we to conclude?

Clearly, facts and truths can someday turn out to be myths and misconceptions.

Considering that Ludwig Wittgenstein only published a single book during his lifetime, he sure exerted considerable influence on his peers. He had confidently believed that in that volume he had single-handedly solved all the problems of philosophy by mathematically reducing them to semantics. He believed there was no longer anything else for the discipline to do—it was kaput, *finis, terminado*, obsolete. It was only after his death that it was discovered that he had completely changed his mind, believing that language was really just a "game" we play and that words could have an endless number of meanings.

The existential and novelist, Jean Paul Sartre, proposed a theory that exalted the endless freedom that is possible for our species. There were no limitations in what was possible, except perhaps just a few social and physical restraints. Otherwise, we are "condemned" to absolute freedom, a condition that is also quite overwhelming and depressing when we consider how unhappy people are with nobody else to blame for their predicament. As he aged, and fell in love with Simone de Beauvoir, he realized there were far more compromises and realistic restraints than he had imagined. He eventually became a full-fledged, card-carrying anarchist, urging his previous followers of freedom to rise up against the oppressive system. And yet, like Wittgenstein and so many other philosophers, his original ideas lived on and flourished—even though their original authors denounced them!

PERVASIVE MYTHS

There are certain myths from the social sciences that have not only permeated our larger culture but also penetrated the core beliefs that guide many of our assumptions and practices. In a few reviews (Armbridge, 2013; Jarrett, 2016), several of the most common misconceptions are mentioned, such as (a) men and women are fundamentally different (from Mars or Venus, respectively) according to objective measures; (b) Rorschach and some other projective tests are actually valid predictors of personality variables; (c) people have dominant learning styles or are left/right brain learners; (d) memory operates as a recording device; (e) violent offenders have diagnosable mental disorders; (f) autism is caused by impaired mirror neurons—or vaccines; (g) the overwhelming majority of domestic violence incidents are perpetrated by men; and (h) mental illness is caused by chemical imbalances in the brain.

One of the most enduring myths of all, perpetuated by members of our profession, is related to the supposed increased risk and prevalence of suicide during the holidays. Every year, as November and December approach, there are stories in the media in which mental health professionals warn the public to be particularly vigilant in observing family members and friends. Two thirds of the published reports that link suicide to the holidays make a false connection between the two when, in fact, the rates actually *decrease* during these months (Annenberg Public Policy Center, 2017; 2019). Typical of these inaccurate claims is one story in which a prominent entertainer was quoted, "This isn't a good time of year for anyone who has lost someone. I lost my mom on the 23rd of December in 1992. Her birthday is on December 1st. That's why people commit suicide around Thanksgiving and Christmas, because that's the time when families come together" (Landrum, 2016).

Perhaps the biggest myth of all, promoted in the media as well as in our profession, is the illusion of control that we have over our mind and bodies. Ehrenreich (2018), a cellular biologist, cynically challenges the whole wellness movement that so passionately advocates faddish diets, exercise regimens, and mindfulness in face of the absolute certainty of declining functioning and eventually death. The concept of the "self" has taken on religious fervor, a worshiping of self-awareness, self-concept, self-regard, self-acceptance, self-affirmation, self-esteem, self-care, and all our therapeutic efforts to promote this deification of self-love. Ehrenreich points out all the ways we've created shrines to ourselves in the form of photos displayed, social media profiles, carefully managed images that are branded, and, of course, the obsession with self in the context of therapy sessions. This obsession with self very often leads to the kind of *self*-scrutiny and *self*-reflection that encourages people to become even more focused on every nuance of internal experience. We end up encouraging people to increase their devotion to being increasingly "true to self," loving oneself, and, in the words of one therapist, coming away "not with anything that is considered universally valid or absolute in a metaphysical sense, but with a heightened and intensified devotion to such individualistic creeds" (Amundson, 2015).

We don't mean to spark arguments or debates with you about any counterevidence you wish to offer supporting any of these ideas, nor are we suggesting that some of these findings don't have kernels of "truth." We are merely saying that they are not nearly as empirically supported as we might believe even though professionals insist on still using them as absolutes.

STAGES OF ACCEPTANCE AND DENIAL

In an examination of how and why some psychological theories ultimately devolve into myths and discredited ideas, Pomeroy (2018) traced six distinct stages in their fall from grace after considerable periods of stubborn resilience in the face of contradictory evidence. As such, he considers psychology, as a discipline, barely a science at all because of the proliferation of unsupported ideas that continue to persist.

First, there is the "flashy finding." Some of them we were forced to learn in Introduction to Psychology classes. The "executive monkey," "planaria and the maze," "compliance shocking," and many other classic studies turned out never to have been replicated reliably. These are mind boggling, dramatic results that change the way we think about the world and ourselves.

The second stage is called "fawning replications" in which negative findings are rejected by prominent journal editors. The scientific peer review process that is considered the gold standard of quality research has been described by Richard Smith, the editor of the *British Medical Journal* as the classic sacred cow ready to be slaughtered. The noted physician and scholar claims that much of what is published is riddled with errors, few of which are ever identified by peer reviewers. He conducted an experiment in which he placed eight deliberate errors into a very brief scientific paper and sent it off to 300 reviewers. The median number of mistakes that were actually identified was two out of the eight. "If peer review was a drug," he reported, "it would never get on the market because we have lots of evidence of adverse effects and don't have evidence of its benefit" (Gorski, 2015). He was referring to how expensive, time consuming, and inefficient the process is, with precious little advantages other than perpetuating an illusion of academic rigor.

In the third stage, a consensus forms. The theory is accepted as truth and makes its way into popular media and self-help books that promote the techniques. True believers hold conferences to glorify the tenants, and exorbitant fees are charged for the privilege of learning the secrets.

The rebuttal is next, the period when the founders of the theory, as well as their disciples, attack their critics, claiming that the conflicting studies were not representative, were biased, or contained methodological errors. They offer other studies, the few that seemed to find some effect, and they recruit the media to defend them and publish these results (which are often not sufficiently rigorous to appear in scholarly journals).

Eventually, in the last stage, with no real solid supportive evidence, the theory dies a slow death—until it is occasionally resuscitated in "zombie" form on the pages of Wikipedia, self-published books, blogs, and practitioners who insist, based on anecdotal reports and their own experi-ence, that it is indeed useful. Besides, their clients tell them it is.

More relevant to our profession was the supposed "science" of phre-nology, or the study of skull shape, which which allegedly predicted person-ality and behavior even though there was no basis in meaningful evidence whatsoever. Another example is John Locke's "blank slate" theory of human development that we are all shaped exclusively by experience, an idea that is utterly ridiculous. There are *still* ideas circulating that stress causes ulcers even though it has long been determined (and earned the investigators a Nobel Prize in 2005) that they are actually the result of bacteria.

Some of us are also old enough to remember when primal therapy and the bestselling book on the approach (Janov, 1970) were all the rage. It was believed that the cure for neuroses and emotional disorders was to re-experience the original trauma and then scream one's bloody head off (so to speak). There was never any empirical evidence to support the basis for this idea, much less its effectiveness, yet the practice continued for decades. As previously mentioned, during the 1980s neurolinguistic pro-gramming took the profession by storm (Bandler & Grinder, 1979). It had a whiff of pseudoscientific rigor since it supposedly relied on neurological mechanisms that allowed therapists to better "access" and influence parts of the brain depending on whether an individual was more susceptible to auditory, visual, or kinesthetic preferences. Alas, after completing hun-dreds of studies investigating the effectiveness of the approach, there was little, if any, evidence to support the claims (Thyer & Pignotti, 2015). It is still being used today by some clinicians.

The same could be said for gay conversion therapy inflicted on people who were told they could change their sexual identity. Once again, there is no reputable research to support this is possible even though, to date, close to one million teenagers have been subjected to the failed treatment and tens of thousands each year are *still* pressured into sessions (Mallory, Brown, & Conron, 2018). There are so many other therapeutic approaches that we could mention in this regard, most of which have been discredited, if not labeled fraudulent. A partial list of such treatments, with minimal or no empirical sup-port, was compiled by Norcross, Koocher, and Garafolo (2006) in their survey of experts in the field (see Table 2.1). We are not saying these treatments didn't help anyone, just that there isn't much (if any) reputable evidence to indicate they do what they say they do. Consider, for example, the number of thera-peutic approaches that are still employed by some practitioners even though they have little solid evidence to support their effectiveness (see Table 2.1).

Perhaps, it is too easy point out how myths and misconceptions have driven the mental health profession through the promulgation of sham

Table 2.1 PARTIAL LIST OF DISCREDITED THERAPIES THAT MAY
STILL BE EMPLOYED

Aromatherapy	Angel therapy
Crystal healing	Rebirthing
Past lives therapy	Future lives therapy
Thought field therapy	Orgone energy accumulator
Treatment of posttraumatic stress disorder from alien abduction	Color therapy
Pyramid restoration energy	Erhard Seminar Training
Age regression methods	Dolphin-assisted therapy
Scared Straight	Double-bind family therapy schizophrenia
Handwriting analysis and interpretation	Catharsis anger treatment

therapies and techniques, shoddy research, and/or the adoption of scientific principles. After all, science often falls short in explaining the therapeutic process—that is, the way we relate to our clients and how our clients relate to us. Despite the challenges and limitations of the scientific and peer review process and the insistence of comparing psychotherapy with medical treatments, the mental health profession has been served well by these debates, discussions, and investigations. For example, Freud may often be perceived as having unusual ideas about sex and relationships between sons and mothers and oral fixations, yet he provided valuable context for understanding defense mechanisms such as denial, projection, and repression that we witness so frequently in human behavior.

Even if we acknowledge that there are some discredited theories and techniques that may undermine our work, there are also other theories and models that have been extremely useful even if they are not easily evaluated through randomized control trials. We end up overemphasizing approaches such as cognitive-behavioral therapy, because the techniques are easily tested, but we ignore the more relational elements that truly make or break the therapy experience because concepts like empathic understanding are not easily addressed or measured in studies.

Ultimately, we have our own cherished beliefs about what works best to help people in the throes of emotional suffering. Many of these assumptions and opinions are indeed grounded in empirical evidence, but others are based on our own experiences that may not (yet) be supported by large-scale investigations. In some cases, these practices may not be justified, or even safe, but in other instances they may be groundbreaking innovations that could revolutionize the field once they are subjected to more rigorous study. Just hope you can tell the difference.

CHAPTER 3

cᴧɔ

How and Why Myths and Misconceptions Endure

We have several psychological terms to describe the entrenched, stubborn beliefs of others who are resistant to changing their minds in the face of overwhelming evidence. These are the clients who persist in certain assumptions that are not only flatly wrong, but consistently get them in trouble. They insist that their problems are not their fault, but rather the result of bad luck, fate, poor genes, meddling family members, or other people, who "just don't understand me."

We also frequently encounter colleagues (and authors) who espouse ideas unsupported by evidence or cite facts that are merely personal opinions (to which we also plead guilty at times). In addition, we've long noticed that it is really, really difficult to get people to change their minds about cherished positions that are both familiar and comfortable. We call this "confirmation bias" or "motivated reasoning."

It is indeed curious why reasoning or logical arguments, supported by clear, overwhelming evidence, is not particularly persuasive or influential. In the case of climate change and global warming, 99% of qualified scientists agree that increases in greenhouse gas emission, droughts, sea levels, and temperature not only definitely indicate this phenomenon exists, but they also attribute these changes to human impact. Interestingly, almost half of Americans, if they believe this is occurring at all, are convinced it will not affect them, now or in the future. Of course, subscribing to this belief allows them (us?) to continue engaging in practices that promote their own short-term self-interest.

Myths, Misconceptions, and Invalid Assumptions of Counseling and Psychotherapy. Jeffrey Kottler and Richard S. Balkin, Oxford University Press (2020). © Oxford University Press.
DOI: 10.1093/oso/9780190090692.001.0001

Any of this sound familiar—as to why therapists might hold onto certain beliefs or practices that don't appear to be grounded in solid evidence? We find it interesting how this can possibly happen, that people could hold beliefs that are inaccurate and likely compromise their effectiveness, if not their survival. Consider, for example, how many people put their health in danger because they refuse to accept some of the most evidenced-based findings—for example, that smoking, obesity, or pollution are lethal; that immunizations protect against deadly diseases; or that the fluoride in our drinking water is not part of a conspiracy to kill us but rather is there to protect our teeth against decay.

THE POWER OF CONFIRMING WHAT WE THINK
WE ALREADY KNOW

As members of the human species, psychotherapists are prone to search for explanations that already confirm preconceptions and sacred cow beliefs about why and how people change. If you are an avid cognitive therapist, it is likely you attribute emotional suffering to disordered thinking. If you are neuropsychologist, then you may instead insist that biochemical and endocrine processes lead to such conditions. If a psychodynamic practitioner, you would prefer to search for causes in early history and unconscious drives. Each of us looks first and foremost at explanations that best jive with our own preferences.

A client consults you for problems at work and in daily life in which he feels little confidence in his ability to get things done. He procrastinates a lot, rarely meets important deadlines, and consistently finds himself in trouble because he is always frantic to catch up. As such, he is highly anxious and worries a lot about things he can't control, especially how others will be disappointed when he doesn't meet his responsibilities. Your immediate first impression? Of course, you haven't met this person and know very little about his situation and the context of his life. Naturally, you are reluctant to form a diagnostic impression based on such limited data. But still, you can hardly avoid offering an initial opinion about what you think might be going on. And this tendency to default toward familiar, comfortable reasoning, and wishful thinking is both natural and unavoidable.

Confirmation bias describes the human tendency to focus on information that supports what we already believe is true. The effect is so powerful that despite overwhelming concrete evidence that the beliefs are inaccurate or unsupported, the opinions are still resistant to change. This is the case even when such beliefs are spectacularly counterproductive, self-destructive, and cost us money and pain (Cipriano & Gruca, 2014). We have certainly seen this operate in the political arena in which constituents continue to support leaders and candidates who are overwhelmingly deceitful, corrupt, abusive, self-serving, and impervious to anything that could possibly change their minds. Financier and industrialist Warren Buffett once observed, "What the human being is best at doing is interpreting all new information so that their prior conclusions remain intact." Or perhaps Hall of Fame baseball player Yogi Berra said it best: "I wouldn't have seen it if I didn't believe it."

Except maybe he didn't say that at all. So many of such amusing anecdotes are attributed to him, mostly because they are the kinds of things he could have said or might have said. But in truth, these sorts of things confirm what we already believe (Gorman & Gorman, 2017). It turns out that people prefer reassurance about their existing beliefs rather than any research that may challenge them.

Compelling myths become truth over time, impervious to any actual evidence that dispute their accuracy. Here are some examples of common popular myths that are actually not much true at all.

- Witches were never burned at the stake after the Salem witch trials. They were, however imprisoned and hanged, and one poor guy was crushed with heavy rocks.
- Paul Revere never single-handedly rode through the American colonies screaming, "The British are coming!" He was one of dozens of such messengers who quietly whispered, "The regulars are coming out." If he had really been screaming his bloody head off, it's obvious he would have immediately been captured.
- A bunch of people never committed suicide on Black Friday after the stock market crash in 1929. There is actually only one documented case in which that happened.
- Real cowboys never wore cowboy hats (they wore bowlers).

We even have a holiday to celebrate when Columbus discovered America, even though Leif Erikson beat him by five centuries. And then there is a bunch of other myths that have endured despite no evidence they were actually true. You can't really see the Great Wall from space. Thomas Edison never invented the lightbulb, Pocahontas didn't fall in love with John Smith, H. G. Wells's *War of the Worlds* radio broadcast never caused mass hysteria, Betsy Ross didn't design and sew the first American flag, the founding fathers (Jefferson, Franklin, and Adams) of America were Christians, and the Puritans came to America to seek religious freedom.

And speaking of religion, there are so many misconceived beliefs that continue within the general population: Buddha was neither a god nor obese; Jesus was a Jewish rabbi, not a Christian; polygamy is not permitted by the Mormon Church; and Islam does not advocate or sanction violence.

Pick a category, *any* category, and you'll find myths and misconceptions that still exist and impact behavior, even though they are absolutely not true. If we look at myths related to human behavior there are just as many that are fallacious. We mention just a few:

- Rorschach tests have absolutely no validity whatsoever in diagnosing personality characteristics or predicting anything meaningful.
- There is no evidence that people have preferred learning styles as visual, auditory, or kinesthetic. It sounds good. It *seems* to make sense. But there's no compelling research to support that different learning styles really exist.
- There is no such thing as being left- or right-brained in terms of dominant learning.
- We only use 10% of our brain (although people really only do use 10% of the features in Microsoft Word).
- You can detect people lying from their body posture or nonverbal cues

We don't know about you, but we have certainly caught ourselves repeating some enticing anecdote or "fact" to a client or classroom and later discovered that it was just a myth that had been shared so often it just seemed to be true. One example is when lecturing about the "bystander effect" in which groups of people disown responsibility for injustices taking place by assuming someone else will do something. It is a pretty compelling, powerful story to demonstrate the dangers of indifference to others' welfare.

On March 13, 1964, at about three in the morning, a young woman was walking to her apartment when a man ambushed her and stabbed her in the back twice. She screamed out, "Oh God! I've been stabbed!" Dozens of neighbors came to their windows to watch the violence but then did nothing to assist her or even call the police. No less than the *New York Times* published an article the next day stating that 38 neighbors were witnesses to her murder and did nothing whatsoever to intervene. This was front-page news around the world for weeks and entered the realm of sacred stories to demonstrate the potentially uncaring nature of our species. The only problem (that we only recently discovered) is that the story was mostly not true at all. In an exposé of the crime and the way it was reported (Gallo, 2015), it was discovered that much of the story was inaccurate despite attempted clarifications and reports by the witnesses. It entered the realm of urban myths as part of reactionary responses to Nazism, oppression of women, and perceptions of violence. But here's the thing: Even after reading about this correction sometimes we "forget" and tell the story anyway because it is so instructive of our own cherished beliefs about activism, advocacy, and collective caring.

SOMETIMES IT'S BETTER TO BE WRONG?

There are many well-educated, affluent, otherwise intelligent people who still hold beliefs that are completely unsupported by any legitimate evidence. They subscribe to fake news from sources that are completely unreliable and biased. They refuse to vaccinate their children because they think it causes autism or believe their astrological sign controls their fate. There are hundreds of such cognitive biases that warp our perceptions of reality and distort the data we take in and interpret according to our whims and preferences (Gilovich, Griffin, & Kahneman, 2002; Haselton, Nettle, & Andrews, 2005; Pohl, 2017). Even though they may distort our perceptions and impact our decisions in critical ways, they also serve important functions helping us deal with too much information flowing in. Biases are simply preferences, and they are present in every single thought and action. They are shortcuts in our thinking that lead to instant assessments and quick decisions, even if they are based on limited or skewed data. Several of these perceptual distortions are described in Table 3.1.

When you review this list of cognitive biases, you may justifiably wonder how we *ever* form any accurate assessment of so-called reality. And keep in mind, this was just a mere fraction of all the other cognitive biases that have been documented and researched.

"Affect heuristic" occurs beyond awareness at an unconscious level, in which our own personal feelings, intuition, life experiences, skew perceptions, and data operate to affirm what we already think we know and understand. Given that most of us subscribe to favored therapeutic models, this would lead us to view our clients issues, as well as what happens in sessions, to conform to preferred templates. This keep things neat and tidy for us so we don't have to invest the hard work necessary to recalibrate the basis for our knowledge on a more regular basis. It also allows us to better conform to the dominant views of our cultural identities, or what scholars refer to as "cultural cognition" (Whiten, 2018).

There are a number of researchers who have been investigating the phenomenon of why people can possibly get away with holding

Table 3.1 A SAMPLING OF COGNITIVE BIASES

Cognitive bias	Description	Example
Optimism bias	Overestimate positive outcomes	Forming unrealistic and unreasonable prognoses beyond what is justified in encouraging faith
Pessimistic bias	Overestimating potential for negative outcomes	Being unduly gloomy and doubtful as a form of protection against disappointment and failure
Belief bias	Using defensive mechanisms of denial and rationalization to protect existing beliefs	Forcing interactions and client behavior to fit into cherished theory and explanations, regardless of whether it is justified
Anchoring	Becoming unduly influenced by first or selective impression	Allowing a client's appearance or initial presentation to foreclose on a more comprehensive view of case
Self-serving bias	Attributing mistakes and failures to external factors to avoid responsibility	Blaming bad luck, client's lack of motivation, family dynamics, the economy, lack of support, and other extraneous variables for poor results
Attentional bias	Assessments and perceptions affected strongly by recurring, intrusive thoughts	Becoming stuck with one particular interpretation that is recursive and self-justifying
Availability heuristic	Decisions and choices are based on "intuition" or whatever seems most convenient or accessible	Explaining and interpreting behavior according to what springs most readily to mind rather than digging more deeply into more complex or alternative possibilities
Bandwagon effect	Following a particular program or action because others do so	Failing to critically evaluate the contextual appropriateness of a decision or intervention because others always do the same thing
Ambiguity effect	Avoiding any options in which important information is missing or incomplete	Settling for a diagnosis that best matches the symptoms available, regardless of whether the information is sufficient
Curse of knowledge	Allowing prior experience and extensive background to prevent deeper exploration of issues	Presuming that one's own understanding of a phenomenon is obvious to everyone else and the only reasonable explanation
Backfire effect	When cherished core beliefs are challenged, they become even more entrenched	"It ain't what you don't know that gets you into trouble," observed Mark Twain, "it's what you know for sure that just ain't so."
Base rate fallacy	Overrelying on the uniqueness and specialness of a case and ignoring general trends and global data	Failing to take into account empirical data to inform and illuminate the meaning and deeper understanding of a client's individual cultural and personal experience

(continued)

Table 3.1 CONTINUED

Cognitive bias	Description	Example
Dunning–Kruger effect	The tendency for beginners to be overconfident in their skills and for experts to minimize their abilities	Evolving to a point of experience and wisdom where extensive knowledge leads to increased doubts and second-guessing
Bystander effect	Assuming that someone or something else will take care of things, letting oneself off the hook	Absolving oneself of responsibility for tasks that are best avoided or disowned, such as referring clients prematurely or assuming that another resource will take care of problems
Focusing effect	Overemphasizing one feature or aspect of an event or narrative to the exclusion of other salient factors	Concentrating too much on attachment disorder, transference, primary trauma, or similar favored phenomenon to an extent that other significant and relevant issues are ignored
Halo effect	Personal attraction and preferences colors and influences one's judgment	The YAVIS syndrome (young, attractive, verbal, intelligent, and successful) explains why young, White, attractive females were preferred and did better in therapy
Illusory correlation	Erroneously attributing a relationship between factors or variables that are actually unrelated	Believing one's favored techniques and interventions make all the difference in producing positive outcomes
Attribution error	Judging others based on their character but oneself based on context or situation	Explaining a mistake or error based on client's resistance or defensiveness but one's own role is excused based on other limitations beyond one's control
Just world hypothesis	Belief in a fair world leads one to think that hard work always pays off and justice prevails in the end	Inaccurately reassuring others that "things will work out in the end" or "people get what they deserve"
Barnum effect	Hearing overgeneralized statements or vague descriptions and imagining that it applies to any personal specific situation	Psychics, astrologers, and sometimes therapists offer nebulous and elusive interpretations or predictions that could apply to almost anyone
Declinism	Remembering and idealizing the past as so much better than the present and possibilities for the future	"I remember the good 'ol days when insurance used to cover 90% of whatever was charged—with no lifetime limit." Sure there were abuses and overdependencies but compared to the situation today . . .
IKEA effect	Just as people fall in love with cheap furniture they assembled themselves, there is a tendency to overvalue those ideas or objects that have been self-created	Believing one's preferred theories, ideas, and approaches are brilliant and better than all others, even when they have limited value

Table 3.1 CONTINUED

Cognitive bias	Description	Example
Sunk cost fallacy	Overinvestment of time, money, or resources makes it difficult to change course and let go of a losing proposition	Emotional overinvestment in a case leads to a desperate commitment to continue a treatment plan that is clearly not working
Bias blind spot	Refusing to accept and acknowledge many of the previously mentioned biases	Claiming to be highly evolved to the extent that one is free of biases, prejudices, blind spots, and cognitive distortions

inaccurate beliefs that, ultimately, could get them killed (Gorman & Gorman, 2017; Mercier & Sperber, 2017; Sloman & Fernbach, 2017). For instance, a sizeable number of people believe that vaccinations that immunize them against life-threatening diseases are part of a government conspiracy to control them. It would appear that evolution would have eliminated those who persist in confirmation bias rather than rational reasoning unless, of course, that such behavior has some functional value—which it does.

There's evidence that people experience a dopamine rush when information they take in supports their own beliefs—even if they're wrong. It turns out that getting along with others is even more important than truth or accurate data processing. This tendency has been called "hypersociability" and is considered essential for so many diverse people to live and work cooperatively with a minimal of conflict. In other words, we tend to develop beliefs, opinions, and practices that, even though they are misguided or downright wrong, persist because they keep us aligned with others who share these assumptions. This also results in what has been called "illusion of explanatory depth" in which we believe we know and understand far more than we do (Rozenblit & Keil, 2010).

How often have you found yourself speaking with absolute authority and confidence about some question that someone asked you when you wonder whether your answer is really true? How definitively do you explain or interpret something to a client when you still feel nagging doubts? When you settle on a diagnosis for a particular case, on a scale of 1 to 10, just how certain you are that this is *completely* accurate? When pressed, we must often admit that so much of what we think (or pretend) we know is really just conjecture, hypotheses, or wild-ass guesses. Yet, as long as others in our circle share our ignorant or inaccurate beliefs, we manage to function just fine, even when operating under wrong-headed ideas. How else could a therapist get away with using obsolete methods decades after they've been proven relatively worthless? Or for that matter, how could followers of a political leader continue to support that individual when confronted with such blatant dishonesty, fraud, and corruption?

This isn't just about self-interest but also about maintaining a position of inclusion in the tribe. Disloyalty or defection from the group beliefs feels terribly dangerous because it means exile. Look at what happened to Sigmund Freud when he dared to speak out against the prevailing wisdom of the time. The Galileos or Socrates of the world are branded as heretics. For his audacity to insist our planet was not the center of the universe, Galileo spent the rest of his life in prison. He remained incredulous that his colleagues could be so ignorant and rigid. "My dear Kepler," he addressed one of his few confidantes in letter dated August 1610, after his conviction by the Catholic Church

> I wish that we might laugh at the remarkable stupidity of the common herd. What do you have to say about the principal philosophers of this academy who are filled with the stubbornness of an asp and do not want to look at either the planets, the moon or the telescope, even though I have freely and deliberately offered them the opportunity a thousand times? Truly, just as the asp stops its ears, so do these philosophers shut their eyes to the light of truth.

MULTIPLE TRUTHS

An unfortunate outcome of early training in mental health disciplines is the notion of a single, unified theory to guide our process of conducting therapy. Early in training, usually during the first semester or two, students are exposed to a multitude of different theories, sometimes one each week. The class serves as a survey of a variety of theories, at least from an historical perspective, and usually ends, regardless of discipline, with an assignment to "select *your* theory." So, after spending just a few months covering psychodynamic, humanistic, cognitive-behavioral, and postmodern approaches, among many others, trainees are advised to se-lect a single approach to guide interventions throughout their career. No pressure, right?

During this exercise, beginners are expected to critically review each of the possibilities, trying it on for size. Of course, the reality during appren-tice years is more likely that you are expected to adopt the favored theory of your instructors and supervisors who definitely have their own preferences about what they think is best for you and your clients.

Throughout the process of exploring, studying, and being tested on the nuances of each conceptual model, students are expected to discern the (stated) differences between the options. This means figuring out

- whether you believe that the role of the unconscious is a major factor in behavior;
- to what extent behavior is predetermined by biological drives;
- whether all human beings have the potential for good and strive toward self-actualization;
- to what degree people reconcile dilemmas in their lives by finding meaning in them; and
- whether psychological distress is primarily the result of dysfunctional beliefs, unresolved conflicts in the past, fractured family dynamics, disordered thinking, unexpressed feelings, impaired relationships, or socially constructed realities.

These are just a *few* of the choices, decisions, and beliefs that must be clarified before a reasonable selection can be made. Interestingly, it turns out that very few clinicians in practice actually rely on a single approach, since that vast majority describe themselves as eclectic and integrative, with only 15% of clinicians claiming to adhere to a single theory (Tasca et al., 2015). This means that trainees are often required, or forced, to begin with one approach because it is reasoned it's unrealistic to expect them to master multiple approaches.

Another pathway often taken is when beginners are reassured that while the initial choice of a model may appear somewhat impulsive or random, each of us tends to gravitate toward one that is most congruent with our values and personality. In other words, you don't really choose a theory; it chooses you!

Although we may lack definitive evidence to support the adoption and use of any particular model with all clients, there is still convincing research that many theories are, in fact, useful. When comparing almost any therapeutic approach to a control group in which no intervention is offered, there is usually an important difference noted in client progress. However, when established theoretical approaches are compared to each other, the actual differences are rather negligible. In other words, despite the frequent insistence that one theory is superior to all others (usually by a dogmatic instructor or supervisor), there isn't actually much evidence that a single approach is always best (Norcross, 2011; Wampold & Imel, 2015).

It is even more ironic that the mental health profession often embraces constructivism and qualitative inquiry to substantiate the various disciplines, yet, in practice, discourages the idea that multiple truths exist (North, 2016). In other words, many clients will improve regardless if you explore their past, focus on distorted beliefs, explore meaning, or reconfigure the family system. There are multiple methods that lead to client improvement, and what is probably more important is your belief in the method you choose (Duncan, 2014; Kottler & Balkin, 2017) as opposed to the notion that there is a single, best way to work with clients.

Although we often tell our clients that there is no single, best way to fix their problems, no definitive answer to the questions that plague them, or no perfect cure for what bothers them, we may still operate as if that is the case in our own thinking and practice. Although the curative factors of psychotherapy are more relational (Kottler & Balkin, 2017; Lambert, 2013), therapists look to theories to provide context for interventions. Having trouble with a client who is resistant to disputing irrational beliefs? Then explore the meaning behind those beliefs. Does the client have difficulty controlling impulsive behavior? Then perhaps examine the unconscious motivations about the behavior. Clinicians likely do this all of the time without even thinking about it—moving from one theory to the next to help a client process, progress, and grow.

Yet it is so often the case that the therapeutic interaction is packed with different versions of relative truth in which the client (a) says one thing but believes another; (b) claims to believe one thing but behaves in a way that is the exact opposite; (c) reports progress or disappointments that is not quite what is observed by others; (d) passionately believes something to be utterly true that is not supported by any reliable evidence; and (e) outright lies about what is going on in his or her life. The reality is that there is no singular truth about hardly anything.

CHANGING HEARTS AND MINDS

"Yes," you agree with a client in the most patient voice you can muster, "I do understand that your husband can sometimes be quite nice to you. But that seems to occur only when he's trying to convince you not to press charges against him for abuse. We've been over this several times before. I've explained to you that given the three previous times you've been hospitalized as a result of him beating you, you remain in danger as long as you stay in the house."

The client looks thoughtful for a moment, but then shakes her head and glances away.

"Look," you try again, "in cases like this, the data are absolutely clear—your husband is not going to change his behavior without serious intervention. How many times do we—do *you*—have to go through this before you realize that you have to protect yourself?"

"I just think he deserves another chance," she insists. "He told me he'll be different this time."

"That's what he told you last time as well. And the time before that. And the . . ."

"But *this* time I think he's really serious. I just need to give him another chance. I need to give *us* another chance. Maybe it's time we stopped these sessions for a while. I've been busy at work so it's really hard for me to even make it over here."

Sound at all familiar? We spent a good part of our days trying our hardest to convince others to surrender ideas that are not in their best interests and adopt alternatives that would be far more useful to them. Much of the time we are also pretty frustrated because it seems to take so much time and effort to make much of an impact. Even when we do manage to change a client's mind that a relationship isn't good for them or that if they keep doing what they're doing, there's only going to be greater heartbreak, the effects don't often last.

There are all sorts of traditions and conventions within our profession that are organized around our own comfort and convenience, as well as efficiency and cost-effectiveness, rather than having maximum therapeutic impact. Our colleagues in social work have long followed the ancient practices employed by most healers around the world in which the help is offered within the client's/patient's home rather than in a designated space offered by the expert. While visiting someone's home, social workers become familiar with the environment, contextual cues are immediately accessible and observable, and a variety of more flexible and creative interventions are possible. Even so, such arrangements are more typical of case work rather than actual therapy sessions.

One of our former students excitedly checked in today, talking about her job working for a therapy agency in which all the sessions take place as home visits. She was describing how this very morning she had conducted one session with a little boy inside the "fort" he had constructed out of blankets in his room, another session with a girl doing "sand tray" play therapy in the garden, and a third session with a child in the park while her mother, who desperately needed self-care time, was allowed to walk laps around them. She talked about the kinds of dramatic changes that had taken place with her clients in this setting that could never have happened so quickly and fluently within an office.

This gets one thinking about how and why the structure of having sessions in our offices has become standard practice. In what way do we imagine that *this* setting is optimal to promote lasting changes in people's lives? Yes, it keeps *us* safer and provides a far more comfortable space for our work. But since when is comfort and convenience associated with change?

"So," the counselor was asked, "do you recommend this sort of treatment?"

She hesitated.

"Let's put it another way. What do you notice, and what have you experienced, that's different about doing therapy this way?"

"Well," she laughed. "This isn't the way I learned to do therapy in school, under highly controlled conditions. It's chaotic and unpredictable. I have to admit it that, for me, I love it! But it isn't for everyone's taste. And certainty not for every client."

The counselor was quick to point out the practical and reality-based disadvantages. It was obviously more expensive. She spent a lot of time in her car traveling from place to place. Her clients were easily distracted by things going on in the house—interruptions, visitors, all kinds of calamity. There was often a lack of privacy, which eroded confidentiality. But most of all, she still could see how asking clients to come to our offices was all about having a "sacred space" for the most intimate and personal conversations.

We mention this example as representative of almost all the issues that we have raised in this book. We present a standard procedure or structure within the profession that is limiting in some ways, perhaps even overly so, and we take a skeptical tone. And yet we wish to offer alternatives and solutions that are informed by reasonable evidence rather than merely relying on convention and tradition.

Dysfunctional, inaccurate, and outdated beliefs are best challenged through honest scrutiny (Barth, 2017). Consider your reaction, and perhaps defensiveness, to things you've just read in these first chapters. Certainly, there were statements that you agree with automatically because they seem so self-evident. How did you notice you reacted to other points that you found troubling or not consistent with your own experience? What parts did you skip altogether or just skim over because you found the material to be irrelevant, boring, or perhaps even a bit disconcerting, if not threatening?

Whereas reading (or listening) to a book like this is often a relatively passive experience, we are hoping for a more active process in which you more carefully and critically consider points that may be at odds with your own beliefs. We wish to urge you to remain open to other possibilities, especially as you delve into the next chapters that directly challenge some of your basic assumptions about what you do and how you do it.

CHAPTER 4

cᐱ⌐

Some Tenuous Assumptions
and Conceptions

We've emphasized that throughout history there are certain assumptions or beliefs that we have mostly accepted as truths, perhaps unwarranted in light of the actual evidence. We mentioned earlier how it was believed that the Agricultural Revolution significantly improved the quality of life among our species. No longer would we have to hunt for our dinner or travel widely to find edible plants since livestock and grains were now within walking distance of our communities. Even though farmers worked double the number of hours than forager/hunters each day, our diets became less varied and more unhealthy. Overcrowding in population centers led to a further erosion of the human capacity for cooperation with the rhythms of Nature. Whereas previously humans lived in the present, now there was a focus within the farming mentality to always plan for uncertainties in the future. Harari (2015) considers this the birth of anxiety in the human condition, the time when uncertainty about droughts, floods, and petulance took center stage.

During periods of upheaval, revolution, conflict, and civil war in human history, it has rarely been about food shortages. "The French Revolution was spearheaded by affluent lawyers," Harari (2015) contends, "not by famished peasants" (p. 102). There are, of course, many such misconceptions about history, myths that have long been perpetuated by those in positions of power to maintain their positions and authority. Religious doctrine has sometimes been active in this regard, leading to widespread conflict between those who subscribe to slightly different belief systems. It turns out

Myths, Misconceptions, and Invalid Assumptions of Counseling and Psychotherapy. Jeffrey Kottler and Richard S. Balkin, Oxford University Press (2020). © Oxford University Press.
DOI: 10.1093/oso/9780190090692.001.0001

that whereas the Romans killed 1,500 Christians, Catholics and Protestants have slaughtered hundreds of thousands in the name of their preferred sect. Then consider the millions of people murdered throughout history in the name of Islam, Judaism, Christianity, Hinduism, Buddhism, not to mention communism, socialism, and democracy.

During more recent times, a number of myths and misconceptions continue to shape not only popular opinion but also public policies. As such we now fear the "wrong" things, which are usually not as great a risk as we might think. Whereas once upon a time the greatest threats to our existence were starvation from famines, plagues, and wars, nowadays people die from eating too much rather than too little and are more likely to take their own lives rather than perish as a result of war, terrorism, or violence. "The average human is far more likely to die from bingeing at McDonald's than from drought, Ebola, or an al-Qaeda attack" (Harari, 2017, p. 2). The vast majority of Americans are overweight or considered obese, significantly reducing their lifespan and leading to all kinds of nasty conditions like high blood pressure, diabetes, heart disease, asthma, gout, joint problems, and gallbladder disease. "Sugar is now more dangerous than gunpowder" (p. 15).

This brief and selected review of historical events applies just as well to our own profession in which certain unassailable beliefs that we will cover later have gone unchallenged. An obvious example is the standardized 50-minute hour. Can you imagine medical professionals deciding ahead of time that *all* their patients will receive a standardized 30-minute examination, regardless of their condition, complaints, history, and needs?

ILLUSIONS OF OVERCONFIDENCE AND CERTAINTY

Let's acknowledge at the outset that much of what we do is in the role of faith healers. We rely on persuasion and influence, suggestibility, and expectations of hope. Some would even say we are essentially shamans cloaked in the guise of scientific precision. We don't mean this in a disparaging or critical way but rather that there is a certain indelible and powerful force that follows a sense of optimism. More than anything else, we are purveyors of hope.

"I just don't see a way out," the client whispers through his tears. "I've tried just about everything. Those drugs don't work—I just can't tolerate the side effects. You're the last resort for me. If this doesn't help me . . . I just don't know what else to do. I just want to give up."

This is the critical moment, or at least *one* significant interaction early in the first meeting. The client showed up for help but with minimal expectations colored by despair. He is desperate for some sort of reassurance, some sign that there is reason for cautious hope. At least, initially, he will not be disappointed.

> I'm so glad you decided to see me [*That's not quite right because you trigger my own feelings of inadequacy*]. The problems you've discussed [*I don't yet understand what they really are*] seem quite common to me [*Actually I've never dealt with something like this before*]. Even though you've been frustrated and discouraged in the past, that doesn't mean you have to continue that way [*Unless, of course, you have some sort of intractable, chronic illness, but let's not go there yet*]. Just the fact that you've reached out to me for help says a lot about your prospects for the future [*I wish that were the case*]. I know that if we work together you'll see noticeable improvements [*Sigh, I hope, I hope*]. It seems to me that much of what you've been experiencing is directly related to some of the trauma you've experienced [*That seems reasonable, as a starting point, but I barely know the guy at this point*]. I think the first thing we need to do is take a more detailed history [*So I can stall a little until I can get a better handle on what's going on*]. Based on what you've shared already it seems apparent that this sort of thing runs in your family [*I don't know if that's really true but it seems reasonable*].

In this example it is apparent the therapist might be relatively inexperienced, but the themes revealed within the internal thoughts and feelings highlight the kind of interpretations, conjectures, hypotheses, and utterances we make, pretending a lot more certainty in their validity that is perhaps justified. It is important that we speak with authority and confidence, at least if we want to have any sort of impact. We are, thus, required to make clear pronouncements about what we believe is going on, but that doesn't necessarily mean that our beliefs are valid and accurate.

We make unwarranted assumptions all the time that are offered as unassailable truths or facts. Here are three different examples of what we mean:

1. *The reason you have this problem with intimacy is because of the compromised attachment you experienced with your mother who was so self-absorbed.* This leads to several questions. Is reality configured in such a way that problems can be reduced to simple cause–effect relationship between two variables? What qualifies exactly as "compromised attachment," and how did you measure its effects? Based on what extensive data and whose report are you determining that the mother was "self-involved?" Further, on what basis did you decide this was excessive?

2. "The reason you showed up for our appointment 15 minutes late again is because of your ambivalence about our work together."
   "Well, no, actually the bus was running late so I missed the transfer . . ."
   "See? You are being defensive about that."
   "No, I'm just trying to explain. . . ."
   "But that's what you do whenever we get close to important issues."
   Of course, the therapist could be perfectly correct with these observations and on target with the interpretations of what happened. On the other hand, she could be overreaching. There is context and history to this interaction that we are missing but the main point is that even if the proclamations are accurate, they are tentative rather than absolute hypotheses and established truths.

3. *The anxiety symptoms you are experiencing are a way to get your attention to deal with the dissatisfaction you are feeling about your job. It's clear they aren't going to go away until you make needed changes.*
   This last one I (Jeffrey) actually said to a client with complete authority and confidence. He totally bought it too and changed jobs as a result. However, it turned out that his furnace leaked, and his symptoms were actually the result of carbon monoxide poisoning.

Once again we mention these examples not to denigrate our authority and expertise but to suggest that a certain modesty, tentativeness, and curiosity may be indicated at times when we seem to be the most certain about our assumptions. It is when we are willing to question, if not challenge, our assumptions and beliefs that we are most inclined to advance the state of our knowledge.

SOME THINGS MOST OF US BELIEVE THAT MIGHT NOT REALLY BE TRUE

Let's consider some additional examples of things that we say or do routinely that may not be as accurate as we prefer.

"I Can Identify the Time When Things Went Bad for Someone and When They Turned Around"

There is a myth circulating in the wider world that we often subscribe to as well. It is the belief that we can identify single moments that were ultimately transformative, for better or worse. We sometimes point to particular conversations, experiences, or events as if they changed every-thing thereafter.

We don't dispute that moments in our lives are not created—or remembered—equally. Of course, particular joyful, evocative, traumatic, or novel experiences become more influential and enduring that those that are routine, expected, or ordinary. Nevertheless, we tell ourselves and others certain stories, little compressed nuggets, that allegedly explain some complex phenomenon like how we came to be a certain way, decided something, or behaved in a particular manner. We may point to one spe-cific thing that supposedly made all the difference. And perhaps it did. But that's only part of the story.

In an interview, comedian Jerry Seinfeld was asked specifically about the single moment he knew he was funny (Kinane, 2018). Now, of course, that's a leading question that presumes that there *is* such a singular mo-ment. He answered by saying, "I remember being very funny, but everyone was funny. I didn't think I was funnier than anybody else, especially when I was young." But then one particular day, during one fateful conversation, a friend said to him, "I think of all of us in the group, you're the funniest, and you could be a comedian if you wanted to be."

Now, is that what *really* happened? Is that all it took for Seinfeld to change the direction of his life and decide to devote himself to a career in entertainment?

Whether true or not, that is what he passionately believes. "And that was the moment I said, 'Okay, I'm going to do it.' That was probably the greatest moment right there."

That makes for a great story, and it may even partially capture his expe-rience, or at least what he remembers about how the process of his career decision unfolded, but we suspect there is a *lot* more to this than the sim-plistic tale. We sometimes do much the same thing when we tell clients the definitive reason why something occurred, why they act a certain way, or why they have their problems in the first place. Once again, it is comforting and convenient to think that way, but as linguist Alfred Korsybski (1941) once pointed out, the map is not really the territory; it is a metaphor to describe the distinction between verbal representations and actual reality.

In a similar vein, Spense (1982) warned therapists long ago that that what clients tell us about their lives ends up being filtered through so many layers, such as (a) what actually occurred, (b) what clients remember about what happened, (c) what is lost when they try to describe this memory with words, (d) what the therapist actually hears from the narrative, (e) how the therapist understands and interprets this description, and (f) how the therapist converts whatever is lost in translation into a verbal summary. It is no wonder that misunderstandings are so common when narrative and historical truth are often somewhat distorted.

Constructivists reassure us that since there is no such thing as absolute truth in the first place, at least with regard to human experience, we should not be overly concerned with such distinctions: The client's view of experience *is* reality as far they are concerned. That's all very well and good, but (and this is a significant *but*) it is also possible that there is a consensual truth that can be confirmed and validated.

"I Can Help Almost Anyone if Given Enough Time"

Therapy is not necessarily helpful for everyone, nor is it useful for every problem. Some people lack the capacity for insight or refuse to take any responsibility for their predicaments. Others are so skeptical or threatened by the prospect that they will do anything to sabotage it. Some prospective clients are so damaged, disordered, or disturbed that almost nothing or nobody could get through to them. It's just the reality that not everyone is a good candidate for what we do.

Even when there is someone who is highly motivated, self-aware, and presenting symptoms that are potentially responsive to treatment, that doesn't mean this person is a good match for *you*. There are compatibility issues to negotiate. Each of us is better at some things than others. We can't possibly connect with everyone, no matter how skilled and experienced. Each of us has specialty areas we excel in and others that we are less than perfectly comfortable. We know this, of course. We recognize this and say we accept this reality and limitation. On the other hand, we often forget and really do believe we can help anyone who walks in the door—and feel disappointed when the person doesn't return.

There are also certain realities related to clinical practice. For those who work in public agencies or community mental health, with long waiting lists of people waiting for services, there are triage procedures in place to screen those individuals who are the best candidates for outpatient, short-term psychotherapy. Others may be referred for medication, inpatient care, or other treatment options. Once therapy has begun, if it is determined that the client is less than motivated or presents symptoms that are not amenable to what is offered, the person may then be referred for some other program. Those of us who have worked in such setting well understand the limits of what we can do when working under limitations of time, resources, and opportunities. We not only know we can't help everyone but also that our work depends on understanding that limitation.

Then there are those practitioners who work in private practice. Their livelihood depends on the ability to fill the days with paying customers. As such, the job requires one to be far more of a generalist, pretty much willing and able to see anyone who walks in the door. The same options, or desire, simply aren't there to refer clients who don't seem like good candidates or who don't make rapid progress.

Imagine a client who confesses doubts and frustration during a session that isn't going well. "I don't think this is helping," she says, with anger seeping into her tone. "I don't like coming here. It just isn't convenient for me right now. I don't know. Maybe I should quit, or at least take some time off for a while."

How therapists respond to this provocation depends as much on their professional setting, specialty, and yes, their own needs, as it does anything related to this client's best interests. You may quibble with us on this, but we would suggest that private practitioners may not be as inclined as agency staff to just agree with the client and terminate the sessions immediately.

Perhaps it would be more honest and convincing if we supplied a personal example. When I (Jeffrey) was in private practice full time, I was desperate to pay my bills and support my family. No matter how many clients (or lack thereof) consulted me each week, I still had to take care of overhead expenses. It was always tenuous and uncertain when new referrals would call. So, more often than not, if a client brought up the issue of termination, I genuinely believed (most of the time) that it wasn't in their best interests (or mine) to end prematurely. Inevitably, I would suggest that we take some time to explore the issues further. I would interpret the resistance and defensiveness as avoidance of significant issues. I would persuade the client to give the sessions more time—and I truly believed that this was absolutely necessary.

Now I work in a county hospital and refugee resettlement agency. There are so many indigent, homeless, traumatized immigrants, asylum seekers, and economically disadvantaged people who desperately need help. And there are so few of us available to help them. By necessity, I no longer believe I can help everyone. I'm quite clear about the limits of what is possible, given the resources available. More often than not, I may rush a client to end our sessions before it is advantageous or refer them elsewhere. Sometimes I feel like a barista trying to simultaneously make several complicated beverages at the same time as I stare out at long line, stretching out the door, of impatient, caffeine-deprived people.

"You Have to Be Completely Open and Honest for Me to Help You"

This is such a lie—or at least a misguided assumption. First, who says that clients are really all that truthful in the first place? They are presenting only what they want us to hear, leaving out important details and context that they either forgot, denied, avoided, or just covered up. At times they don't even know what really happened or not, creating stories that are as much fantasy as any semblance of reality. And there's often no way we can tell the difference (Kottler, 2010; Kottler & Carlson, 2011).

It's interesting to consider that it may not even matter much of the time if we really know and understand what occurred. It might not even be all that important that clients talk about what's bothering them, at least out loud: They can talk around things or about things in a general way and still do the important work inside their heads and hearts. That, after all, is the basis for some hypnotic inductions, eye movement desensitization, imagery techniques, and other methods. Also, any of us who have ever been in therapy as clients know full well that there are all kinds of mental conversations that take place in the company of therapists that they never hear out loud. That is one of the more remarkable aspects of the process: Clients may only spend an hour a week in the therapist's office, yet they continue a mental dialogue all throughout the week.

"The Influence in Therapy Sessions Only Travels in One Direction"

All the while we are doing our best to persuade clients to do our bidding, follow our lead, listen carefully to what we offer to them, they are working just as hard to convince us of their own perspective. This is mostly about agreeing with them that their problems are the result of others' behavior, that they don't really need help in the first place, and that this therapy stuff won't take very long nor be very difficult.

Then there is all the subtle, indirect influence taking place. Our buttons are pushed. Our unresolved issues are triggered. A parallel process is taking place wherein during some of the time we are talking to our clients, we are also talking to ourselves. And not infrequently, clients say things to us that send us off into a whole other realm of self-reflection and personal scrutiny, whether that occurs during the hour or in the days that follow.

"I just can't get over how helpless I feel watching my father deteriorate like that. He used to be such a powerful figure in my life, and now he's reduced to an incoherent invalid. I wish I could do so much more for him but . . ."

It's at this point that I (Jeffrey) stopped listening. I think that more than 5 minutes must have elapsed before I noticed that I completely lost the thread of what the client was saying. I went off into my own world, thinking about my own father who had a stroke many years ago. It wasn't just that this client sparked a connection that I felt to my own situation but rather that he was teaching me something that I hadn't quite realized before. I had to visibly shake my head to bring myself back into the moment, resolving that I'd get back to my own thoughts and feelings at a later time. But I also couldn't help realizing, with a certain amount of guilt, that whether my client was getting something out of this session or not, it certainly had a powerful effect on me.

"Our Sessions Together Are the Reason Why You've Improved and Things Have Gotten So Much Better for You"

We aren't suggesting that the work that occurs isn't important, significant, or even critical; otherwise, what's the purpose of therapy anyway? The main goal is actually to promote what happens *after* the client walks out the door. Talking doesn't do much good if it isn't translated into action.

However, we need to be careful of *attribution error*, or being quick either to take credit for the success that happens in therapy or to blame ourselves for the client's lack of progress. Over the past few decades, various attribution errors by clinicians were outlined because of misdiagnosis, misidentification of causes or influences of behavior, or misunderstanding of cultural factors, such as race and poverty (Chapman & Watson, 1999; Dumont & Leconte, 1987; Nafisi & Stanley, 2007; Toporek, 2002). Although we have some insights into attribution errors by students, we really have no idea how often these occur in practice.

Probably at some point in time you have had a fever and took some type of fever-reducing medicine. After a brief time, your aches and pains dissipated, and your temperature dropped to something close to 98.6. When the medicine wears off in about 6 to 8 hours, maybe you take another dose until your temperature is no longer rising and you are feeling better. In this instance, you can tie the brief reprieve you have from fever symptoms to the medicine you are taking. There appears to be a cause and effect— one that is U.S. Food and Drug–approved and demonstrated through randomized controlled trials. We can say with some degree of certainty that the medicine works.

However, can we say the same about our sessions? Do clients always leave a session better than when they came in? Actually, sometimes the opposite happens. A client comes into session in a relatively good mood but during the course of the session brings up some serious, traumatic past issues. The client might cry in anquish. At the end of the session, you are working with the person to regain composure and send him back out to the real world. As the client is leaving you might say, "You worked really hard today." As he forces an appreciative smile, you both feel this was a solid session, but he is now leaving the interaction even more distressed than when he first arrived. When you see him again the following week, you might notice a turning point in the therapy, and the client seems really committed to the process. No doubt you are thinking that your sessions are moving the client toward significant progress.

But what if the client does not improve? What if the next week the client unexpectedly cancels the session? At this point, you wonder if you will ever see him again. Is this sudden, unexpected termination attributed to your sessions? If client progress is attributed to your sessions, should a lack of progress also be related to your sessions? Clients who demonstrate progress in sessions, and even make plans to transfer the lessons to the real world, may fall short or not follow through at all. We do not always know why. No doubt you have had clients make promises and commitments in therapy, appear motivated to accomplish a task or goal, make plans, and even role-play the scenario and process worst-case scenarios. The client appears ready, and there is little doubt in your mind that she is going to back out. And yet, when it comes time to act, she does nothing and repeats the same self-defeating behaviors. This failure to transfer learning is part of what we originally learned when studying the research process.

You might recall (or you might have blocked it out) the various ways we try to prove that something is better or worse. We call this *experimental validity*, and there are two major types: internal and external. Internal experimental validity (the most commonly discussed) is where we try to demonstrate that any change that occurs is due to the intervention and not some other factor. For example, community mental health centers are often so busy that they have a waiting list. In a representative example of a wait-listed study, Ehrenreich-May et al. (2017) compared adolescents being treated for depression and anxiety over a period of 8 weeks to those on a wait-list. It is typical in such studies that the clients receiving treatment show fewer depressive or anxious symptoms compared to those on the wait-list. But what is often overlooked is that usually *both* groups improve. Adolescents on the wait-list experienced decreases in their symptoms; they started to get better without any intervention (except signing up for the wait-list), but their progress was just not as noticeable as in those receiving 8 weeks of therapy. So, that leads to the question regarding whether the interventions work. And the answer is that sure they do, and they work faster than doing nothing at all. But that does not negate the fact that doing nothing at all also works, just at a slower pace. In this respect, time is often a threat to internal experimental validity because things tend to get better simply due to the passage of time.

"What We Do During Our Sessions Makes All the Difference"

Not only is the actual intervention used in a session under question, but the actual session itself can be challenged. External experimental validity addresses the very nature of the study—the setting in which it was conducted. Sometimes the context is so removed from the real world that applying what is observed has very little relationship to what occurs in the real world. Consider what happens when working with individuals who struggle with substance use and addiction in a residential treatment setting. We tend to see a high percentage of relapse—40% to 60% according to the National Institute on Drug Abuse (2018). What we know about substance use treatment is that relapse does not necessarily constitute a treatment failure. However, why is it such a high percentage? On one hand, the likelihood of relapse for individuals with substance use disorders is not unlike individuals who suffer from other chronic health problems (e.g., hypertension, asthma) and struggle to maintain their treatment regimen (National Institute on Drug Abuse, 2018). On the other hand, the treatment one receives in a residential treatment program is unlike the issues one encounters in the real world. The pressure to maintain sobriety when institutionalized is quite different than what an individual faces once outside of the treatment setting. That is one reason why a major focus of inpatient treatment is in preparing individuals to maintain sobriety outside of treatment.

We could make similar comparisons to the traditional therapy session conducted in an office. Conversations can be intimate, private, and confidential. Yet even with sophisticated techniques such as systematic desensitization, empty chair, role play, psychodrama, and other evocative techniques, there is no substitute for real-world experiences, and thus a traditional therapy session necessarily limits our ability to prepare our clients to address real-world challenges.

"I'm a Better Therapist Than Most Others You Could Have Seen."

This is called the illusory superiority effect or Lake Wobegon effect, named after the *Prairie Home Companion* radio show where Garrison Keillor always ended this show by saying "and all children are above average." Indeed, the vast majority of therapists, approaching 90% of those surveyed, consider themselves better than average compared to their peers (Sapyta, Reimer, & Bickman, 2005). This isn't that different from similar studies that asked people to compare their driving ability to that of others on the road; once again, almost everyone said they were better than everyone else.

It would seem that we are not very good at, or perhaps not very honest in, assessing our own competence. No matter how confident and self-assured we might appear, that seems to have little relationship to actual performance. If anything, there is often a negative correlation between how vehemently someone proclaims their extraordinary skills and their actual effectiveness (Trivers, 2011). Those practitioners who are inclined to sing their own praises most loudly are also those who are most insecure.

Another variation of this theme is the stubborn belief that one's particular allegiance to a theory or approach is better than what everyone else is doing. As we are certainly aware, there are well over 400 different conceptual paradigms that have been identified, and most practitioners believe their choice is superior to other options available, even though there is no compelling evidence to support this assertion (Wampold, 2018; Wampold & Imel, 2015). Complicating matters further is that the vast majority of clinicians actually identify as integrative, pragmatic, or eclectic, preferring to combine features from several theoretical traditions (Prochaska & Norcross, 2018). They either hone in on so-called common factors or decide to rely on whatever method or strategy would appear to be most useful at any point in time. Of course, all this is based on self-reports, which are notoriously unreliable: In other words, what therapists say they do behind closed doors is not necessarily the same as what we might actually witness.

The reality is that we may actually be doing more harm by holding so strongly to certain beliefs. When we express certainty to clients about what is going on in their lives, we ultimately assert power and dominance over the client. These feelings are even reinforced biologically: We experience an increase in the neurotransmitter dopamine, and the areas of the brain's pleasure centers that are activated are the same as those activated by illicit drugs (Lehrer, 2008). If our feelings of certainty are more like an addiction, we might have a hard time relinquishing those feelings or even keeping them in check with our clients.

EMBRACING UNCERTAINTY

Ultimately, uncertainty might have some distinct advantages. Although we may sometimes apologize for the answers to questions that escape us or feel defensive when confronted with the limits of our knowledge or expertise, there is also a certain honor in embracing our cautious doubts. In fact, we empower our clients when we enter into a collaborative relationship and allow clients to take control of their own decisions (Amundsen et al., 1993; S. Smith & Macduff, 2017). Whereas certainty can affect the working alliance and power within the therapeutic relationship, embracing the ambiguity of the therapeutic process may humanize us to our clients and help us to better understand their novel experiences. The factors that contribute to our certainty—our expertise, experiences, training, and reliance on research—are not infallible. Although abandoning these factors would be foolhardy, as they contribute to our understanding of clients and the therapeutic process, we can all be duped by claims of knowledge and expertise, including our own.

CHAPTER 5

⚬⁓⚬

If Research Is So Important, Why Do We
Often Ignore the Results?

We have known for decades that smoking causes cancer, obesity leads to heart disease and early death, and that texting while driving dramatically increases the risk of an accident, yet people still persist in these obviously harmful activities regardless of the devastating consequences. We know that depression is the single most dangerous condition that results in lost productivity, reduced quality of life, and early death: one million people take their own lives each year, and the incidence of suicide is dramatically increasing. This major health concern receives only the tiniest fraction of support and resources compared to other problems.

Heart failure is one of major causes of death, killing one in every four people in the United States. There has been consistent and overwhelming evidence that a certain package of treatments that include medication, procedures, and collaborations result in impressive survival rates. Yet these findings have not yet found their way into mainstream practice.

Billions and billions of dollars are spent each year on research, yet an estimated 85% of the results are completely ignored (Chalmers & Glasziou, 2009). Furthermore, the average delay between the publication of a study with significant and groundbreaking results and putting the ideas into practice is about 17 years (Morris, Wooding, & Grant, 2011).

It would appear that despite the passionate devotion that we articulate about the importance of research, not only with respect to general health issues but also the practice of psychotherapy, we rarely seem to pay much attention to the results of these studies, at least in a timely manner.

Myths, Misconceptions, and Invalid Assumptions of Counseling and Psychotherapy. Jeffrey A. Kottler and Richard S. Balkin, Oxford University Press (2020). © Oxford University Press.
DOI: 10.1093/oso/9780190090692.001.0001

Practitioners may become comfortable with what is already familiar and within their domain of experience, reluctant to introduce some newfangled method that supposedly renders the status quo obsolete.

We talk constantly about valuing, even worshiping research. But do we really? Our own beliefs and skepticism about new information and the extent to which we may be willing to change or alter how we practice can be a major impediment to using research findings (Balkin & Kleist, 2017; Retsas, 2000). Consider the extent to which research findings are disputed or disregarded based on convenience, culture, and minority opinion. Although all of us were required to take the obligatory research courses in college and graduate school, very few therapists ever actually undertake any systematic studies once they are in practice. In addition, organizations may be reluctant to alter established protocols so new research can be implemented. Clinicians, as well, find it challenging to change old habits (just like our clients). As just one example, there has been little change in the way substance use and addictions have been treated during the past decades. Even though protocols for managing chemical withdrawal have advanced, treatment is still heavily dependent upon group therapy and support groups for maintenance (Stevens & Smith, 2018).

We discussed earlier the illusion of certainty and the challenge of changing one's perspective or point of view in light of contradictory evidence that may conflict with favored theories. It's inconvenient, uncomfortable, and sometimes exhausting to change one's mind about something, given that it requires innumerable adjustments. Long ago it was discovered how cognitive dissonance explains why people dig in their heels and stubbornly hold onto particular beliefs, even in the face of overwhelming evidence that it isn't valid. Of course, we see this not only in the political arena but also within our own profession. One example is related to the fervent belief that psychoeducational methods would be optimal strategies to permanently reduce drug addiction or other risky behavior. Students would be shown a warning film, listen to a talk by a police officer, or receive a pamphlet warning about the dangers of premarital sex, yet these well intentioned efforts had little effect whatsoever.

Consider policies related to abstinence-only education, renamed as sexual risk-avoidance to sound more benign. Over $2 billion has been committed to implement these programs even though there is absolutely no evidence that they have any impact on delaying initiation of sexual intercourse or changing risky sexual behaviors for adolescents (Santelli et al., 2017). Some religious-based schools and universities even ask their students to sign a contract upon admission, stating that they vow, upon pain of expulsion (if not being condemned to an eternity in hell), that they will not engage in sex during their tenure at the institution. It turns out that such purity pledges actually *increase* the risk of pregnancy and sexually transmitted diseases since students don't have access to birth control or condoms! This isn't all that surprising considering that only 3% of Americans wait until marriage to have sex, and the vast majority of pledgers break their promises, leading to increased guilt, shame, depression, and anxiety (Paik, Sanchagrin, & Heimer, 2016).

The decision to continually fund and advocate for an ineffective program does not make much sense. But, of course, the program is not implemented because it really works, but rather because it sounds good to constituents and parents. People like the *idea* of it even if there is no basis in reality. And what's not to like? The idea that teen pregnancy could be prevented if we just tell adolescents to "say no to temptation" would accomplish the goal of reducing teen pregnancy but also fall into line as a moral victory. When the theory is challenged, data are collected, and findings show the ineffectiveness of the program, people become passionate or even angry at the notion that the program is a failure.

SIMPLE SOLUTIONS AND COMPLEX PROBLEMS

Much like the issue of abstinence education, society tends to focus on simple, singular solutions for complex, multifaceted problems. We have all heard anecdotes about schools that demonstrated higher student achievement and reductions in student misbehaviors when the administration required uniforms for all of the students. It was also alleged to reduce the stigma attached to lower economic students. These are actually mostly urban legends that hide the true results, which indicate that rigid dress codes like this have negligible impact on improving students' achievement or significantly alter their behavior (Brunsma, 2004). Once again the myth is perpetuated because it seems like such an easy fix for such difficult set of problems: Just change what students wear to school—and voila!—better discipline and supposedly improved performance.

There are so many other examples within the social science literature that describe initiatives to solve complex puzzles with a quick, simple answer or action. Just as abstinence programs do not appreciably change students' behavior, neither do moments of silence or prayer make much difference. And perhaps the most feeble, simplistic solution of all to reduce drug use among teenagers: "Just say *no* to drugs!"

LIMITATIONS OF THE SCIENTIFIC METHOD

It would seem that part of the problem with our research is, well, our research. Perhaps we believe that we can solve complex problems with simple solutions because we have devised a way to address, evaluate, and solve society's ills. Astrophysicist Ethan Siegel (2018) investigated the contributing factors that oversimplify and wrongly endorse simple solutions to complex problems. Besides outright fraud (e.g., falsifying results to obtain the desired findings), Siegel indicated that we can easily fall prey to self-deception when we prioritize results that support our beliefs and gloss over discrepant findings or findings that challenge our belief system. We are also vulnerable to what he referred to as "motivated reasoning," when we choose to believe the more persuasive message as opposed to what evidence clearly indicates. The denial of global warming is one such example since if this reality is accepted, it would mean acknowledging the uncomfortable and inconvenient consequences that the planet is falling apart in such a way that we will have to make some adjustments.

Motivated and biased reasoning during a research investigation is so impervious to influence precisely because it is designed to protect us against uncomfortable and undesirable conclusions. In its variant forms, researchers recognize and acknowledge literature and studies that support their hypotheses and then cherry-pick examples and data that support their preferred conclusion and publish only positive results. In studies of antidepressant medications for example, 98% of those that report positive results end up published whereas less than half of those with negative outcomes ever find the light of day. And even when the primary results were considered negative by the U.S. Food and Drug Administration, the researchers simply changed their criteria to consider only the secondary outcomes that were more favorable (Carroll, 2018). It's easy to fool oneself when you are the easiest person to fool and have an incentive and unconscious desire to do so.

We also see situations where a minority opinion or lone wolf influences public perception with a charismatic, albeit ill-conceived viewpoint on an important. The belief that autism is linked to vaccines is based on a well-known case of documented, scientific fraud, but when powerful political or media figures continue to publicize this misinformation, it gains traction despite the fraudulent nature of the science behind it. Despite the discrepant data, people choose to believe what is convenient and what supports their own preconceived notions. In essence, even the most rigorous scientific procedures do not protect the public from fraud, motivated reasoning, or self-deception.

Research studies in our scientific endeavor are particularly skewed and suspect given the biased samples that have been employed—namely, mostly relatively privileged, educated, Western individuals. How do we hope to generalize our findings to the larger world when something like 90% of the samples upon which studies are based were culled from mostly American college students? One of the most prominent publications, *Journal of Personality and Social Psychology*, included articles in which 96% of those samples were from Western, educated participants, and two thirds of them were American (Henrich, Heine, & Norenzayan, 2010). How, then, do we truly know and understand the experiences of those from remote areas, from the underclass, and from all over the world when so many of the studies are based on students attending Introduction to Psychology classes who were required to participate to receive credit? This is more than a little problematic when attempting to generalize to the larger population (Hanel & Vione, 2016)—unless, of course, we are only treating American college students.

In social science research, we also run into the problem of replication. It's been estimated that only about half of the studies published in psychology journals are actually replicable (Open Science Collaboration, 2015). The most common defense of this disappointing results is to attribute the inconsistencies to variabilities in samples. Although this is a legitimate concern, it turns out that diversity of a sample appears to have minimal effects on the lack of replicated results (Yong, 2018). In other words, we often think that limits to generalizability—the application of research findings across a population—are because people are so diverse and studies are often limited by participants who are more alike than different. But that is not really the case. Rather, research findings lack generalizability not because of the people included or not included in the study but because the phenomenon being tested is simply not that stable in the first place. As one example that is quite familiar, about half of those who attempt treatment for substance use end up eventually relapsing (National Institute of Drug Abuse, 2018). Making predictions is tough, even in the most controlled studies, leading to the conclusion that that human behavior might just be more inconsistent than when we like to think. This is both disconcerting and disappointing, considering that one of the functions of research is make accurate predictions.

A team of 186 researchers have worked together to test this claim by replicating 28 seminal studies in psychology using a sample size of over 15,300 participants—60 times the number of participants from the original studies (Yong, 2018). For example, in a refutation of one popular myth based on a widely cited study, it was found that smiling doesn't really make people feel any better (Sleek, 2018). Results from studies that have been cited in psychology textbooks and used to justify practice in fields, as well as in advertising and political science, might not be true at all. It's also been difficult to replicate other classic studies such as the claim that posing in a power position (wider stance with hands on hips) makes one feel bolder and more assertive, revising answers on an exam improves performance, or that being reminded about money makes people more selfish (Jarrett, 2016).

To add to the uncertainty about what we truly know and understand based on research, the vast majority of published studies in the social sciences are correlational rather than experimental. They aren't so much testing anything as looking for relationships between factors that are assumed to be connected in some way. Predictions are made based on assumed cause—effect phenomena such as disordered eating and depression or increased mindfulness and reduced anxiety. This means that our favorite ideas may not be as well supported as we prefer to believe.

We don't wish to imply that research in general, or the scientific method in particular, is not absolutely essential for the advancement and viability of our profession. It's just important to keep in mind that the system of scientific inquiry used in social sciences was not devised and refined by social scientists but rather by the physical sciences. In the early conceptualizations of contemporary mental health, it was considered imperative that the field was linked to the precision of the biological sciences to gain respectability from the scientific community. Behaviorism took it a step further by applying the scientific method to investigate such principles as positive and negative reinforcement, punishment, and operant conditioning. These same scientific principles are used today, suggesting that the mechanisms of human behavior and mental health can be evaluated and tested in the same way as the physical sciences. Unfortunately, issues of human error, confirmation bias, motivated reasoning, and participant selection are much easier phenomena to control in the physical sciences than the social sciences because of the intrinsically unpredictable and inconsistent nature of human behavior.

HOW MUCH DO WE VALUE RESEARCH?

Raise your hand if you can honestly say you read each paragraph, much less each section, of an experimental study in an academic journal. Okay, Rick says he does, but then he teaches advanced research classes for a living. Jeffrey, on the other hand, admits that most of the time he checks out the abstract, and if it looks interesting, he skips right to the discussion, sometimes just to the conclusions. He rarely, if ever, does anything more than scan the methods section and usually skips the tables altogether, even though these could very likely be the most important part of the whole article. Although he confesses to a certain shame in this negligence, Jeffrey suspects he isn't the only one who reviews articles somewhat less critically and thoroughly than they may perhaps deserve.

All of scientific research is predicated on a position of not knowing, of holding assumptions and beliefs in check, so that we may remain open to actual observations and evidence as it unfolds. It is this curiosity and suspension of certainty that allows us to make new discoveries. We embrace a position of ignorance—or, using the Latin injunction of all scientific inquiry, *ignoramus* (We do not know)—that permits critical, objective, careful gathering of data. As such, there are few, if any, theories that are considered the ultimate and final truth. Likewise, it is the admission of doubt and uncertainty that leads to further and more advanced investigations. Once we think we truly *know* something, we cease looking for deeper, more robust answers to questions that concern us.

Columbus believed, insisting until this death, that he had discovered an island off the coast of East Asia since he couldn't conceive of the very idea he had run aground on an unknown continent. History is littered with so many other such accidental discoveries while the individual was looking elsewhere. Gunpowder was invented while Daoist alchemists were searching for the secret of life. The microwave, X-rays, anesthesia, chemotherapy, antibiotics, rubber, Teflon, superglue, and even "corn flakes" were all discovered when the scientist was busy looking for something else.

Whatever lapses and mistakes that have occurred in research efforts from the past, we wonder if things will get much better, given the inattention and shortcuts that are now prevalent. Jeffrey teaches in a medical school where the majority of students don't bother to attend classes in person any longer but rather watch the lectures at fast forward speed on their mobile devices at home. Some students even wait until a week before exams to watch *all* the presentations together. Before we become too critical of this practice we'd have to admit that many among us do the same thing right before its time to submit continuing education credits to renew a license.

In a study across 24 academic institutions, Arum and Roksa (2011) found that undergraduate students spend about half as much time studying than they did in the 1960s, with less than 2 hours per day studying alone. Although students still maintain about a B+ grade point average, their mastery of critical thinking skills have significantly eroded. Consider, then, how these trends continue throughout graduate school. It is hard to demonstrate a value for research when professionals are less than enthused about becoming responsible and discerning consumers of research. Certainly the ways we access and digest knowledge is evolving, and this has particular consequences, for better and for worse. Ultimately, we all seek more accurate and revealing information regarding whether what we are doing is useful helpful to others.

DO WE REALLY KNOW IF—AND WHEN— WE HELP ANYONE?

I'm just so appreciative for all you've done for me! This has been an amazing experience and I'm so grateful for everything I've learned from you. I just don't know what I'd have done, or where I'd be, without your help. Probably homeless or something. [Laughs] Seriously, though, the changes that I've experienced since we've been talking together have been remarkable. Everyone tells me that I don't even seem like the same person. I feel so much calmer. And because of you, I have a clearer idea of where I'm headed. So, I guess there's no reason for me to keep coming here anymore. I've accomplished everything that I wanted in our work together—and even more than I expected. Of course, I'll call again if I ever need any more help in the future. Thanks once again.

Sounds like a pretty successful outcome, doesn't it? This would be music to our ears, confirmation that every one of the treatment goals had been reached. The client is leaving far better off than when he first arrived. In addition, he recognizes these significant changes and can readily express this gratitude. He also seems to be highly motivated to continue the work on his own after the sessions ended. He exudes confidence and seems fully prepared to handle whatever else comes his way.

The only question, however, is how do we know that *any* of this is really true? What if we told you that, in fact, according to reports from this person's family, he is worse than ever. He is still actively using drugs. He is still hanging out with the same losers who got him involved in criminal enterprises. Although he claims to be working, it turns out that he was actually fired from his job a few weeks earlier. He spends most of his time getting high, staying up all night, and sleeping until noon.

We have all sorts of ways we attempt to assess the effects of our interventions. We use anxiety or depression scales, symptom checklists, surveys, follow-up calls, and reports on frequency of target behaviors. Most of them rely on either therapist observations or self-reports by the client.

That is certainly useful information, but the accuracy of these assessments might very well be skewed, biased, distorted, or even fictitious.

We can all think of clients we saw for a period of time, absolutely convinced beyond any doubt, that they responded well to our interventions and made spectacular progress. But then, at some later time, we heard reports from reliable witnesses that this person had relapsed. What we once believed was a solid cure turned out to be what seems like it was waste of time—so far, anyway. The end of the story has yet to be written.

Likewise, there are clients we've seen who we were convinced were abject failures. They dropped out of treatment after just a few sessions and seemed quite dissatisfied with what we offered them. Then we heard reports at some later time that they actually made significant changes immediately after the sessions ended abruptly.

I (Jeffrey) literally ran into someone like that this week! I know people use that expression all the time, meaning "recently" or "not too long ago," but I precisely mean on Sunday (and this is Tuesday). And by "literally running into someone" I mean that exactly as described. I was visiting family back in Michigan where I used to have a private practice 30 years ago and had since moved away. I had gone for a run along a narrow pathway when I brushed into a guy running the opposite direction.

"Kottler? Are you Dr. Kottler?" the guy called out. At least I think he did. So I stopped abruptly and turned around to face him. I didn't recognize him.

"Do you know who I am?" he asked.

I smiled but shook my head.

"I was one of your clients. A long time ago. You probably wouldn't remember me."

I shrugged.

"And I only saw you one time." He laughed at that. "And I didn't even stay for the whole session."

Now I was intrigued. I studied his face but still didn't recognize him. Perhaps not surprising after so many years. And apparently I only saw him for a single session.

"Round peg in a square hole."

"Excuse me?" I responded, more confused than ever. I started to wonder if it might be better for me to just continue on my run.

"Round peg in a square hole," he repeated. For just a moment I suppressed a giggle, thinking maybe this was a secret agent code. Maybe he mistook me for a spy. Then he explained, "That's what you said to me."

"Uh huh." Somehow I had some vague memory that was triggered.

"I came to see you because I was unhappy at work. Depressed actually. You had only met me for a few minutes, but once you heard about what

I was doing, and after I told you about myself, you said to me that I was round peg in a square hole. That I didn't belong there. That's all you said to me. I was so disappointed that I left. We didn't even finish the session."

Oops. I guess I blew that one. Time to excuse myself and move on. But then he broke out in this huge grin.

"That's *exactly* what I needed to hear. I thought about it over and over. I've even told this story to a hundred different people. I mentioned it to someone the other day, how what you said to me made all the difference. Can I just shake your hand? I've thought about you for years but never thought I'd ever see you again."

I held out my hand but he gave me an affectionate hug and held me at arm's length. He just shook his head back and forth, squeezed my arm, and then ran in the direction to which he'd been heading.

Apparently I had imagined this session had been an awkward mistake, a premature termination in which he didn't even make it through the hour. Perhaps he had left disappointed as well. But it actually turned out this had been a turning point for him, "exactly what he needed." It had been a spectacular success even though I chalked it up as a failure.

What are we to make from such episodes in which the people we think we failed end up recovered and those we believe lived happily ever after end up a wreck? Part of the problem is that positive outcomes in therapy are not easily defined, or rather they can be identified in so many different ways. We often rely on the client's reported level of satisfaction or sometimes as measurable reduction in specific symptoms. We could also consider the therapist's own assessment of progress. Other programs just consider regular attendance of sessions as evidence of commitment. Alternatively, we could use measures of improved interpersonal engagement or the quality of the therapeutic alliance. There are various structural measures that consider the extent to which mandated policies and procedures were followed. There are process measures that look primarily at compliance and completion of programs. And then there are the familiar outcome measures that use rating scales to determine specific changes in target behaviors. Obviously, a more comprehensive, integrative evaluation would provide more complete and meaningful information to better inform our practice (Brown, Scholle, & Azur, 2014).

We also have to consider the circumstances and context in which therapy takes place. Motivation plays an important role in any therapeutic endeavor, especially when we compare those who desperately reached out for help on their own versus those mandated by the court or blackmailed by a significant other. In addition, it is clear that some disorders and complaints are easier to treat (adjustment reactions, uncomplicated grief, etc.) versus those that represent more chronic, intractable conditions (personality disorders, psychotic conditions, bipolar disorder, etc.). After all, some positive outcomes are just the result of maintenance and support to ensure compliance to medication whereas others require considerable effort that still result in poor prognoses.

UNRELIABILITY AND INACCURACY OF OUTCOME MEASURES

Not only are there a variety of therapeutic outcomes to consider, but there are so many different measurements they are too numerous to list. There are hundreds of different checklists, questionnaires, and protocols to supposedly determine treatment outcomes even if they are not all that meaningful in terms of actually assessing what really happened during the experience (Liebherz, Schmidt, & Rabung, 2016). Everyone talks a good game about the importance of measuring the impact of what we do, but there are also practical implications to this. Researchers like Scott Miller (S. D. Miller, Hubble, Chow, & Seidel, 2015) advocate the use of rating forms after each session, asking clients the extent to which they felt heard and understood, the satisfaction they felt talking about issue they considered important, and whether the therapist's approach was a good fit for their desired goals. That all sounds great but to what extent is this desirable, if even possible, in the reality of daily practice?

Imagine, for example, a session is coming to a close. For some time the therapist has suspected that there may be a history of sexual and physical abuse in a client's background that is still having a significant impact on her ability to establish and maintain intimacy in her relationships. She has been twice divorced because she managed to choose men who were verbally and physically abusive. She has huge issues of mistrust in friendships. The therapy has proceeded slowly, in fits and starts, because of her caution and concerns that she didn't feel safe.

Although the client had been hinting at past trauma, until this particular session she had been unwilling to talk about what happened. During a tearful confession, she shared, for the first time with anyone, what her father and uncle had done to her when she was 11 years old. This also led into a detailed description of the suffering she experienced in her previous marriage, the brutal attacks directed her way, some of which led her to seek medical care. Finally, with just a few minutes left, she disclosed how desperately she wanted to trust her therapist but found it difficult. As they both stood up, she initiated a cautious embrace.

Now, after this moment, can you picture yourself asking the client to fill out a client feedback form?

We don't mean to imply that systematic measurement of progress is not important, just that the kinds of contrived, overstructured research instruments that are favored by academics are not necessarily useful or practical in the real world, especially when what they measure may not really be all that meaningful.

It is one thing for researchers to collect data to meet their own needs and quite another to interrupt the process of what is going on in a therapeutic relationship to collect such data. Is it really necessary to ask a client, after an intense, emotionally charged session, to sit down and complete a feedback form? And aren't questions related to feeling understood or allowing clients to talk about what they prefer essential in the grand scheme of things—for all clients, all the time?

There have been attempts to measure changes in coping skills, personality attributes, self-esteem, reduction of symptoms, depression or anxiety scales, session rating scales, functional status, client satisfaction, global health, behavior checklists, and overall well-being. From these measures, we can conclude a few things (Balkin & Juhnke, 2018; Kottler & Balkin, 2017):

1. Most measures tend to be fairly accurate in helping clinicians assess a variety of client outcomes of interest such as depression, anxiety, the working alliance, etc.
2. Most assessment instrument are overreliant on self-report, and that is a problem for clients who are wise, experienced with treatment, or simply manipulative.
3. When clinicians are filling out instruments on their clients, there is a lot of variability between what clients perceive and experience compared to what their therapists report.

Regardless of perceived inaccuracies or limitations of assessment instruments, the problems encountered with them are tied to misuse as opposed to their psychometric properties. In other words, how clinicians use the instruments is usually more important than the work that went into developing them in the first place. Any such instrument represents just a single source of data but is not necessarily a decisive indicator or clinical judgment. They do provide supportive evidence that may be useful but they do not replace the clinician's own clinical judgment.

CLINICAL, PRACTICAL, AND STATISTICAL SIGNIFICANCE

To muddy things even further, not only do we have multiple definitions of client outcomes, but we also have different ways of determining the significance of any particular research finding. There can be *large*, measurable differences between two different treatments, but that doesn't necessarily mean that these results are useful to us; likewise, there can also be *small* differences between two different treatments, and that doesn't necessarily mean that these results are not useful to us. For example, Balkin, Harris, Freeman, and Huntington (2014) evaluated how individuals struggle with forgiveness and found a statistically significant difference between clinical and nonclinical participants. In other words, individuals who were receiving counseling services were more likely to struggle with issues of forgiveness and conflict than individuals not receiving counseling services. So, while this finding was identified as significant and meaningful, from a clinical standpoint, such a finding is really not that surprising. Relationship difficulties are a common reason for people to seek counseling, so, of course, people in counseling reported more problems in this area. These concepts are explained with some additional examples and a summary in Figure 5.1.

Sometimes we use research and assessment tools to make important clinical decisions. Is a client so at risk for self-harm that she requires hospitalization? Is a client capable of adult living skills and self-care? Is this manifestation of depression potentially responsive to medication? Should this person be referred for neurological exam? These types of decisions are often based on some criteria, and when the client meets that standard we refer to this as *clinical significance* (Thompson, 2002). Sometimes these decisions are more objective, such as using a cutoff score on an assessment, and sometimes these decisions are based on a subjective feeling about the client. In other words, what one therapist determines as clinically significant may or may not be what another professional believes is most meaningful and important.

Practical significance refers to the magnitude of differences between groups or the degree of a relationship between variables. We often have guidelines to describe small, medium, and large differences or relationships. We also have a variety of effect sizes, and a lot of debate on the best effect size to use. There are also problems with respect to the method for calculating the size of the effect in meta-analyses, often relying on incomplete data or combining data from studies that used very different research designs (Hoyt & Del Re, 2018). And when we identify an effect as large, medium, or small, that determination is often based on a guideline that

	Statistical Significance	Practical Significance	Clinical Significance
Definition	A statement of probability expressed through a statistical test that an observable difference or relationship is occurring outside of the realm of chance. This is generally expressed as a percentage (i.e., p-value) of confidence in the result. Statistical significance represents confidence that the results would be replicated.	The magnitude of differences or the magnitude of a relationship that actually exists. This is expressed quantitatively as either a standard deviation or percentage of variance.	An evaluation of the importance of a finding. This evaluation is based on what the researcher knows of the context and circumstances to which the finding is applied.
Example 1: Integrative Care (Lenz et al., 2018).	Clients receiving collaborative, integrative care from their primary care physical and a licensed mental health professional demonstrated statistically significantly more progress than clients who received treatment outside of an integrated care setting.	The actual magnitude of the difference was .31 of 1 standard deviation unit—a rather small effect.	When placed in a medical context, this effect is actually twice that of many well-established medical protocols.
Example 2: Struggles with forgiveness and conflict between clinical vs. nonclinical participants (Balkin et al., 2014).	Clients receiving counseling demonstrated statistically significantly more distress with issues of forgiveness and conflict than participants not receiving counseling services.	There was a moderate difference between participants who received counseling services versus those who did not, accounting for 11.5% of the variance in the model.	The finding is not all that importantly as we would expect individuals in counseling to have more distress and issues of conflict than individuals who are not in counseling.

Figure 5.1. Statistical, practical, and clinical significance.

might be quite old (e.g., Cohen, 1988) that has very little relevance to our own research interests. Most often researchers rely on arbitrary guidelines to discuss the importance of a finding rather than making a case as to why the results are important.

Of course *statistical significance* is among the most popular and favored method of revealing the relevance of research. It implies numerical precision and exactness, such as .05 level of probability. It is a common belief that when researchers describe findings as "statistically significant," that is somehow a stupendous declaration that is both important and impressive.

"Integrative care" has become the rage in recent years, offering mental health services within the context of primary care. Increasingly, funding has been provided to train therapists to work more collaboratively in multidisciplinary teams since this increases the likelihood patients will be referred for mental health services. Lenz, Dell'Aquila, and Balkin (2018) studied the effects of integrated primary and behavioral healthcare (IPBH). They evaluated 260 articles and found 36 randomized, controlled studies detailing the effects of IPBH. With millions of dollars of funding going toward training clinicians in IPBH, you'd expect a pretty substantial effect. There was indeed a statistically significant effect, meaning that there was a likelihood of repeating these results with a similar sample and effect size, But what about the practical significance? The actual effect was .31 of one standard deviation unit—a rather insignificant, if not meaningless, endorsement of this program. To put this into perspective, if you were to graph this, the actual difference would be hardly discernible to the naked eye. Yet, placed into the proper context, maybe this is clinically significant. This effect size is more than double that of well-established medical recommendations for using aspirin to prevent a future heart attack (Lenz et al., 2018; Leucht, Helfer, Gartlehner, & Davis, 2015). Many physicians routinely make this recommendation when treating patients with heart disease. So, while the practical significance may seem negligible, sometimes any edge to that could increase the likelihood of success is important, especially in a discipline where success seems hard to track.

This is especially true in the use of suicide measures. Balkin and Juhnke (2018) noted standardized instruments used to evaluate client suicidality are extremely poor predictors, often identifying clients as suicidal when they are not (false positive) or misidentifying clients as not suicidal when they are (false negative). So, why use them at all? Because of the clinical significance. Although instruments like these sometimes provide data that are not very helpful, sometimes they *do* provide useful information. Suicidality is one of those issues where even a small amount of data is better than none at all. So, if we can increase the likelihood of identifying a suicidal client, even by only a slight degree, that could very well be clinically important.

Statistical significance is highly influenced and shaped by factors that artificially bolster the effect sizes. For example, when the sample size is large (10,000 vs. 100 participants), there is more likely to have statistically significant findings, even when the differences or relationships are relatively small (Balkin & Kleist, 2017; Balkin & Sheperis, 2011). After all, statistical significance is just a statement of probability—the likelihood that an event would happen again under similar circumstances. But as we discussed earlier, about half of the findings from experimental studies in psychology may not even be replicable, rendering any measurement of statistical significance moot.

Some noted academic journals have banned the reporting of null hypothesis statistical tests altogether due to the arbitrary nature of how such tests are reported (Valentine, Aloe, & Lau, 2015). For example, most statistical tests are deemed important when the result is statistically significant (i.e., reported as $p < .05$), but Rosnow and Rosenthal (1989) famously challenged this statement, arguing, "Surely, God loves .06 nearly as much as .05" (p. 1277). Once again, the relevance of statistical tests likely lies in how they are interpreted and used, not in the tests themselves.

EVIDENCE-BASED VERSUS EMPIRICALLY SUPPORTED TREATMENTS

Let's review the most basic premise of any medical or mental health treatment. If someone is diagnosed with throat cancer and seeks the care of an oncologist, there may indeed be some debate about the optimal dosage and length of radiation to ensure that the disease is completely eradicated. Regardless of the problem, everyone wants the most efficient, brief, and minimally invasive procedure that also minimizes cost, time, and side effects.

In the case of psychotherapy, there has been strong push during the past several decades to develop effective treatments in the most brief and effective manner to control the dosage at maximum effect. We have adopted terms to describe how we comply with this standard. Empirically supported treatments refer to specific techniques and strategies that reduce symptoms based on well-controlled studies. The term *evidence-based practice*, however, can apply to *any* evidence that may affect client outcomes, including anecdotal, intuitive, or experiential sources that are still subjected to some degree of methodological rigor. Once again, the use of flashy, influential words might feed into our motivational reasoning, but the rationale for why we do what we do is often based on flawed results that are not replicable. So, why do we put so much stock in these terms and the science behind what we do?

Mental health facilities, insurance companies, and funding agencies demand accountability and cost-effectiveness. But if we had to go to court and truly defend our choices and actions, the evidence may be considered suspect and insubstantial, at least by some reasonable standards. The reality is that most of the time in sessions we are flying by the seat of our pants, so to speak. The client says or does something, and we instantly react. If questioned afterward why we selected that particular response or intervention, we could surely make up some reason to justify the choice, but the truth of the matter is that we are usually not altogether certain. Given that we are often allotted just a few seconds to form some sort of interpretation and response, it isn't all that surprising that we appear to operate in impulsive, automatic ways even if these habits have been shaped over time by training, feedback, testing, and refinement.

The more experience we accumulate over time, presumably the better informed our choices and actions are. What might appear to be spontaneous, impulsive, or intuitive reactions are actually just cognitive shortcuts that abbreviate the time lag between action and reaction. Beginners tend to slow down this process, careful to proceed through each sequential step of perception, interpretation, meaning making, review of options, and selection of choice, followed by cautious implementation.

With all of these issues in mind, the validation of what we do is often evidence-based, although not necessarily empirically supported. In an era where there is such pressure to demonstrate our effectiveness, we often rely on research that falls short of doing what it is supposed to do—namely, clearly support that our services help people in ways that are significant and measurable. We work within a system that embraces Sir Francis Galton's sentiment that everything can be measured. While that is an extraordinary premise on which behavioral health is built, it is hard to prove. Suffice to say that evidence-based treatment is not necessarily empirically supported. Understanding this discrepancy is important in communicating accountability to stakeholders as well as clients. They want to know that we are using strategies that go beyond what you can get if you were just venting to a close friend or family member; that is, clients want assurance that they are seeking out professional counseling services for a good reason.

MAYBE THIS IS AS GOOD AS IT GETS

We live during a time when people are in a hurry to get things done. There is a demand for 5-minute yoga and 7-minute workout regimens. People take courses in speed reading and sign up for speed dating. There are mobile applications for 3-minute mindfulness exercises. Self-help books promise things like "10 minutes to become a better manager." Likewise, the therapy profession has been under pressure to reduce the amount of time it takes to reduce or cure presenting complaints, especially via specifically measurable outcomes. We recall one case in which a patient was admitted to a psychiatric unit complaining of more than a dozen poisonous snakes inside his stomach. He was discharged once the number of snakes reported by the patient was reduced by 80%. Besides, clients are impatient and want immediate results. This has never been more evident considering that the average adult attention span has diminished from 12 to 8 seconds in the last decade (McSpadden, 2015). For a comparison, even goldfish can focus for 9 seconds without losing interest, meaning that we are have now devolved to the level of a gnat.

Given the pressure we feel to make a difference as quickly as possible and to make instant decisions in the moment to respond to clients, it is clear that our actions may not be as scientifically informed and justified as we might prefer. Yet, we also view mental health as an area that can always be advanced to improve the services provided to clients. By linking what we do to similar methods used in the physical sciences and insisting on similar quality and rigor, we attempt to validate our profession and practice. Of course, there is a lot of error, but we might have to accept that. The scientific method does indeed fall short when explaining how and why psychotherapy works, but it has survived the test of time and is rooted in our own scientific tradition. This might be as good as it gets.

But if we tell the public that our methods lack validity, we will likely help no one (and put ourselves out of business). And the reality is that we are effective, and we do help people, just not for the reasons we think. Just like our treatment strategies and interventions, research is a tool, and it should not be used as a sole basis of decision-making but rather as another source of information to be considered in the collective, holistic care of clients. We cannot be certain about everything we do. We can't even agree on what qualifies as an expert or master therapist as it is certainly not related to knowledge or even experience (Hill, Spiegel, Hoffman, Kivlighan, & Gelso, 2017; Kottler & Carlson, 2015). We even have trouble at times agreeing on what constitutes a negative outcome or failure. We often focus on the benefits of treatment: For example, did the client show a reduction of symptoms or accomplished stated goals, such as maintaining sobriety or feeling less depressed or anxious. We are even encouraged to develop measurable objectives in a treatment plan. But these practices may not address what the client really wants from therapy. Even positive outcomes, like decreases in depressive symptoms, might not resonate with the client and may lead the client to feel therapy was not successful, despite the objectives measured. The whole idea of what constitutes success or failure is up for debate, as we explore in the next chapter.

CHAPTER 6

⌀⌀

When Therapy Fails

First, the good news.

Yes, indeed. Although you may have been prepared to skip this chapter altogether, reluctant to read even more about the discouraging, perhaps detrimental, effects of therapy, we view the discussion about failure to be one of the most significant, and even uplifting, aspects of our exploration.

Let's begin with an acknowledgment, once again, that therapy efforts rarely "fail" in the sense that our clients don't receive *anything* meaningful and helpful after their investment of time, effort, and resources. Sometimes clients don't get everything they want from the experience, but it is relatively rare that they leave worse off than when they came. The research exploring client satisfaction is quite dated, with more recent studies focusing on how to evaluate client satisfaction within the varied contexts in which it takes place (Timulak & Koenig, 2017). Regardless of the type of treatment, client symptomology, and therapist style, 9 out of 10 times people are generally pretty satisfied with their experiences and the outcomes (Lilienfeld, 2007).

With that said, we also wish to point out that it is precisely by acknowledging and studying the times when things don't go as planned or the results are not what was desired that we have most optimal opportunities to learn from our mistakes and improve our effectiveness in the future. In the words of Oscar Wilde, "experience is simply the name we give our mistakes."

It is for this reason that Jeffrey has devoted much of his life and career studying the phenomenon of failure in therapy, as well as how practitioners

Myths, Misconceptions, and Invalid Assumptions of Counseling and Psychotherapy. Jeffrey A. Kottler and Richard S. Balkin, Oxford University Press (2020). © Oxford University Press.
DOI: 10.1093/oso/9780190090692.001.0001

make sense of those experiences (Kottler, 1993, 2012, 2017, 2018, 2019; Kottler & Blau, 1989; Kottler & Carlson, 2002). This unabating interest (some would say obsession) stems directly from the dramatic discrepancy between the public pronouncements of (over)confidence that so often occurs in case conference, case reports, and supervision sessions compared to the internal feelings of doubt, uncertainty, and confusion that are sometimes far more accurate.

It just hasn't been very safe for us to talk about our mistakes and failures. Admitting errors or misjudgments leads to censures, shaming, and even litigation, demotion, or loss of one's job. There are, thus, very good reasons for denying, disowning, or at least ignoring failures whenever possible or whenever you can get away with it. The consequence of doing so, however, is a lost opportunity to significantly improve one's clinical skills.

NOW THE BAD NEWS

We've frequently assumed—and have been reassured accordingly—that therapy is a relatively benign treatment: Even if there are times that it doesn't appear to help very much, it doesn't seem to do much harm. We suppose the qualifier *relatively* might be accurate if we compare the talking cure to far more intrusive interventions such as brain surgery or the side effects of radiation or chemotherapy for cancer. But that doesn't mean that what we do is necessarily harmless during those times when clients don't improve. In fact, sometimes they do end up worse off after attending sessions even though this is actually rarely reported for the previously mentioned reasons (Bowie, McLeod, & McCleod, 2016; Cuijpers et al., 2018). However, keep in mind when negative effects do occur, it is most likely when clients perceive an absence of collaboration and care from the therapist (Bowie et al., 2016).

Cognitive-behavior therapy (CBT) is one of the most carefully standardized and manualized treatments in our repertoire. It has been consistently described as the "gold standard" of clinical intervention (David, Cristea, & Hofmann, 2018). Over 7,000 randomized controlled trials (RCTs) or protocols appear in library databases (e.g., PsycInfo, Academic Search) on CBT. Google it as a search term and you get 150,000,000 items listed. It is one of the options that is most easily trained and supervised to ensure compliance to the protocols. It has also been rigorously researched, and its outcomes, meticulously measured. In addition, the results have been impressive, with outcomes compared to those of many drug treatments, without the annoying side effects (Lenz, Haktanir, & Callender, 2017)—no tremors, blurred vision, dry mouth, hypertension, or constipation. It is for this reason that CBT has been described as revolutionizing mental health-care, "allowing psychologists to alchemize therapy from an art into a science" (Jarrett, 2018). David et al. (2018), in fact, argue that "no other form of psychotherapy has been shown to be systematically superior to CBT" (p. 1).

But that's not to say there aren't adverse effects for some people. And it is absolutely imperative that we get a better sense not only of when therapeutic interventions are most effective but also of when they fail or make things worse. This honest self-scrutiny is so much more difficult when one's overconfidence leads to blindness, a virtually universal phenomenon that plagues everyone in the human race. This overconfidence effect is what leads 84% of Frenchmen to believe they are better-than-average lovers, 93% of American students to assert they are better-than-average drivers, and three fourths of college faculty to claim they are in the top 25% of teaching performance. In other words, we are not very good at assessing our own competence accurately and are prone to overestimating our skills (Gilovich, Griffin, & Kahneman, 2002; Kahneman, 2011; Larrick, Burson, & Soll, 2007; McManus, Rakovshik, Kennerley, Fennell, & Westbrook, 2012).

In one study of experienced, passionate, and committed cognitive-behavior therapists, investigators found some disconcerting reports during their interviews (Schermuly-Haupt, Linden, & Rush, 2018). Participants were asked to discuss a recent case, usually presenting symptoms of depression, anxiety, or personality disorder and that had lasted at least 10 sessions. They were asked to consider whether their clients expressed difficulty with a number of negative side effects of their sessions, including increased anxiety, marked deterioration, increased family conflict, or the development of new irritating conditions. Even though the therapists had a vested interest in minimizing such deleterious results from their treatment, 43% of them admitted their clients experienced such undesirable and unanticipated outcomes. Many of these conditions were considered "severe" and lasted weeks, if not months afterwards. They included suicidal ideation, relationship breakups, social isolation and withdrawal, and feelings of shame and guilt.

The results of these interviews were actually surprising for the participants because prior to the conversations, three fourths of them said they could not think of a client who had experienced negative outcomes from their treatment. It was only after digging deeply into a case that they considered—and acknowledged—that not all was as it seemed. In many instances, the increased distress was explained, or justified, as an inevitable or necessary part of the treatment. Admittedly there have been times we have said things to clients like:

- "Sometimes you have to become worse before you become better."
- "These symptoms are your body's way of getting your attention to address these problems."
- "Increased pain and suffering are part of the process of confronting your dysfunctional behavior."
- "It's natural and normal that you would struggle more as you adapt to a new way of being."

Truthfully, we actually believe these reassurances and explanations (most of the time). But we also can't help but consider that perhaps denial and rationalizations may also be playing a role in the failure to recognize the times when things are not going as well as we'd like to believe.

It is important to note, first, that the researchers were careful to mention the results from their study might be skewed because they depended exclusively on the memories and recall of the therapists, admittedly unreliable and perhaps biased. Second, some of the clients were on psychoactive medications that could have also accounted for some of their side effects. Nevertheless, it is certainly interesting, and potentially useful, for us to consider more carefully the potential harm from even our most standardized and safest treatments. You may recall a time when you offered (what you believed was) the most gentle observation, a sensitively framed explanation, or carefully modulated interpretation and then noted with horror how the client became ballistically furious and stormed out of the room. You were left astounded by the unexpected response.

TRUTHFUL INFORMED CONSENT

We are supposed to thoroughly inform clients about the potentially deleterious effects, limitations, or unintended consequences of any treatment. Rereading the previous statement, we are struck by the noble intention and ethical reasons for providing more detailed informed consent but are also reminded of how this could undermine, if not, sabotage the kind of treatment that depends so much on optimistic expectations, faith, and unbridled trust in the process. After all, we are in the business of selling hope. Imagine, for instance, if we announced in the first session all the potential side effects the way drug companies are required to do in their advertisements. One diabetic medication, for example, lists the following possible consequences of their treatment: dehydration, urinary infection, yeast infection of the penis, kidney problems, low blood sugar, difficulty breathing, swelling of the lips, hives, vomiting, diarrhea, dizziness, confusion, vaginal odor, and, of course, death. Probably not the best way to inspire confidence.

If we were going to be completely honest and forthcoming with new clients, warning them about the possible impact of their decision to seek therapeutic assistance, it might sound something like the following:

> Although psychotherapy is generally considered a relatively safe treatment you should be warned that any of the following conditions could result from your experience.

- You will find that favored coping strategies that served you well in the past are no longer effective, requiring you to learn completely new and different ways of dealing with personal issues.
- Many of your relationships will become altered dramatically and may even abruptly end with family members or friends who feel threatened by the changes you undergo.
- You will likely become more self-absorbed, perhaps focusing excessively on yourself to the detriment of existing relationships, as well as increasing your (over)sensitivity to what is going on around you.
- You will sometimes leave sessions feeling extremely upset, agitated, bewildered, and perhaps feeling misunderstood.
- You will become increasingly aware of painful, shameful, uncomfortable experiences that you have worked hard to ignore or bury.
- You may seriously question whether it is indeed worth the time, money, energy, and commitment to dredge up all the painful stuff you would much prefer to leave alone.
- You will become far more psychologically sophisticated and informed. This will increase your awareness of all the stupid, annoying, dysfunctional, self-destructive behavior on the part of those you know most intimately.
- You will no longer feel satisfied with certain mediocre standards for yourself and others, now expecting, if not demanding, greater intimacy, openness, and honesty.
- You may develop dependency feelings toward your therapist, which could lead to disturbing, uncomfortable fantasies.

- You could become increasingly addicted to deeper levels of intimacy in all your relationships, leading to increased disappointment and frustration when others can't meet those needs.
- Whatever progress you make could come to a crashing end and relapse after you stop your sessions.

It really shouldn't be that surprising that therapy has (at least) temporary negative effects, given all the stuff we stir up during sessions. We ask clients to look at their most uncomfortable, distressing issues. We challenge and confront their current dysfunctional coping strategies. We urge them to look at the things that they have been successfully avoiding most of their lives. We require them to do things that they've never done before and likely do not do very well. It is inevitable that they will feel a certain frustration and discomfort with initial progress that does not meet their unrealistic expectations. Plus, there will be all kinds of confusing and uncomfortable feelings they will experience that are directed toward their therapist.

WHEN THERAPY ISN'T HELPFUL

If CBT, one of the most well-researched and refined methodologies, can occasionally result in casualties, there are other procedures that are potentially far more harmful at times. Consider how during previous eras supposedly well-regarded treatments for emotional suffering produced all kinds of collateral suffering such as lobotomies, shock treatments, bloodletting, exorcism, strait jackets, and ice baths, to mention a few. It leads one to wonder what we might be doing these days that will someday be discredited as fraudulent or dangerous.

In a provocative article several years ago, Barlow (2010) brought attention to the possible side effects of therapy, especially therapeutic practices that force compliance to a method that may not be consistent with what people can handle. He mentioned exposure therapies as one especially disruptive set of interventions since a number of clients with agoraphobia or panic disorder ended up far worse as a result. But Barlow saved some of his most pointed blame for critical incident stress debriefing (CISD).

As you may recall CISD used to be all the rage, requiring firefighters, law enforcement officers, and emergency personnel to undergo mandatory group sharing of their reactions to disturbing, traumatic, or terrifying situations that they survived. It seemed to make logical sense that such professionals should be given the opportunity to talk about their lingering symptoms and fears, as well as reaping the benefits of a structured group therapy experience. Certainly some people are good candidates for such a program, especially those who are ready to talk about negative feelings, but in certain professions, such behavior is neither normative nor even appropriate given the prevailing culture.

CISD, along with other trauma therapies, are likely not as helpful as we might believe. The problems extend beyond the harmful effects of therapy and encompass what is viewed as effective. Reflecting back to the previous chapter on the gold standard of research, the RCT, most studies using RCT focus on effects in which the interventions are brief. Shedler (2017) noted that RCTs utilize brief interventions because, otherwise, there would not be a way to conduct the research. Most RCTs in psychology are eight sessions or less. However, it takes 40 sessions for about 75% of clients to demonstrate meaningful progress in therapy. That's about a year of therapy! So, even though RCTs may demonstrate progress, it is often brief and lacks documentation demonstrating long-term benefits.

Ultimately, there is a lot of research on therapies that take advantage of RCTs, thereby purporting to be evidence-based, empirically supported, and efficacious but are actually ineffective or even harmful. Such potentially harmful therapies have been extensively documented (Cummings & O'Donohue, 2008; Lilienfeld, 2007; Norcross, Koocher, & Garofalo, 2006; Thomason, 2010) and include many commonly used strategies:

- Attachment therapies (e.g., rebirthing)
- Eye movement desensitization and reprocessing
- Treatment for dissociative identity disorder
- Crisis counseling
- Mindfulness interventions
- Meditation
- Critical incident stress debriefing
- Scared Straight interventions
- Boot camp interventions for conduct disorder
- Energy or thought field therapies
- Jungian dream work

Researchers have done a fairly good job operationalizing treatment progress and outcomes, but the documentation of treatment failure remains fairly opaque due, in part, to the ambiguity of what constitutes a treatment failure. For example, treatment failure could easily be operationalized as a continuing of worsening of current symptoms. But then how do we account for the decrease in current symptoms but the appearance of *new* disruptive symptoms?

Myron first sought help because of problems in his marriage. He had been described by his wife as too passive, withdrawn, and disengaged, although he preferred to think of himself as easy-going. Myron was a likeable guy, after all, and was happy deferring to others when they appeared to have strong preferences—and his wife tended to be rather controlling and highly opinionated at times.

After only a few sessions devoted to learning increased assertive behavior, there was clear, specific, and measurable improvement according to the evaluation criteria. Myron was even more commanding and definitive in sessions after a while, arguing with the therapist over disagreements. This was clearly a success case, at least in terms of transforming the initial symptoms into supposedly more functional behavior.

Alas, Myron didn't necessarily feel much better after his sessions ended—even though the therapist seemed pretty pleased with the result. Yes, he could now more readily stand up for himself, both at home and at work, but this created an assortment of new and different problems for him. It turns out his wife was not at all happy with the new Myron whom she now found to be unreasonably argumentative at times. Even more concerning, Myron didn't much like himself either. Yes, he now had some new skills that were the result of treating the initial complaints, but the unintended consequence of these changes is that he felt increasingly anxious and out of sorts. He was reluctant to return to the therapist so instead consulted with a physician who prescribed antidepressants to treat his new symptoms.

BLIND TO OUR FAILURES

It turns out that therapists are generally not very diligent or proficient at acknowledging when sessions aren't going according to the preferred plan. And when the problems are eventually recognized, clinicians often don't directly address the issues (Bowie, McLeod, & McLeod, 2016). Sometimes this is the result of clients unduly blaming themselves for not making sufficient progress; they are reluctant to provide accurate feedback about their dissatisfaction.

Rather than an all-or-nothing phenomenon, there is actually a continuum of bad therapy that is sometimes difficult to assess. If a client doesn't return after a single session, is that a treatment failure or, rather, a success because perhaps the client already got what was needed (Hoyt, et al., 2018; Talmon, 1990)?

Surprisingly, there are all kinds of different conceptions of what constitutes a failure in therapy. Although negative outcomes are usually considered "official" by the therapist's assessment, many would agree that it is actually the *client's* judgment that matters the most. Yet the criteria for such a determination can include a number of different variables such as the perceived strength of the relational alliance, the accuracy and validity of the therapist's assumptions, and/or the personal characteristics of either the client (motivation, resistance, faith) or the therapist (rigidity, confidence, narcissism) (Kottler & Carlson, 2002).

The assessment of progress becomes muddled even further when there is a difference of opinion between the participants.

THERAPIST: "It seems like that you've had a breakthrough in a way, now that you realize what you've been doing that has been most problematic."
CLIENT: "I wouldn't put it that way at all."
THERAPIST: "No?"
CLIENT: "If anything, I feel worse."
THERAPIST: "As we've discussed, it's normal that you're going to feel uncomfortable and anxious when letting go of what's familiar and trying something new."
CLIENT: "But what I'm saying is that it's really not working for me."
THERAPIST: "You mean not working quite *yet.*"
CLIENT: "No, I mean I don't really like where this is going at all."
THERAPIST: "So, you'd like us to move in a different direction altogether?"

In this brief interaction it's clear that the therapist misinterpreted what the client was saying after several consecutive responses, until such time that she realized that she had to let go of where she was pushing him and instead try something else. In one sense she made some strategic mistakes, exacerbated by her stubbornness to push even harder when the client was providing feedback that he didn't care for what was happening or at least the pace of the progress. And yet, finally, the therapist realized it was time to let go, to accept that this approach wasn't appropriate, or that perhaps the timing wasn't optimal.

Is this a therapy failure just because the therapist made some mistakes in timing and execution? Assuredly no. Because they had a good relationship, one that felt safe enough for the client to disagree and redirect the focus. They would now be able to salvage the misunderstanding and simply try something else. As long as they keep experimenting and trying different things, there is just a learning process for both of them. A true failure would occur only after one or both of them gave up in frustration or disappointment.

Making mistakes really isn't the problem that leads to an ultimate treatment failure. Clients are remarkably forgiving of remarks that fall flat, jokes that aren't funny, interpretations that miss the mark, strategies that don't help, recommendations that don't work out—as long as we have established a relationship that is trustworthy, respectful, and strong (Kottler & Balkin, 2017; Timulak & Keough, 2017). They will be patient with us and allow us our occasional indulgences, assuming they sense we have their best interests in mind and that we are doing our absolute best to help them.

POSSIBLE CAUSES OF FAILURE

If it isn't a mistake, or even a few of them, that ultimately and inevitably lead to failures, what then are the most common identifiable causes? We've grouped them according to four main themes, beginning with the most frequent source that is actually related to what clients bring to the sessions. If they are poorly motivated ("My mother sent me") or have wildly unrealistic expectations ("It's your job to fix me"), then it's likely the outcome will be less than optimal. If clients present entrenched, complex, intractable symptoms that are part of some organic condition, psychotic process, or impulse or addictive disorder, then the prognoses also isn't that great. If they have some florid personality disturbance, poor capacity for insight, or some hidden or disguised reason to sabotage the treatment, obviously things will be much more challenging in sessions. So despite the belief that everything depends on us, what we do and say, the most important determinant of outcome very much depends on the client (Duncan, 2014; Lambert, 2013).

However. Yes, of course, there is a qualifier because we don't mean to leave you hanging. The second best predictor of failure is connected to what the therapist brings or doesn't bring to the encounter. If clinicians also have unrealistic goals for a case, related to being a "savior" with the power to fix all problems, then disappointment is also highly likely. Sure, it is important to be hopeful, confident, and optimistic, but within realistic parameters. Sometimes we move too quickly or slowly, at a pace that may be convenient or comfortable for us but not necessarily suitable for the client's readiness.

There are times when we do make mistakes in the timing or execution of an intervention, even catastrophic ones that drive the client away and prematurely end the treatment. Just think about all the clients who never returned after a few sessions and why that might be the case; it wasn't always because they were cured. No matter how well trained, experienced, and prepared we might be, we will misdiagnose certain conditions, bungle interventions, or lose clients because of what is perceived as an insensitive or hurtful remark. This could be a single incident but is often the consequence of some unresolved countertransference issue.

There are famous examples in history of negligent inattention to details and opportunities that resulted in disaster. The video rental company Blockbuster was once offered the chance to buy Netflix for next to nothing and declined. In the 15th century, the Byzantines built an impregnable fortress but left one of their gates open for the invading Turks. Likewise the Great Wall of China stands 20 feet tall and is 16 feet thick and 4,000 miles long to keep out the invading Mongols, but the invaders just bribed a guard to open a gate for them.

There are also interactive effects that capture dysfunctional dynamics between and within the relationship. Sometimes clients and therapists are incompatible because of vast differences in style, values, personality, or limitations of the treatment approach. We often say that we know we can't help everyone, but deep down inside we might really believe that it is possible.

Finally, there are variables completely unrelated to the client, therapist, relationship, or approach and are influenced by external factors that are *way* outside of our control. If the client operates in a toxic family structure, a sabotaging peer group, or an environment that undermines the therapeutic growth, then progress can be stalled. If there are financial or other issues that are going on behind the scenes, that can also exert negative effects. This is the explanation of failure that we like the most because it lets us off the hook for responsibility. After all, there's only so much we can do when factors outside our control exert their sabotaging influences.

ACKNOWLEDGING MISTAKES AND EMBRACING FAILURE

Writer Truman Capote's early life was described as a nightmare. His mother was an alcoholic, and his father, mostly absent. He was a mediocre student and eventually followed in his mother's path as an addict. Yet he once remarked that "failure was the condiment that gives success its flavor." Capote believed that the trials and tribulations of his life, the disappointments and setbacks, were valuable experiences that allowed him to better develop his craft into a singular clear vision.

Maybe it's not so much a good idea to embrace or celebrate failure as much as to acknowledge negative outcomes as useful learning opportunities, as valuable feedback that allows us to make needed adjustments. There are, after all, many gifts that failure can offer us *if* we incorporate the lessons in such a way that they encourage greater flexibility. Viewed in this way, mistakes or failures are data that we take to heart and decode in such a way that we can figure out alternatives that may be more helpful. In that regard, they often promote deep reflection and self-scrutiny about what exactly went wrong and why. Although we will never find definitive answers to those questions, the very process of considering what happened and how things went awry encourages us to become more flexible. This means letting go of what is familiar, comfortable, and has worked consistently in the past and, instead, to experiment with something novel and far more creative.

In most aspects of life, failure stimulates change. When something doesn't work, when we've tried an approach several times with the same disappointing results, we have little reasonable choice but to abandon that strategy in favor of another alternative. The therapist presses his client to revisit a past trauma, but every attempt to do so ends up in dramatic decompensation. The client begins sobbing, losing control and all hope. The rest of the session involves reassembling her before she walks back into the world.

After three successive attempts to address the unresolved trauma that the therapist really does believe is at the heart of the client's problems, he finally jettisons that idea completely. He had some assistance to do so when the client informed him she would not return if he tried pushing her in that direction again. Even though the therapist might be correct in his assumptions about what is going on, it still doesn't make much difference if the client isn't on board. And it's been pretty clear after three tries that she is not nearly ready for this.

At this point, the therapist started wondering why it took him so long to catch on to his mistakes and correct them. He admits he had been stubborn in assuming that because digging into past traumas had worked for many other clients, it surely would be helpful for this one as well. And frankly, after abandoning this approach, he didn't have a clear idea of what to try next. It was only after confessing this to the client that together they were able to collaborate and discuss some viable alternatives.

In many of its manifestations, when processed critically, honestly, and reflectively, failure often leads to change and potential growth. The classic example is the case of Steve Jobs who suffered a series of disastrous failures with his Lisa Project and NeXT Computers and was unceremoniously fired from Apple by his own board of directors when sales plummeted. But he learned from his mistakes by spending time considering the ways his own rigidity, arrogance, and overconfidence led to his fall. He accepted (partial) responsibility for his errors in judgment, spent his years in exile at Pixar learning about a completely different corporate culture that nurtured creativity and then returned to Apple to save the company.

Perhaps the trajectory of Abraham Lincoln's failed career is even more impressive in its dismal record. After losing his first election for the Illinois state legislature, followed by a crushed love life and nervous breakdown, he proceeded to lose a remarkable number of elections for the U.S. House of Representatives (twice) and the Senate (twice). The guy just wouldn't quit! We suppose we could make the case that he was a slow learner, but eventually he caught on to the formula that finally got him elected to higher office. Even more important, through his disappointments and defeats, he eventually developed a unique, confident vision for himself as a leader.

Once again, the disappointing initial outcomes did not lead to ultimate failure in politics, business, or therapy, but rather the decision to pay close attention to the useful information provided regarding what is not working very well brought about ultimate success. Just as with Jobs or Lincoln, initial setbacks can increase one's resolve and foster even greater experimentation innovation. Much depends on how those experiences with failure are processed internally to allow the person to pivot in other directions that may produce quite different results.

PROCESSING FAILURES

We offer several ways that therapists can benefit from close scrutiny of their mistakes and even qualified failures by reviewing a series of reflective questions (Kottler, 2012). This works best when you first become aware there is some intractable difficulty that doesn't seem to be improving in the sessions.

What Are the Signs That Therapy Isn't (or Wasn't) Working?

This brings to mind the importance of continuously monitoring and assessing progress and checking the relative satisfaction of clients during every facet of the process. We've mentioned previously how some researchers like Scott Miller, Barry Duncan, and others advocate doing this through systematic questionnaires after each meeting. We find that approach somewhat formal and artificial for our tastes, and we prefer simply to ask on a regular basis how things are going and what could be done to make the experience more fruitful.

Questions can be framed using plural pronouns to emphasize shared responsibility for outcomes:

"What are *we* doing together that is less helpful than you would prefer?"
"What do you wish *we* would do more often that would be more helpful to you?

The main idea is that we want continuous, ongoing, direct feedback from clients as to what is working best for them, at least as they report their experiences. Of course, clients don't necessarily know what is best for them, nor are their stated preferences always in their own best interests.

Nevertheless, it is imperative we have a sense of which interventions have been most and least effective. It helps to step back and take a systematic inventory of what has been happening thus far. Specifically this means tracking carefully *exactly* what we've tried that has consistently been helpful, as well as what has fallen flat. This may seem rather obvious, but, as mentioned, we are often blind to our mistakes; otherwise, we wouldn't repeat them.

Related to this honest assessment, it's important to identify the turning point when things started slipping downward or out of control. At what point did you first notice that things were not proceeding as they should, or as you hoped? What were some earlier signs of this that you missed?

What Secondary Gains Is the Client "Celebrating" as a Result of the Failure Thus Far?

We are referring to the benefits that clients "enjoy" as a result of remaining stuck or even sabotaging their progress in sessions. When they consider the consequences of improving or the amount of work actually required, it may seem far preferable just to pretend to want to change without actually having to do so. Change for them will mean taking greater responsibility for their lives, surrendering excuses for why they aren't getting what they say they want most, and cease blaming others for their misery.

This means that until such time that we can help clients to acknowledge their payoffs and realize that any benefits from avoiding change have awful side effects, they will continue to undermine the work done. One favored means of altering this predicament occurs when we can bring those secondary gains out of the shadows so they must own them. It's much harder to get away with such defenses once they are clearly aware of them. Once someone realizes that the guilt she is tenaciously holding onto actually enables her to continue engaging in the self-defeating behavior, it no longer works quite as well.

How Has the Problem Been Defined in a Way That It Cannot Be Resolved?

It has always been a popular strategy within our profession to adjust goals when efforts are less than desireable. When the outcome doesn't match expectations, we just alter the objectives and redefine what constitutes a success. "Okay, then," the therapist might suggest, "since it seems impractical at this time for you to think about getting out of the relationship for all the reasons you mentioned, how about instead we look at how you can better meet a few of your most important needs within the relationship, at least until such time as you feel more prepared to make more definitive plans?"

Various therapeutic approaches have different names for this more flexible conceptualization of problems, such as "reframing," "looking for exceptions," or "alternative outcomes." Regardless of the term preferred, we sometimes end up in trouble when we accept the client's definition of the problem or when we have been far too ambitious or unrealistic in planning treatment goals. That signals that it's time to consider other ways of looking at what might be a successful outcome if measured in a different way.

"Yes, it's true," the therapist agrees once again with the client, "although you said you were going to announce to your husband that the marriage is over and you want a divorce, instead you decided that you're not ready for that dramatic step yet for all kinds of good reasons. So, as an alternative, it would seem that it's better for now that you try to establish a more open line of communication with him. That means that you didn't so much fail to follow through on what you said you wanted to as to adjust your goals for the present time. That seems perfectly reasonable."

Voila! A success rather than a failure.

How Have I Been Attempting to Disown Responsibility for What Is Going On?

The question of claiming responsibility is a tough one, especially since we are often inclined to blame the client when things aren't working out very well. We call it resistance, defensiveness, lack of motivation, transference, or whatever other excuses we can make to imply that lack of progress is not our fault.

And yet, there is something empowering that happens when we do acknowledge our own role in the impasse or conflict. We tell couples all the time that relational problems are *always* an interactive effect, so why would that be any different with respect to what happens in therapy? Once we are willing and able to identify what we have been doing or not doing that is making things worse, we are in a far better position to change the pattern. But that can only happen if we are willing and able to see ourselves more clearly.

Here are some examples from each of us when we tend to characteristically have difficulties in therapy, supervision, or teaching.

> *Jeffrey*: My experience and overconfidence sometimes get in the way. I sometimes fail to see each client as a totally unique individual, with his or her own special set of circumstances, issues, background, and life experiences. I make assumptions based on my initial assessment and diagnostic impression, which also leads me to overgeneralize or operate on autopilot: "Oh yeah, it's another one of *those* types of cases again."
>
> Then there's my impatience, my need for clients to move at my preferred pace. I get triggered when clients backslide or move too slowly, feeling like it is a reflection of my own inadequacy, ignorance, or incompetence. As such, I push clients too hard, too fast.
>
> *Rick*: My formative development as a clinician came from working 7 years in acute care psychiatric hospitalization. Clients generally stayed 2 weeks, and then they were discharged, usually to a lesser level care in outpatient treatment. So, therapy from my perspective was a lot like surgery—brief and intense but with a lot of focus on jump-starting the healing process. When working outside of this setting, sometimes I needed to slow down and facilitate a gentler approach. In the hospital, a client may get angry, but I would still see them the next day: They couldn't escape me. Yet in other settings, if I pushed clients at the same, hurried pace, they would likely not return.

What Have I Been Expecting That Is Unrealistic or Beyond the Person's Ability?

Not only do clients bring wildly unrealistic expectations to therapy, but we also have ambitions that are out of line with reality. Despite protestations to the contrary, sometimes we do believe we can "save" people or at least "cure" them. Sometimes our enthusiasm, optimism, and deep caring leads us to promise things that we can't deliver. Sometimes we underestimate or misdiagnose the nature of the client's difficulties, finding that after several sessions we just scratched the surface of what was really going on.

Rule number 1 when helping someone with almost anything: Don't ask them to do something that they are yet ready or willing to do. That is a recipe for disappointment.

One intern described a case in supervision in which her client, a guy in his 30s who was extremely co-dependent on his mother. He lived at home, and his mother controlled every aspect of his life. She even called to make his appointments.

The intern was concerned about breaking this pattern that kept the man stuck. "Don't you think I should tell him that I won't schedule any more sessions with him until he calls to make his own appointment?" she asked, quite reasonably.

"That's a great idea," the supervisor replied. "It would indeed help him to take more responsibility for his life and get him into take more responsibility for the sessions."

The intern nodded her head enthusiastically, pleased with her idea and even more so that her supervisor approved.

"Unfortunately," the supervisor continued, "you can ask him to do that, but it's been pretty clear that he likely won't comply. Several times previously you've asked him to confirm his prior appointments, and he hasn't managed to do so, always ready with excuses. So even though this is a sound idea you are probably asking him to do something that he isn't able, or ready, to do quite yet. This is a setup for failure."

The supervisor then negotiated with the intern an intermediate, more realistic and attainable objective, one that she was absolutely certain that the client could accomplish.

Of course, we must balance unbridled optimism with the power of faith: Sometimes people *are* able to do remarkable things that we, and they, thought were beyond them.

Who Has an Interest in Sabotaging the Treatment?

We don't mean to offer more excuses, but there are truly limits to what we can do an hour each week compared to everything else that happens in a client's life. No matter how skilled or forceful we might be during a session, once the client walks out the door we no longer have any control over their actions. We can assign (or negotiate) homework assignments, solicit promises regarding forbidden activities, involve family members in the process, schedule follow-up texts or calls—heck, we could even hire a detective to follow the person around in daily life, and that *still* wouldn't prevent lapses or continued dysfunction.

When clients begin therapy, it is often threatening to significant others in their world. It likely means the changes this person will undergo requires adjustments on behalf of family and friends. It makes people uncomfortable when one person in the group stops drinking, drugging, overeating, or engaging in reckless behavior when they would prefer to continue such actions. It is much easier to undermine the outlier, the rebel, the one among them who is determined to change, rather than having to invest the hard work themselves.

It's, therefore, important that even if we don't involve others directly in the treatment, we at least deal with underlying systemic forces that are operating. Otherwise, whatever progress that is made during sessions quickly unravels once the client walks out the door.

What in *Me* Is Getting in the Way of Being More Effective?

Whether you prefer to call this countertransference, unresolved personal issues, or simply blind spots, there is little doubt that we are sometimes triggered by what clients bring to sessions or even by their own characteristics or behavior. For those still participating in weekly supervision, hopefully these issues are identified and worked through or at least carefully monitored.

Even with the most careful self-scrutiny and supervision, it is still inevitable that certain personal qualities, habits, and characteristics of our style will compromise our ability to help everyone in our care. This is one of those statements we hear or read that is universally acknowledged. We've heard ourselves say that exact same thing to beginners hundreds of times. That doesn't mean, however, we actually always believe it. Sometimes we "forget," imagine ourselves as infallible, or at least inflate our sense of power.

These questions help us to confront the limits of what we can do, given that therapy is a collaborative enterprise in which we have far less control than we'd prefer to admit. It is precisely during the supposed failures that we are forced, or at least provided an opportunity, to see these disappointments as gifts to improve our performance in the future. This is our growth edge. Our clients become our most profound teachers, showing us pathways that we'd never considered previously.

CHAPTER 7

✧

How We *Really* Learn to Do Therapy

In the preceding chapter we ended our discussion by mentioning one of the most neglected aspects of professional development: how our clients become our greatest teachers. It happens to be one of the most pervasive beliefs of our profession that the best way to learn to do therapy is to read books like this, attend lectures and seminars, follow the curriculum as dictated by accreditation standards, write papers and take tests, study for licensing exams, accumulate continuing education through workshops and online programs, and participate in supervision. Certainly these training experiences provide an important foundation by teaching the basic concepts and skills. The myth, however, is that this is truly what creates and sustains an excellent practitioner.

WHAT YOU NEVER LEARNED IN GRADUATE SCHOOL

Students in any professional training program often complain they are relatively unprepared for the realities of practice. Law students learn almost nothing directly related to actually working as a lawyer. Beginners in almost every field feel like they may very well have learned the theory and basic concepts of their discipline but not how to navigate practical challenges. Likewise, one of the most consistent grievances of psychotherapy students is that they say they weren't adequately prepared to run a private practice, operate a business, or deal with the usual political squabbles that operate in agencies or organizations. Faculty usually plead guilty to these charges,

Myths, Misconceptions, and Invalid Assumptions of Counseling and Psychotherapy. Jeffrey A. Kottler and Richard S. Balkin, Oxford University Press (2020). © Oxford University Press.
DOI: 10.1093/oso/9780190090692.001.0001

claiming it is not really their jobs to teach beginners these sorts of things but rather to help them to develop a professional identity.

It turns out there are all kinds of important things we never learned in graduate school, which especially neglect certain realities that have become perpetuated as myths guaranteed to disappoint us (Kottler, 2015b, 2018a). We would have received the distinct impression from training programs that when faced with a problem, clinical challenge, or decision point, there are only four choices like on a multiple choice exam—and only one correct answer. Only later do we eventually debunk this myth since, in fact, there are often limitless choices and perhaps none (or all) of them are reasonable options.

There are other myths that we are similarly forced to confront. The answers we are most desperate to find are usually not found in books (or online). We take ourselves way too seriously. You will never, ever feel good enough. Despite your education, license, and extensive experience, your family will still not take you seriously. Who you are is as important as what you do. And, as mentioned previously, our failures teach us as much, if not more, than our successes.

The holes in our education were not all bad news since there have also been some pleasant surprises. Who knew how much fun it would be to have a window into people's most private lives, secrets, and intimate confessions? We had little idea of the power and sense of control we'd feel understanding why people behave the ways they do. We may have anticipated a degree of satisfaction making a difference in people's lives but perhaps could not have predicted how this would promote growth in our own personal development. We later learned how challenging, and yet stimulating, it is to have our personal issues triggered by what our clients bring to sessions. Then there are the incredibly captivating and poignant stories that clients share with us. We had no idea what an honor it would become to join people on their journeys during times when they were most desperate. The pure intensity and drama of the interactions that occur in sessions may also have been a bit of a surprise. Eventually we discovered the greatest benefit of all—that being a therapist teaches us to be far more contemplative, analytic, and reflective in all the aspects of our lives. This could lead to the belief, or rather myth, that we really do understand our clients and can identify the definitive causes of their troubles.

THE MYTH OF UNDERSTANDING OUR CLIENTS

"I'm depressed," the client begins his story. "I've been that way for as long as I can remember."

There are certain questions that immediately come to mind, helping us to narrow the possibilities of an accurate diagnosis, followed by the corresponding suggested treatment protocol. "When did you first become aware that you were depressed? What does depression mean to you? How often and when do you feel this way? What are the specific sensations and symptoms that you are experiencing? Which medications are you taking? How are you sleeping? What about your appetite? Sexual interest? What physical ailments or medical conditions have bothered you? Who else in your family has been depressed? When is a time when you *aren't* depressed? How do your loved ones respond to you when you feel the worst? What have you tried that seems to make you feel better? What have you tried repeatedly that has failed to be helpful at all?" And so on. The whole idea of this line of questioning is that, in the end, we will presumably understand the particular type of depression (if that's what it really is), as well as its origin.

This is the sort of speculative inquiry that is routinely discussed in supervision and case conferences. After having conducted a 50- (or 90-) minute intake interview, we are often allotted a few minutes to describe and capsulize the case, followed by a diagnosis and treatment plan. The supervisor, or others in attendance, will then offer their own critical comments, perhaps challenging the case formulation and arguing about what is "really" going on. This has always struck us as living in a sort of fantasy world in which we all pretend like there is a "truth" attached to each case, one that we can discover.

"I notice that you didn't mention the obvious maternal attachment breach that was evident in the client's history," one supervisor points out during the discussion. "After all, he . . ."

"What about the embedded micro-aggressions that have been metabolized throughout his childhood?" another supervisor argues. "This is another instance in which cultural scripts have obviously . . ."

"Obviously?" a third participant interjects. "Not so obvious to me. I'm far more concerned about the pervasive systemic dysfunction within the family. The florid co-dependency issues must be addressed before going deeper into the secondary causes of the depression."

"Secondary causes?" the intern repeats, furiously writing down all the contradictory input. "What secondary causes? I mean, what *are* secondary causes?"

Everyone turns in surprise at this question. "Why, of course, these must be addressed before the tertiary factors come into play."

All around the table others are shaking their heads in frustration or perhaps disagreement. It's hard to tell because everyone seems to have a different opinion. And each of them seems to be utterly confident and self-assured in their pronouncements.

We've usually found debates and analyses like this to be interesting, if not stimulating in some ways. Yet we've also been puzzled how even the most expert and experienced figures in the room speak with such authority about someone they've not only never met but have heard only a very limited history and a summary description of. How do any of them know *that* is what is really going on? Do they have access to some sort of brain scans, blood tests, spinal fluid, or genetic markers that reveal the underlying disorder? Did they administer a half dozen psychometric instruments that have clearly demonstrated validity to reveal significant data? Did they secretly interview all the significant others in the client's world to collect additional information?

Regardless of the formulation that is initially created after the first few sessions, we rarely have found it to be completely accurate and comprehensive. More often than not, the first impression turned out to be quite truncated and imperfect. Of course, the client presented the story in such a way to minimize certain features. He left out things that were viewed as irrelevant or perhaps didn't give an optimal impression. In some cases, he exaggerated quite a bit, ignored certain details, and "forgot" to include some significant context. Okay, in a few instances he sort of lied a little bit. After all, be barely knows this person who wants all the lurid secrets of his life.

Back to our original question. After spending such limited time with someone we just met; someone who is, almost by definition, a little confused, disturbed, and overwhelmed; someone whose recollections are distorted, perhaps fragmented by trauma or anxiety; and someone who wants more than anything for us to like him and see him in the best possible light, how on earth are we supposed to know and understand what's really going on?

THE MYTH OF CAUSE AND EFFECTS

One thing for sure: We are going to read and understand our clients a lot better in the future, thanks to advances in technology. John and Julie Gottman (2018) have been doing research for years, hooking couples up to equipment that reads their micro-expressions and physiological responses to predict their prognosis, as well as to lower the emotional threshold in sessions. People are choosing to wear mobile devices, implants, or watches that reveal the most subtle changes in respiration, moods, and physiological functioning.

Neuroscientists and technology companies have been developing new ways to measure emotional responses through pupil dilation, infrared thermal images, speech patterns, voice spectral colorations and modulations, and carbon dioxide in breath exhalations, all of which reveal underlying, hidden, unconscious, innermost emotional states like fear, aggression, attraction, and joy (e.g., Armory & Vuilleumier, 2013; Mauss & Robonson, 2009). While there are legitimate fears that privacy will be compromised once our chemical signatures are so easily revealed, this will also make us more accurate empaths, better able to recognize what clients are actually feeling, even when they don't know themselves or can't put the sensations into words. Nevertheless, we still insist this will rarely be sufficient to arrive at a definitive singular cause for any emotional disorder.

We frequently speak in the language of causality. Of course, very rarely does mental health research demonstrate both a consistent time sequence and a control for extraneous variables to indicate causal relationship (Balkin & Kleist, 2018). Yet, that does not keep us from saying things like, "Your early trauma caused many of the problems you have today," or "Your reliance on comfort foods is the main self-soothing defense to protect you from rejection," or "If you stopped badgering your daughter all the time, she wouldn't act out as much." Some of these hypotheses may indeed have some influence or impact, but they are hardly the only factors at play.

Epidemiologists consider several criteria to determine *possible* causality with respect to conditions or diseases. The strength and consistency of the association between supposed cause and effect are important. If every single time ($n = 14+$), a client arrives late to a session, it was preceded by an argument at home, this may lead one to conclude there *may* be a correlation. If within a group session everyone seems to get along and support one another quite well, unless one particular participant makes an appearance, in which case arguments and conflicts take over, this might lead us to conclude there *might* be a connection. Notice, that we were careful to use the words *might* and *may* in these assumptions.

It's also important to consider some specific result, whether an infection or behavior change, that supposedly occurred as a result of the alleged cause, one that definitely preceded the outcome. Epidemiologists also love to test the gradient of the variable; that is, the greater the exposure, the larger the effect. The relationship has to be considered plausible within existing knowledge: It has to make sense within the parameters of scientific investigation. Ideally, this relationship can be replicated under experimental conditions. Saying that smoking causes cancer is an example of a phenomenon that meets these conditions.

We see this phenomenon in therapy too, such as when working with clients who are struggling with issues of conflict and forgiveness. The likelihood of reconciling with someone who has caused pain or harm in some way is linked to the extent to which an offender has expressed remorse and changed behavior. In other words, the most influential factor in deciding whether someone reconciles is external to what is going on in therapy and really outside the control of both the client and the therapist (Balkin, Perepiczka, Sowell, Cumi, & Gnilka, 2016).

As we've pointed out previously, the majority of social science research is correlational—that is, the examination of relationships between two or more variables. This has been an issue of contention in the field, but these critiques might be misguided. When we examine how phenomena relate and interact with each other, we do gain a deeper understanding of the underlying process.

It is human nature to make quick inferences based on limited data. Such intuitive or instantaneous decisions contribute to the likelihood that we would survive long enough to pass on our genetic material to our offspring. Our ancestors who hesitated too long to process information were usually clubbed or speared to death or devoured by a predator. We are thus hardwired to make rapid assessments of situations and then act on them. There is no time for doubt or recriminations.

Science, on the other hand, is based on a degree of uncertainty, especially with complex phenomena. As we discussed in the previous chapter, everything is based on hypothesis testing that is designed to test statistically significant differences between variables. There are confidence levels that only go as far as 99%, and the custom is to stick with the more achievable 95%. In other words, we are never absolutely certain about anything. We never accept a "truth" but just reject the null hypothesis.

LIFE IS NOT A MULTIPLE CHOICE EXAM, WITH ONLY FOUR CHOICES, ONE OF WHICH IS CORRECT

1. A client comes to see you complaining of symptoms of sleep disruption, fatigue, lethargy, appetite loss, anxiety, social withdrawal, difficulty concentrating, and incessant worrying. The correct diagnosis of this condition is
   a. generalized anxiety disorder.
   b. posttraumatic stress disorder.
   c. bipolar disorder.
   d. thyroid dysfunction.

2. The best choice of an intervention to address severe obsessive compulsive disorder is
   a. exposure and prevention therapy.
   b. cognitive therapy.
   c. a serotonin reuptake inhibitor.
   d. a residential inpatient structured program.

The best answers to these questions is, of course, "It depends." Any of these responses could be correct, as could all of them, or none of them.

At some point in our academic work, we were expected to learn the content of various courses, and then tested on our supposed mastery of this information. We memorized the cranial nerves or learned the names of artists, titled works, and significant features of a paintings and sculptures. We were required to recognize the supposed "correct" answers to questions that allegedly demonstrated our learning. Once in graduate school, the ideas may have been far more complex and elusive, but we were still required, at times, to recognize the correct theorist associated with a particular conceptual framework or identify the best definition of a defense mechanism. The key point we are making is that from our high school years all the way through our licensing exams and continuing education evaluations, we are tested on our knowledge based on the idea (surely a myth) that there are only a few choices and that the correct one can be reliably determined.

Once graduated, we'd sit in a session with a new client and feel absolutely flooded with options about what to do or say at any moment of time, with little notion that any one of these choices is better than the others. Often the conclusion is that "none of the above" or "all of the above" might be more appropriate. As such, we were unprepared for the realities of therapeutic practice, namely, that life in general and therapy in particular does not lend itself whatsoever to multiple choice structures.

Sure, this type of testing is convenient and easier for both students, faculty, and administrators. Since these instruments don't actually measure much depth of learning, they are simple to grade and reduce performance to a single score. Even though this has become a familiar and popular device for assessing learning outcomes, it is also appropriate mostly for lower order and well-defined content. This is not exactly a description we would apply to learning therapy knowledge and skills.

The other disadvantages and limitations of multiple choice exams have been mostly ignored because of cost-effectiveness. The actual validity of the instrument is compromised in so many ways beyond its limited focus on specific, correct answers (as determined by the test constructor). Although multiple choice items can be written to assess higher order learning such as analytic or evaluative understanding, far more often they just assess basic lower level grasp of memory or comprehension. In addition, the bias of these tests are well-documented and likely present a disadvantage to a number of groups. The behavior of test takers is also suspect because the optimal strategy encourages guessing during those instances when you can eliminate a single option or two. When stymied altogether, a student may very well make random guesses. Most important for our purposes is that problem-solving and complex reasoning, two critical skills in our profession, are usually not assessed whatsoever. Finally, there is a matter of interpretation related to some of the questions and answers, since response options may seem ambiguous or confusing. This further erodes the meaningfulness of results since answers are only evaluated as all or nothing, with no partial credit given for reflective, nuanced responses. On a geology exam, for example, students were asked to select the strongest force on Earth:

a. Sedimentary rock
b. Igneous rock
c. Quartzite
d. Granite

One student crossed out all the answers supplied and wrote, "LOVE" at the bottom of the page. Needless to say, no credit was given.

WHAT ABOUT ACCREDITATION STANDARDS?

Objective type exams are often used simply because they are the most expedient way to assess whether a particular course offering meets mandated standards established by the discipline. And such accreditation status is absolutely critical for a program in social work, psychology, counseling, family therapy, or other fields to be considered legitimate and reputable. Thus, regardless of the students served; institutional mission; community needs; faculty preferences, interests, and specialties; or administrative control and resources, we are expected to include certain requirements in training that cover particular content. There are specific categories, subcategories, and demarcations within disciplines that are prescribed without exception. This has long been considered the optimal means by which a profession and the programs that prepare clinicians maintain acceptable standards of training.

There has traditionally been a rigid power hierarchy within mental health, depending on one's degree, such as MD, DO, RN, PA, MS., MA, PhD, and so on. If the professions that "own" psychotherapy (social work, psychology, counseling, family therapy, psychiatry) ever wanted to be taken seriously by their counterparts, it was imperative that they standardize their training and accreditation requirements. Until such a movement (which is still ongoing in some states), almost anyone could (can) call themselves a counselor or therapist. It is about popular reputation. Thus, certain clothing brands like Gucci, Dior, and Hermes or automobile manufacturers like Tesla, Mercedes, or Rolls Royce are respected and coveted because of their image as the best, whether that is true or not.

Then the war began. There is considerable disagreement about who fired the first shot across the bow to begin this century-long battle that has resulted in many casualties. Some would say social work was responsible once they required that a professional had to obtain a terminal degree only in that discipline to prepare their graduates. Psychology decided to fight back by introducing their own rules that one had to graduate from one of their sanctioned programs, plus secure a similar internship, before allowed to teach in their programs. Not to be left out, marriage and family therapists, mental health counselors, and rehabilitation counselors all jumped into the fray with their own restrictive rules. The current state of affairs is that we are now all partitioned into specific professional guilds, even if much of what we do is quite similar, if not identical. Needless to say, this is all quite confusing for consumers, and even more so for a prospective candidate, who seeks to become a therapist but can't figure out the best pathway for doing so.

These territorial policies are not really intended to improve the quality of training as much as they are supposed to maintain "pure" professional identity. Yet interdisciplinary collaboration is not only the norm but absolutely essential in the real world in which mental health professionals all work cooperatively in both inpatient and outpatient settings. It's just as important for social workers to have a strong background in psychology as it is for psychologists to be trained in basic social work practices. Likewise, counselors, family therapists, and psychiatric nurses all rely heavily on other disciplines as a knowledge base. This is clearly all about protectionism, and it definitely limits both the scope of practice and competence areas of all mental health professionals. If you were truly interested in producing the most qualified, expert therapists, why wouldn't you recruit psychologists, social workers, psychiatrists, counselors, and family therapists to work together toward this goal?

Policies related to accreditation and licensure tend to be overly bureaucratic. Even though I (Jeffrey) have been licensed as a psychologist, family therapist, or counselor in a handful of states, I am no longer eligible for licensure where I live because the state doesn't have reciprocity with the jurisdictions in which I've resided; They require me to have attended an American Psychology Association–accredited program and internship even though such things didn't yet widely exist when I graduated over 45 years ago. I am also required to take courses that I actually regularly teach and for which I've written the textbooks. Such reports are very common among our colleagues, especially during a time when we are more mobile than ever in the pursuit of different professional opportunities.

Professional organizations sing the praises of accreditation for therapist preparation programs, at both the masters and doctoral levels. They say such recognition makes a statement that the curriculum and faculty meet minimal standards, as well as make it easier to seek licensure or certification after graduation. It also serves important legitimacy functions given that some institutions may offer programs that are not consistent with generally accepted standards. Thus, the American Psychological Association, National Association of Social Workers, Council for Accreditation of Counseling and Related Educational Programs, American Association of Marriage and Family Therapy, American Association of Sex Educators, Counselors, and Therapists, and American Rehabilitation Counselors Association, among others, all have standards for their accredited programs that include very specific mandates for which courses that are offered, qualifications of faculty, student retention policies, number of supervision hours required, and so on. They all require departments to undertake a laborious self-study, host a site visit by an accreditation team, and submit a report to a committee for review, all of which is intended to ensure that the quality of education is maintained. Of course, these standards are defined and described according to some fairly rigid criteria that clearly value some things over others as ascribed by the powers of those in charge. Obviously there has been a movement toward including anything that can be empirically supported and supposedly evidence-based. Thousands of articles have been published on accreditation in various scholarly journals in the various mental health disciplines, mostly discussing the importance and value of the process. What's interesting, however is that the research demonstrating a link between accreditation and competent practice or clinical excellence is scant to nonexistent.

In writing about whether accreditation truly improves the quality of medical education, Al Alwan (2012) makes several points that are equally applicable to the preparation of therapists. First, they require mandatory adherence to standards that are developed primarily on homogeneous geographic/cultural regions, most notably urban, Westernized locales. They fail to take into account the vast differences in institutional mission and goals; student composition and interests; faculty philosophy, strengths, resources, and approaches; community needs; program specialties; or geographical and cultural norms for the area.

There is no clear evidence that professionals who graduate from accredited programs are significantly better than those who do not, even if it would seem, intuitively, this should be the case. In a discourse analysis of accreditation standards in health, it was discovered that the descriptions, metaphors, and values embedded in the language emphasize strict adherence to certain practices related to competence, outcomes, skills, and knowledge, but almost never related to the empathic and compassionate care of clients and patients (Whitehead, Kuper, Freeman, Grundland, & Webster, 2014).

What is often assessed in such comparisons is knowledge rather than actual clinical performance in sessions. Why is this the case? Consider how such research would be conducted. First, there is the difficulty of defining and objectively measuring clinical excellence. Then, who would complete such an process? Having therapists complete a self-report measure on how excellent they think they were in a session is neither very accurate nor meaningful. It is also the case that clients are not necessarily the best judge of what happened, except to say they were satisfied. Having a client complete a measure of the therapist's performance and then linking the assessments to the clinician's qualifications and accreditation standards would be highly problematic. Would the therapist have only one client complete the measure, or would some type of aggregate score be composed from multiple clients—some who like the therapist and some who might possibly despise the therapist? And then would it be possible to identify enough clients from enough therapists to have sufficient representation? These complications help explain why it isn't realistically possible to show definitively that accreditation necessarily leads to better functioning.

Specializations Within Standards

In addition to the accreditation is the distinction of specializations within each of the professions. We have specializations in addictions, gender issues, career counseling, supervision, gerontology, children/adolescents, family therapy, college counseling, school counseling, and every theoretical framework imaginable. The current state of disciplinary specialization is ridiculous, often pushing out the foundational knowledge of one field to promote (and limit) one's own professional identity (Duer, 2005). We talk a lot about the importance of diversity and respecting cultural differences, yet the inflexible standards of accreditation often fails to recognize and/ or acknowledge the important role played by regional and local geography, jurisdictional licensing, student composition, client needs, institutional policies and goals, budget and resources, and faculty composition and phi- losophy, not to mention innovative and creative ideas. When an institution requires that a degree program be limited to a certain number of credits, the state licensing board mandates that certain subjects be offered, and then the accreditation body requires a long list of required courses, there is almost no space or option for electives, specialties, or areas of interest and expertise.

STANDARDS WITHIN STANDARDS

One would imagine that professional standards, by definition, would ap- pear to have clear face validity but that doesn't necessarily lead to improved quality of education. For instance, every profession has standards related to things like cultural competency, assessment, addictions, group work, family systems, trauma, and so on. Most of these were developed as a type of pet project from a designated division or specialty of an association or because some committee thought it was a good idea to include.

Once again, there is no evidence that competencies published by various mental health associations translate to improved outcomes. Considerable research is done on the designated competencies themselves in which graduates complete surveys to determine their mastery of par- ticular training standards. With various divisions, associations, and spe- cial interest groups within each major mental health association, there are hundreds of standards that cannot possibly be addressed adequately in a finite hours of training. The counseling profession, for example, has dozens of different divisions based on interests, specialty, and population. When school counselors were surveyed, they reported they felt unpre- pared to address LGBTQ issues so a standard was created to require this among their members (Shi & Doud, 2017). Dobmeier and Reiner (2012) surveyed graduates from accredited counseling (Council for Accreditation of Counseling and Related Educational Programs [CACREP]) programs and found that the interns reported feeling perfectly competent in implementing the "spirituality competencies" from the Association for Spiritual, Ethical, and Religious Values in Counseling (ASERVIC). That's all very nice, but they also discovered that among the respondents, the vast majority were completely unaware that such competencies existed in the first place. Hagedorn (2009) identified competencies in treating sexual addiction and that mental health professionals were ill-prepared in their training.

Almost every year, some new mandated requirement or standard is added to the pile. If brain plasticity and neuropsychotherapy become the rage, then this becomes a new standard of competence. It isn't just the professional associations that are deciding what should be required in training standards since licensing boards have their own demands, many of which vary greatly across state or provincial lines. Depending on one's location and professional identity, it may be considered essential to meet standards related to aging clients, refugee trauma, school shootings, opioid addiction, autism, hypnosis, play therapy, or an assortment of other topics. It all gives the distinct public impression that we are unprepared to deal with all kinds of specific disorders, populations, and conditions.

THE KILLING OF THE UNIQUE PROGRAM

One intended consequence of pervasive accreditation is the standardization of programs that are all composed of the same identical features, regardless of the location, context, interests, and needs. In many accredited master degree programs, for example, there are so many required courses that there is no room for electives whatsoever. Unique and customized training cultures have been discouraged, if not wiped out.

Gergen (2000) classified cultural world views according to three primary traditions. In the romantic view, such values as passion, creativity, intuition, playfulness, and depth of self become primary guiding forces that shape curriculum and practices. This would be familiar in programs that are person-centered, humanistic, or organized around object relations or self-theory. The modernist tradition is all about logic, rational discourse, empiricism, and evidence-based knowledge that are common nowadays, especially in programs that emphasize cognitive-behavior therapy and other empirically supported treatments. These are both quite different from postmodern world views that can represent quite a departure from more traditional priorities and perspectives, teaching narrative, feminist, and other approaches that break down traditional hierarchies of power. Yet despite these differences in philosophy, approach, and focus, they are all expected to contain essentially the same curricular offerings. We claim to have a deep respect for and valuing of plurality, multiculturalism, and diversity, yet we are forced to comply to a fairly singular vision of what therapist preparation should look like according to consensual standards.

One could argue that each training program has its own unique culture, based on the composition of faculty and students, institutional goals and purpose, geographical location, community values, jurisdictional licensing, instructor philosophies and theoretical orientations, and even tenure and promotion requirements that drive faculty priorities and time commitments. Some programs are more didactic, others more experiential. Some favor traditional teaching and evaluation methods while others are embedded in more postmodern views. Then there is the impact of faculty relationships among one another and with students. Perhaps more than anything else, this shapes the culture of a department, establishing norms related to sanctioned behavior. For example, departments that are conflicted and fractured model such behavior to their students, creating an oppressive culture that is excessively rule bound.

Then there is all the diversity in institutional mission and priorities and how that impacts any universal national standards. Compare, for example, the differences between a program housed in a research-oriented, grant-funded, urban, public university and a small, private, professional school in a rural setting. Or consider the differences that would be manifest in faculty who are largely psychodynamic in orientation versus those who espouse feminist/social constructivist philosophy. Obviously, they would emphasize unique and specialized content and varied styles in how they would prepare/teach/train/grow their graduates.

We are by no means denigrating accreditation standards for the purposes of eliminating them or merely challenging the myth that they are indelible universal truths handed down to us by divine authority. Who could argue against requiring all licensed practitioners to have developed certain basic competencies prior to letting them loose on the public?

Accreditation standards and competencies do indeed streamline training, making it more difficult for various programs to differentiate themselves, especially when standards are so comprehensive. Keep in mind that most masters programs are around 30 credits, and yet within our field, although that used to be the standard, it rose to 36 credits, then 42, 48, and 60 hours to cover all the requirements.

Innovative programs that feature more cutting-edge and contemporary approaches are severely limited in how they may construct their curricular offerings. Instead, all accredited programs are expected to stick to the standard content, meet or exceed the defined competencies, and demonstrate that students can pass required exams (Peterson, 2004). The number of the different places where psychotherapy and counseling programs are housed is staggering and includes medical schools, public research universities, small regional universities, private colleges, seminaries, religious institutions, for-profit online companies, and professional schools. Then consider all the different departments in which these programs are located: psychology, human services, family studies, education, counseling, psychiatry, sociology, social work, human relations, clinical studies, health, on and on. Each of them has their own unique traditions, rituals, priorities, and values, which are often surrendered in the pursuit of homogenized standards of competence.

HOW ACCREDITATION MIGHT BE MORE USEFUL

It is easy to conclude that our collective mental health professions are overly standardized with no real link as to how the standards improve the services provided. However, standards do guarantee that important components of training are covered. The public should feel reassured and protected by that. Likewise, prospective students are well informed about which programs meet professional standards and are most recognized as legitimate. The choices are often bewildering to sort through, weighing costs and potential benefits.

A prospective student first tries to figure out whether she wants to be a social worker, psychologist, counselor, family therapist, or whatever. Then she tries to figure out which degree is best, given what she thinks she wants to do. Still confused, she decides to check out which programs in one field—counseling, for example—are nationally accredited. But then, to her surprise, she discovered that Harvard University has some type of related program, but it isn't accredited. She wonders, "Does that mean it isn't good enough to qualify? Or rather that they are so prestigious they don't need to bother with external approval?"

Next she consults a list of nationally accredited programs and finds one that is part of a profitable chain of mostly online or hybrid programs. "If it received this accreditation, does that mean that its better than the ones that did not?" she asks herself, still utterly confused. Finally, she finds a program that is four times the cost of her local public university, but it seems from their literature that it can be completed in half the time. Finally, in exasperation, she decides there's just too many choices and options to make an informed decision. She can't even settle on the "right" discipline, must less the kind of program that might fit her needs that she can't yet quite define.

This might seem like an exaggeration, but this is not an unusual journey for someone who is considering joining our profession but isn't sure where to begin. Although we are contradicting some of our earlier arguments (because we are both so ambivalent and conflicted), we so value the benefits of accreditation because graduating from such a program tells prospective clients, employers, doctoral programs, and licensing boards that a degree met certain standards and covered what is considered required content. It is a consumer protection process that is designed to enhance the reputation of the program and reassure others that a graduate meets or exceeds what is considered minimal levels of competence.

OUR CLIENTS ARE OUR BEST TEACHERS

Accreditation agencies give us the impression that everything a therapist really needs to know is contained in the required coursework they have selected, plus the extracurricular direct experiences in the field. Oversight is handled by instructors and supervisors who are also considered to be the sole and ultimate authorities on what is needed. Whatever was missing in these training experiences is supposedly picked up along the way through the required continuing education programs offered by "accredited providers." Scholarly articles, books, and online content can be selected to fill in gaps, although such material is hardly "accredited" except for the glowing quotes by recognizable figures on the back cover. Presumably, if someone famous or an authority on the subject wrote a review of the book, the publisher would find some complementary quote that proclaims its important contributions. We agree this is hardly the most compelling way to convince prospective readers that a book is worthwhile.

Ultimately, it is our clients who teach us the most about which interventions and strategies will likely produce (cause) the most beneficial effects—that is, if we are paying attention. We enter every session and approach every client with a number of preconceptions about the therapeutic process, our role and preferred approach, and what is most helpful. We tend to stick with what is tried and true or at least what appears to have been most useful in the past. We are most comfortable with what is most familiar to us, just like our clients. We much prefer to follow the patterns that have worked previously. Keep in mind, once again, that we aren't as well informed as we think we are about these sorts of things.

In a previous project (Kottler & Carlson, 2006), two dozen prominent theorists were asked to identify the client who had the most influence on them, the one who impacted them in a profound way, either personally or professionally. Naturally, some of the individuals identified times that a particular client triggered them in some way, opened up old wounds, or brought their attention to some unresolved issue. What was most interesting, however, were the number of times these famous therapists,

responsible for developing major paradigm shifts in the ways we conceptualize our work, pointed to specific clients they considered responsible for
their seminal ideas. It was during their sessions with this client that they
realized their previous approach was obsolete or limited, requiring them
to develop a completely new way of conceptualizing the process, as well as
developing alternative methods to make a greater difference.

These stories may have been oversimplifications in many ways but they
still illustrate how our clients are ultimately the ones who shape our growth
and development. Of course. this is only the case if we listen to them with a
truly open mind, surrendering many of our preconceptions that lead us to
fit them into an existing mold.

Among those theorists who identified a client instrumental in helping
them shape their distinctive conceptual framework, several described a
sort of empathic transcendence that opened up new avenues during their
journeys to find their own distinctive voice. The depth of the relationship
they experienced encouraged them to explore the power of the alliance as
the single most important force in their work. In some cases, it was the high
intensity of emotional arousal in a session that led them to consider alternative ways to manage the drama, as well as to process what occurred in a
new way. Other theorists were required to collapse their usual boundaries
related to time and space parameters to operate far more flexibly and cre-
atively, given that their usual and prior methods proved worthless with a
particular client. They were forced to invent something altogether novel to
address challenges they'd never encountered before.

It is perhaps not surprising that the client some influential theorists
identified was the one who clearly validated their most cherished beliefs
about the process. They were grateful that these particular clients confirmed their significant ideas. Michael Yapko (2006) remembered a client
who was instrumental in helping him to challenge the myths related to
false recovered memories. Alan Marlatt (2006) recalled a client who helped
him to refine his revolutionary ideas around treating addictions as behavior
disorders rather than as a disease. Bradford Keeney (2006) encountered a
client who sparked a new-found interest in the ancient traditions of indigenous healing practices. Robert Neimeyer (2006) and Albert Ellis (2006)
both pointed to particular cases that challenged their existing conceptual frameworks, leading them to develop new paradigms that shaped
our profession (constructivist and rational emotive, respectively). Ellis, in
particular, confessed, "It was largely as a result of working with her that
I developed the concept of 'unconditional acceptance,' meaning accepting
others no matter what they do or how disturbed they might be" (p. 69).
This was absolutely critical for him in learning to become more patient and
tolerant of his frustrations.

One of the ways by which we can become more open to learning from our clients is to refrain from routinely using diagnostic templates and relying solely on prior experiences to view current issues. Instead of employing the traditional decision trees and limited options from the *Diagnostic and Statistical Manual* that provide names for what we encounter, there are a series of curious questions (to borrow the phrase from narrative therapy) we might ask ourselves.

1. *What is the client's story?* This, of course, refers to the initial presentation, with all the rich details provided in the narrative. We listen carefully with hovering attention, interrupting only when necessary to flesh out the descriptions of what happened.
2. *What is the client's experience?* What are all the varied reactions and responses the client has as a result of what happened or what she is dealing with? What does she wish us to know that others don't seem to grasp? What are some features of the experience that are most difficult to articulate?
3. *What does the client think is going on?* What is the client's own theory and ideas regarding what is wrong and what needs to be done to fix it? It's not that we will agree to this plan but rather that we must initially acknowledge that we heard clearly this initial opinion, however irrational or ill-formed.
4. *What seems to be going on?* Appearances can indeed by deceiving so we try to try to form only tentative assumptions about what may be happening.
5. *What is the consensual name for this?* So far we have resisted jumping to a diagnostic conclusion, but it does help to settle on a tentative label that might typically be assigned to the particular configuration of symptoms.
6. *What else could it be?* This is where we loosen things up, refusing to foreclose on other possibilities that could also explain the phenomenon.
7. *What has the client already tried?* Clients are experts on their own experience. Prior to seeing a therapist, they have already exhausted everything they can possibly think of to deal with their problems. They have likely repeated their favorite strategies innumerable times, no matter how often they fail. It is thus useful to make a list of all the things that are certain to be a waste of time.
8. *What has been working so far?* Among all the strategies that have been attempted so far, what has be at least a little helpful or useful?
9. *What treatment might work best?* As a starting point, we formulate a very tentative plan, one that is fluid and flexible, continuously updated, and informed by the client's reactions and input.

STRATEGIES FOR SELF-SUPERVISION

It is a reality for most of us that we don't receive the supervision we need most during those times that are most critical. The point of maximum confusion is during the session itself, followed, second, by the moments after the client walks out the door. Yet alas, there is nobody observing us from behind one-way mirrors and rarely someone available immediately afterwards to debrief us. So perhaps days later we are left to try to reassemble what we believe happened during a session, providing limited and skewed information. Since it's likely these consultations occur after considerable time has elapsed, they are scheduled according to convenience and standing appointments rather than pressing needs.

In addition, it may not feel safe to be completely honest and disclosing if the supervisor is in a position of power or authority who decides on promotions, endorsements, recommendations, salary raises, or even if you get to keep your job. This is especially true if we want to process something that happened revealing our ignorance, neglect, or miscues. Although we can profit the most from those instances when we may have screwed up and need to be challenged in some way, this only turns out to be helpful when the supervisor is perceived as essentially supportive and encouraging rather than overly critical and punishing (Lizzio, Wilson, & Que, 2009).

For those who have been operating as professionals for some time, it is entirely possible there is actually no ongoing supervision whatsoever, except for the token continuing education programs that are routinely completed. It is rare, if ever, that anyone ever actually observes us in action. We are pretty much left to our own devices to figure out what we might be doing wrong, or what we could do better.

Although it is imperative that we receive ongoing training, development, and supervision if we ever hope to improve our effectiveness, it is a myth that all of this takes place in formal supervision. Many continuing education programs are a joke. During mandated ethics continuing education, members in the audience play with their mobile devices or try to sneak out early. Those who remain often nod off in boredom. Hardly anyone is in a very good mood whenever they are required to do things that don't appear meaningful or personally relevant. Since a good chunk of continuing education units can be accumulated online, participants barely pay attention just enough to pass the required test at the end. Sometimes people run the programs while doing other work assignments or simultaneously watching other, more entertaining videos. Let's just agree that these programs are not as engaging or useful as they were designed to be.

The reality is that most of the time we are learning by the seat of our pants, so to speak, hopefully adding to our repertoire and skill set by paying close attention to what our clients are teaching us. Books such as this one can sometimes offer a few new ideas or, hopefully, challenge us to consider alternative ways of conceptualizing our work. Likewise, watching videos of master practitioners or attending conferences that feature live demonstrations can also be enlightening and stimulating. In the grand scheme of things, these experiences are somewhat rare and infrequent compared to the daily challenges and problem we face that leave us uncertain or bewildered.

In the end, we mostly supervise ourselves.

If this is truly the case, and we urge you to consider this premise for yourself, then the important question is how we can do that more effectively and consistently so that we don't just end up (a) deceiving ourselves by justifying actions that are less than useful, (b) making the same mistakes over and over because they are familiar and comfortable, and (c) being lazy and operating on autopilot. There are actually several ways we might hold ourselves more accountable and push ourselves to be more innovative, as well as learn from our clients' instruction. We don't advocate this as a substitute for supervision by qualified experts, nor do we wish to neglect the usefulness of *meaningful* continuing education, advanced education, and spirited case conferences. We do, however, offer some modest suggestions for ways we could do a better job of critically examining and altering our own behavior.

SOME DIFFICULT PERSONAL QUESTIONS

Let's begin with ourselves, usually the most obvious and productive place to start the process. Whether you call it countertransference, projective identification, displaced feelings, personal triggers, or the more benign, "emotional involvement," there is little doubt there are times we get sucked into the drama of a client's story and experiences. Sometimes these feelings are simply the result of empathic resonance and deep caring, but other times they represent an exaggerated, distorted, or quite personal reaction that is based on our own unresolved issues and vulnerable soft spots.

Hopefully, we have worked on our own personal struggles in therapy as clients or certainly these issues have come up in prior supervision, but what makes them "core" issues is that they remain with us, more or less, throughout our lives. Whereas "civilians" are readily able to bury these prior disturbances, therapists are unable to hide from them since they regularly crop up in disguised or varied forms during sessions.

What Still Haunts You the Most?

No matter how often or how long someone has worked in therapy on core issues, there are always remnants that are left untouched, tender spots that are carefully guarded. For us, it may be feelings of inadequacy, never feeling good enough, or smart enough, or worthy enough. It helps explain why we've been so compulsively productive and achievement oriented. It also accounts for why we could become so easily defensive when clients don't improve (or students don't learn) as rapidly as we think they should (if we were more capable).

In What Ways Are You Not Fully Functioning?

This is a tough one. It requires brutal honesty regarding our own limitations and weaknesses. Personal coaches are big on asking corporate executives to agree to a 360-degree assessment process in which a representative sample of co-workers, employees, family members, friends, and others are asked to provide feedback on behaviors and characteristics that are both highly appreciated and productive and self-defeating and off-putting (Lovett & Robertson, 2017). Comprehensive interviews are conducted with key personnel and significant others, asking about strengths and weaknesses, as well as the best constructive advice they could offer. All of these data are then organized into a comprehensive report that is intended to help the person to improve performance and functioning.

Wouldn't it be something if we all had access to such rich and useful data about ourselves? Each of us really does have the opportunity to initiate our own such investigation by asking those with whom we work what suggestions, feedback, and constructive ideas they could offer us? All of this is predicated on the degree of honesty, sensitivity, and specificity of the feedback. It is critical that we have access to the most accurate data on the situational and contextual impact of our behavior, always an everchanging phenomenon depending on the client, complaints, goals, alliance, and stage of the process.

What Are Some Aspects of Your Lifestyle That Are Unhealthy?

Ideally, we hope to model for our clients precisely those behaviors and actions that we consider to be most adaptive and in their best interests. Given that emotional disturbances have a direct connection to lifestyle patterns like diet and exercise, as well as conscientiousness with regard to healthy habits, we are in the business of urging people to become more mindful about the daily choices they make. Obviously we can be more convincing and persuasive when we engage in those same actions ourselves.

When our own sleep and eating patterns are consistent and measured, when we refrain from excessive consumption of drugs or alcohol, when our finances and spending patterns are restrained and responsible, when we prioritize intimacy in our personal relationships, when we—well, you get the picture: It is imperative that we examine our own behavior for evidence of the same sorts of dysfunctions and self-defeating consequences that we target with our clients.

How Do You "Medicate" Yourself?

This is one of those questions that we frequently ask our clients, directly or indirectly, when we are interested in identifying their coping mechanisms to deal with disruptive symptoms. Most commonly, we assess for drug and alcohol use, self-soothing behavior that has annoying side effects, and other habits that are not in one's best interests. It is during such inquiries that we cannot help but consider our own patterns that may be less than beneficial.

William Glasser (1976) once advocated substituting "positive addictions" for those that have terribly destructive side effects. Certainly compulsive exercise, excessive focus on social media or time spent playing online games, or similar entrenched habits are better than heroin or cocaine to deal with daily stressors; however, they can still result in undesirable collateral effects such as neglect of other areas of our lives. And then, of course, our overdevotion and excessive commitment to work can become a form of self-medication itself, a place to hide from things we may wish to avoid or to fill an emptiness missing in some part of our lives related to intimacy, boredom, or lack of meaning.

What Are the Lies You Tell Yourself?

For therapy to work best, it is desirable that the participants practice a sort of scrupulous honesty and frankness. This is an evolutionary process as trust is built and clients feel like they can be more forthcoming about their deepest secrets and feelings. Likewise, we start out somewhat cautious and careful, not wanting to push too hard in the beginning or scare clients away by being overly direct and revealing. It is one of the jobs of the profession that we are "truth tellers," willing to tell people the things that they've been unwilling or unable to accept about themselves previously. For instance, we might challenge a client with something like the following:

> Perhaps one reason why you can't seem to maintain a romantic relationship for longer than a few months is because you demand expectations from others that are virtually impossible for them to meet. I notice that you sometimes do that with me in sessions when you fully expect that I'm going to simply fix you in a matter of a few hours. Then you become frustrated and angry with me. When I try to point this out, you start to pout and withdraw. This is *exactly* the sort of pattern you've described happens with your partners.

This is potentially powerful stuff, pointing out through immediacy some repetitive behavior that is at the heart of a client's issues. We identify and challenge self-deceptions and lies, at least those we believe people can handle at the time. But this also leads us to consider the lies we tell ourselves, at least if we are willing to be congruent. After all, we are known to fool ourselves far better than we deceive others. Being able to do so actually provides an evolutionary advantage since if we can lie to ourselves it makes it far easier to sell such lies to others (M. K. Smith, Trivers, & von Hippel, 2017). As we've noticed in the political arena, some individuals actually appear to believe the lies and "alterative facts" they tell and thus become absolutely resistant to ever confronting a semblance of reality related to global warming, economic prosperity for the marginalized and dispossessed, or the contributions of immigrants. Such overconfidence in one's distorted beliefs and myths is actually known to increase one's popularity and social success, even when others suspect exaggerations and deceptions (Murphy, Barlow, & von Hippel, 2018).

How often have you caught yourself saying something to a client about denying or minimizing some problematic behavior and realized you sometimes do much the same thing? We find ourselves pointing out the ways that people externalize blame for their problems or attribute causes that absolve them of responsibility. Or they rationalize why they do self-destructive things, providing lame excuses. Or they make up reasons for poor performance that allow them to continue behaving in that way.

This is another one of the ways that our clients become our greatest teachers, in this case with regard to our own personal growth and professional development. It may sometimes be the case that we hear colleagues (or ourselves) attributing negative outcomes in cases (or our own personal lives) to circumstances that let them (or us) off the hook. Since we are smart and clever, it isn't that difficult to attribute relapses to family dysfunction, toxic peer groups, poor motivation, lack of time and resources, or the client's own ambivalence.

What Do Your Fantasies Reveal During Sessions?

This is a favorite question because it uncovers so much about our inner lives, priorities, distractions, unfulfilled desires, and demons. Let's agree that even the best among us cannot possibly remain completely present and focused 100% of the time, even during the most compelling and poignant disclosures. Our minds are constantly drifting, sometimes triggered by something the clients says or does, or just as often by something rumbling inside of us. Given that humans spend half their waking moments daydreaming, and during the most demanding and complicated tasks, we still lose focus 30% of the time, it is inevitable that we are thinking about all kinds of things unrelated to the conversations in sessions. There's also evidence that the more our minds wander, the more likely we are unsatisfied or unhappy with some aspect of our lives (Killingsworth & Gilbert, 2010).

The average daydream or fantasy lasts about 14 seconds or so—brief, intermittent, flowing in and out of the present, and numbering over 2,000 during a typical day. Do the math: There has to be dozens of such lapses during every session. So, here's the question: When you leave the room, where do you typically go in your head? We find this endlessly interesting to consider the places we tend to revisit over and over.

What Is It About These Questions That You Find Most Threatening?

This is our final question and the one that is potentially the most revealing. Which questions did you skip altogether or just write off as irrelevant? The problem with self-supervision is that it is too easy to escape the issues we may find most uncomfortable. That, of course, is why our profession exists in the first place—to assist people in this journey of self-discovery and healing because it is so difficult to do on one's own.

REVIEWING AND CRITICALLY EXAMINING CLINICAL BEHAVIOR

Whereas previously we have discussed ways we may improve our professional functioning via the lessons we learn from our clients and facilitated through greater self-scrutiny, we wish to end this discussion by providing some reminders that relate more specifically to clinical skills and behavior.

First, and perhaps most important, the single best predictor of excellence in any domain and discipline is the intense commitment and desire to become truly exceptional. This begins with what is happening inside our own heads before, during, and after sessions. It is precisely the willingness to admit when you are feeling lost or confused, when you've reached an impasse, and when you acknowledge mistakes and weaknesses that you create the opportunity to correct and improve your skills. It would be lovely if we could recognize difficulties as they are occurring, but this is often unlikely when in the throes of intense interactions. Sometimes when we think and process too much we miss what is actually happening in the moment.

One of the strategies that therapists teach their clients is to become far more reflective about their own behavior, observing themselves carefully and noting the effects of choices that they make. This often takes the form of paying closer attention to actions that have previously been automatic rather than intentional. In a similar vein, we could all profit from listening and watching ourselves more critically, monitoring the internal noise that takes place at times, and identifying and confronting certain biases or preconceptions that are evident.

Finally, it is important to recognize and acknowledge the limits of any sort of self-monitoring and self-supervision, especially when we are blind to aspects of ourselves that others may find off-putting. That's why it is so important that we consult with more experienced colleagues about cases, as well as our own behavior. And that is also why it is so useful for us to work on our personal issues in our own therapy since it is almost a certainty that we must accept that we will never feel good enough.

YOU'LL NEVER FEEL GOOD ENOUGH

The ultimate myth that was first introduced to us in graduate school goes something like this, as first presented by one of our early supervisors or instructors:

> Look at me. I'm really good at this therapy business, aren't I? It appears like I know what I'm doing almost all of the time. I know things, lots of things, that you don't know. I appear poised, confident, in control almost all of the time. I know the answers to your questions. I've read books, lots of them, really challenging ones too. I know big words and fancy terms for concepts that you barely comprehend. I've got cool-sounding names for almost any human behavior or condition—and I act like they are always accurate. I've told you about so many cases in which I knew exactly what to do to fix people. I've given you

the impression that whatever comes my way, or whomever walks in my office, I know just what to do to help them.

And [Here it comes!] . . .eventually, with enough training, workshops, and degrees, someday you might be like me and feel good enough to help almost anyone.

Good luck with that.

We are pretty certain that we aren't the only ones who feel lost at times, who screw up and say or do the wrong thing, who feel like no matter how hard we work at this stuff we'll never be good enough or at least as good as the models we've seen. But then again, the circumstances and context of our sessions don't much resemble the "performances" we see dramatized on a stage.

Even though we've mentioned that the vast majority of practitioners (9 out of 10) describe themselves as better than their peers, there must be something else going on that that is still not enough and will never be enough. There is just so much uncertainty related to the work we do. No matter what actions we take, which technique we employ, or even what interpretation we offer, there is almost always some lingering doubt about other alternatives that might have been more useful or accurate. How are we ever to really know what is best?

We acknowledge that there are some among us who are not particularly troubled by all this. They just shrug, do the best they can, and move on to the next case. You do the best you can with what you know and understand at the time. Sometimes you hit the bullseye (or at least appear to), and other times you miss the target completely. Oh well.

We suspect that it's the rare therapist indeed who can just shrug of all the doubts and uncertainty, completely unbothered by the idea that we sometimes have no clue what's going on, no defensible rationale for why we intervened in a particular way, and no real understanding of what happened in a session or why. Heck, maybe it's not even important that we fully comprehend these things; maybe it's sufficient that whatever we do produces some sort of desired changes even if we can't always explain why.

Most of us don't understand how electricity works, but we can operate a light switch. We don't really understand how an airplane weighing a million pounds can manage to lift off the ground and fly yet we readily entrust our faith in these winged tubes of steel. Likewise we hear things about displacement of water to maintain buoyancy of an ocean liner that weighs millions of pounds and somehow manages to float, but that doesn't mean we understand how that works. Or we take scientists word that things like atoms or molecules exist, but we've never seen them and never will. All of these assumptions are embedded in a certain kind of faith. And so it is that we have the conviction that what we do is helpful to people most of the time even though we may not really understand what is happening or why. Of course, that doesn't stop us from making things up. "Yes," we might tell a client with perfect sincerity and confidence, "it does seem like your dream of falling through the ice and landing in the arms of a robotic mermaid expresses a wish to have a supportive partner, but it also signals a deep insecurity about your own ability to manage your affairs."

It isn't the content of these interpretations that we wish to emphasize as much as the confidence with which the therapist might offer them as truth. Of course, they are mere hypotheses, or even wild guesses, but they are often pronounced as if they are irrefutable nuggets of ultimate wisdom.

As we've highlighted, when we were first introduced to the profession, our instructors would frequently announce certain "facts" or "truths" as if they were irrefutable when they were actually just opinions that were informed by somewhat skewed experience. We may sometimes be as guilty as anyone else in presenting our favored and cherished beliefs as if they are just as valid and useful for everyone else. Because we are aware of this, we are also sneakier than some others when we qualify such statements with seeming cautious qualifications:

> "There is some evidence to indicate . . ."
> "Many of the therapists we've interviewed . . ."
> "I've found in numerous instances . . ."
> "There is a body of research to support . . ."
> "Experience tells us . . ."
> "As you are probably already aware . . ."
> "There are countless studies and overwhelming evidence to. . ." (Okay, this one goes way too far.)

ACCEPTING THAT WE WILL NEVER BE GOOD ENOUGH

The important question is how do we function in the world if we don't know enough and will never be good enough? How do we operate when we aren't totally sure how our tools work, much less which one is the best choice? How do we reconcile the need of our clients for perfect understanding of their problems with the reality that this is impossible? How do we continue to comply to consensual standards of our profession like the "intake interview" or "50-minute hour" (see Chapter 8 and 9 of this volume) when they are based on convenience or myths, rather than any solid evidential support?

There are times when greater experience in the field also results in acceptance of a degree of ignorance, blind spots, and limitations that are inevitable. But the wisdom that accompanies such a realization can actually increase our ability and confidence over time. With that said, of course, age, maturity, and experience can contribute to *perceived* mastery of clinical skills, flexibility in professional orientation and identity, improved clinical judgment and decision-making, and greater focus on relational engagement in sessions, but that *doesn't* mean that the quality or effectiveness of treatment is better (Dawson, 2018).

So, here's the good news. So what if we never reach the standards of excellence that we ultimately desire? So what if we don't know everything we possibly could or wield our therapeutic wand with the ultimate skill of a wizard? You can still fix things even if you don't completely understand how they work. And you can help people without understanding them.

Sure, it's preferable, and useful, for our clients to *feel* like we understand them, at least better than some others in their world. It's not this all-or-nothing sort of thing but rather that we have a reasonable grasp of important parts of who they are, at least those aspects that appear to be related to whatever is bothering them.

CHAPTER 8

✧

Intake Interviews—The "Real" Problem and the Best Way to Fix It

"How would you describe your major problems that are most bothersome?"

"When do your symptoms seem to be most disturbing?"

"How have you noticed that your moods, behavior, and relationships have changed since the appearance of these problems?"

"What can you tell me about your family history? Who else in your family has struggled with similar difficulties?"

"What medical conditions have you experienced?"

"What about medications, drugs, or alcohol use?"

"Tell me about your current living situation."

"Describe how you spend a typical day."

These are just a few of the questions we might ask during a first meeting with a client who is feeling highly anxious, uncertain, overwhelmed, and desperate for immediate relief. In addition, during internship one of our supervisors required us to address 20 other questions during the initial meeting, including things like, "What brought you to ask for help now?" "What do you expect and want from these sessions?" "Who else knows you are coming for help and how do they feel about that?" "What has it been like for you to seek other forms of assistance or guidance in the past to deal with these troubles?" "What has worked best for you, and what has proven a waste of time?" And toward the end: "What has this been like for you so far?"

Myths, Misconceptions, and Invalid Assumptions of Counseling and Psychotherapy. Jeffrey A. Kottler and Richard S. Balkin, Oxford University Press (2020). © Oxford University Press.
DOI: 10.1093/oso/9780190090692.001.0001

A RIDICULOUSLY BRIEF PERIOD OF TIME TO FORM A WORKING DIAGNOSIS AND A VIABLE PLAN

We can almost never recall a first session with a client in which we felt anything but confused. There is not only so much territory to cover but also many obligatory tasks to complete, so much information to collect, and so many possible causes and explanations for the difficulties that it is hard to imagine that *anyone* could feel completely settled on a diagnosis and treatment plan. Many clients find it challenging to provide a coherent narrative of what they are experiencing, much less what they think it means. They stammer answers that don't often make sense. They respond with a shrug to queries that must surely have definitive replies. They avoid answering some questions altogether, seeming to prefer remaining secretive. Each of their disclosures leads to a dozen other questions regarding greater specificity or representative examples. The more deeply we delve into this initial exploration, the more mysterious it all appears.

In most clinical settings a first meeting with a client is often extended as a double session. Review boards allow this sort of thing and reimburse for it because they recognize it takes a bit longer than an hour to complete all the information that must be gathered, determine a differential diagnosis, and then construct a treatment plan, as well as outcome goals that are measurable and attainable within the allocated protocol. This means that during an intake interview, we are required to accomplish several crucial tasks (Mears, 2016; Poole & Higgo, 2017; Sommers-Flanagan & Sommers-Flanagan, 2017).

1. *Elicit a description of chief complaints and presenting problems including, but not limited to, symptoms, life disruptions, collateral damage, and effects on daily functioning.* We also want to know who referred the client and why this person is seeking help at this time. Is this a voluntary choice to get help, mandated by some external authority, or perhaps coercion by a family member who threatens far worse consequences?

   Whatever the client reports to be the main problem may not be nearly as significant as other issues fermenting in the background. When the client says he is "depressed and lonely," is that really the best descriptor of his condition, or is that just a convenient label that minimizes the complexity of his experience? We are left to sort all this out, all the while we are rushing through the dozens of other items on the assessment protocol.

2. *Explore the history of the presenting issues including family background, sociocultural context for their manifestation, relevant legal issues, precipitating*

influences that may involve previous emotional disturbances and their re-sponsiveness to various treatments. Specifically, we want to know about previous emotional problems, their effects and consequences, and course of progress.

In an ideal world, we would be allocated several months to uncover all these salient details, intervening variables, and especially the cultural context of the client's experiences. When the client says her family is from Syria originally but they identify as Assyrians, a host of follow-up questions must necessarily emerge. She explains that she is a descendent of the oldest civilization from that region. She also clarifies that her people are Christian, rather than Muslim, and that they have dealt with oppression and discrimination from almost every other group. She also explains that seeing a therapist is not common, and she must keep the relationship a secret from her family. Maybe you can learn more about these contextual factors a bit later, but for now you've got to move on to assessing her current functioning.

3. *Conduct a mental status exam to assess the person's cognitive and emotional functioning, current stressors, and ability to reason and respond appropriately.* Let's be honest about the relative accuracy and relevancy of a 10-minute test of memory and thinking processes. Such an examination is probably useful as a rough picture of brain dysfunction or psychotic processes but is otherwise pretty worthless for finding out much about the client's personal style of reasoning and emotional coping strategies.

If there is time and adequate resources, we could administer a battery of tests for looking at personality features, intelligence, perceptual reasoning, verbal comprehension, processing speed, brain functioning, symptom checklists, and other behavioral indicators. Unfortunately, there is rarely the opportunity for most of us to rely on these extensive, expensive, and time-consuming batteries. We are mostly required to take shortcuts and rely on the intake interview to elicit these data solely from observation and client reports. Needless to say, the information we gather is necessarily less than comprehensive and accurate.

4. *Collect a thorough medical history that includes any organic diseases, prior physical disabilities, medication history, and drug and alcohol use.* Sometimes we have access to files forwarded to us from referral sources, but that is likely the exception rather than the rule. Nonmedical practitioners also don't have sufficient training and background to truly understand and decode the prior workups. Considering that something like 15% of all medical diagnoses aren't accurate in the first place, coupled with 50%

of patients not understanding what the physician told them was wrong, the reports we may receive can just as easily lead to misinterpretations as further clarity.

"My doctor says I have serious depression and so she gave me a drug called 'fluvomine' or 'fluxomime' or something like that."

"Do you mean fluvoxamine? Does it say Lovox on the bottle?"

"Um, I'm not sure. Maybe."

"And what did you tell the doctor exactly about what was wrong?"

"Just that I was upset because Miguel told me that his promotion means we have to move again. And that means we have to start all over. We've done this so many times already that I just don't know . . ."

"Wait a minute. Stop for a moment. Are you saying that's what you told the doctor, and she gave you this prescription for depression?"

"Sure. What else could it be?"

What else indeed?

Of course, we know that antidepressant medications are a \$10 billion industry, second only to statins as the most prescribed medications in the United State. One in 10 patients who visit their primary care physician will leave with a prescription for antidepressant meds. In addition, roughly half of all those who are taking those drugs aren't actually benefiting from their effects, unless they "enjoy" the annoying side effects of drowsiness, nausea, constipation, dry mouth, dizziness, and weight gain (B. L. Smith, 2012; Santarsieri & Schwartz, 2015).

As often as not, our brief medical inquiry determines that our clients have been put on medications they really don't need. An even more compelling example is related to the use of benzodiazepines and other sedatives to treat reports of anxiety and insomnia. All a patient has to do is say to a doctor "I'm not sleeping well," or "I feel stressed," and they are likely to become among the half of all Americans over the age of 12 who regularly take painkillers, tranquilizers, or sedatives. And that doesn't include those who self-prescribe cannabis or other drugs to manage their discomfort.

So, what does this leave us with? More confusion and uncertainty. Plus more pressure to perpetuate the myth that an intake session can truly hone in on what's wrong and what to do to fix it.

5. *Conduct a suicide assessment to determine potential for self-harm.* Okay, so this is optional but should be completed for our most desperate clients. But we still do some sort of risk assessment with every client who walks in the door. Sure, it's important to determine if they are a potential danger to themselves or others. But within this first contact, we still

make predictions regarding the likelihood that this person will return for another session or just how good a candidate we believe he is for what we do and how we do it.

To save time (the clock is ticking), you may decide to collect as much of these data as possible on forms you distribute ahead of time, but you will still be required to review all the material. Since clients often minimize or exaggerate things, if not "forget," to include significant information, some digging into each of this areas is essential. Then, while the client is staring at you and asks for your initial assessment of what's going on and what will happen next, you stall a little until you can construct some explanation that sounds both reasonable and realistic, but still doesn't directly contradict or challenge the client's own unrealistic expectations.

JUST A FEW MORE THINGS

Oh yeah, we forgot. You also have to persuade the client to return for another session now that you have collected all the information that is helpful for *you*. That means some actual counseling must take place, something clients can take with them when they leave to demonstrate that the enterprise is worth their time. After all, if you could list the single most important goal of any first interview, one that stands about the rest, it would certainly be to make sure the client returns for a second time; otherwise, we can't do much good. And then we have to complete all these tasks within just an hour or two.

As mentioned, before this first interview ends, the client fully expects, if not demands, that you actually *do something* to make things better. This could be a simple as reassurance and support, mentioning that you are now a partner during this difficult journey. It often involves giving a name, however tentative, to whatever is bothering the person. In some cases it is appropriate to offer immediate therapeutic advice, even if the client is not yet ready to act decisively. All of this can be capsulized as the meeting comes to an end:

I'm so glad you decided to consult with me during this time when you need support and encouragement. It would appear that these symptoms are directly related to some losses you've experienced recently, including the new responsibilities you have at work, the health problems of your aging parents, and the uncertainty you feel from the mixed messages you are now getting from your partner. The anxiety you've been feelings seems normal and appropriate, given the pressure you are under. This seems to be the sort of reactive anxiety that responds well to therapy without the need for any medication. But let's see how things go and we can reassess later. I'd like to suggest that we begin right away with making some small shifts and adjustments in some things you've been doing already that have not been helping and may actually be making things worse.

In this example, the therapist tries to hit each of the important points, using the plural pronoun, "we," as often as possible to signify collaboration. The therapist covers herself by presenting the initial diagnosis and possible causes in tentative language, yet also with reassurance and confidence, as if to say, "No worries. We've got this! Whatever is going on, we will figure it out together."

Once the client finally walks out the door, then the *real* panic sets in because you have to compile all these incomplete data, rambling and incoherent stories, seemingly random assortment of symptoms and complaints into a diagnostic entity that appears to hold some, if not most, of what was described. Then, in the few minutes you have before the next appointment (unless it's been scheduled right afterward, in which case you have to try and remember most of what happened at the end of the day when everything blurs together), you have to compile a treatment plan, complete with objectives for each session.

If you are an intern or under close supervision, in your next case consultation, you will be expected to explain and defend all of this, presenting the case as if you really do understand what is going on with this person and what will likely best prove helpful.

Now, does that sound like a ridiculous, if not impossible, task? How are we supposed to do all that with someone we just met for an hour or two?

Such is the illusion that we are like doctors who can administer a few tests; draw some blood, urine, and/or saliva samples; listen to the heart and lungs; if necessary, order a scan; pronounce a definitive diagnosis; and then prescribe medication or recommend surgery to fix the problem. Within general medical practice, physicians are usually wrong in their diagnostic assessments about 15% of the time (Brush, Sherbino, & Norman, 2017; Graber, 2013). Physicians even tend to be overly optimistic in their predictions of patient recovery for those in intensive care. In one study physicians in the intensive care unit predicted that three fourths of their patients would fully recover when, in fact, only 60% did so (Soliman et al., 2018). And this was with access to the best and latest technological innovations in their field.

WHEN INTAKE SPECIALISTS DISAGREE

Danny, a 14-year-old adolescent, was admitted to an inpatient crisis unit because of behavior that was described as both defiant and oppositional. He had a history of sexually acting out at school, was running away from home, and using alcohol and methamphetamines.

During a meeting with Danny's parents, they described their son as a rather introverted with few friends. He seemed to prefer spending most of his time alone whenever he had a choice. His parents seemed to respect his wishes and mostly left him to his own devices since he was doing reasonably well in school. It was in the last few months, however, that he had hooked up with a new group of friends. At first, the boy's parents were delighted that he finally developed some kind of social life yet they noticed that since he'd been hanging out with these other boys, Danny's behavior dramatically changed.

"Changed how?" the therapist asked.

"Well," Danny's mother replied after a thoughtful pause, "for one thing he dresses differently now. We're not even sure where he got these clothes since we did not buy them for him."

"But that's not all," Danny's father added. "He's just, I don't know, a lot more emotional. He seems angry all the time. He argues with us about everything. Then he started talking back to his teachers. It got to the point they suspended him."

The therapist noticed that the mother seemed far more upset about something else they hadn't yet mentioned and so cued her to continue.

"He's been just acting really strange lately," she said.

"Strange how?"

She looked at her husband and he nodded. "I noticed he's been sneaking into our bedroom and stealing my makeup, blush, eyeliner, lipstick. When we confronted him about that he denied it. At first. But then he started crying and said he thought he might be gay."

"I told him he's not gay," the father interrupted. "He's just confused."

"Anyway," the mother continued, "he doesn't listen to us anymore. He doesn't listen to anyone. He stays out late at night. One time he was missing for 3 days, and we were so worried about him. We didn't know what to do. Then, well, then things got a lot worse."

The therapist had already heard from school authorities about this incident that had gotten him suspended for an indefinite period. Danny had been discovered in the bathroom performing oral sex on another boy.

"That was the last straw," the mother said with a sigh. "That's why we brought him here to you. Because we don't know what else to do."

Along with this initial intake interview, Danny was also examined by the admitting psychiatrist who diagnosed the patient with oppositional defiant disorder. He also tested the boy for drug use and found residual effects of marijuana and methamphetamines. Danny also admitted to passing out from alcohol a few times each week.

Danny seemed to make solid progress during 2 weeks of intensive treatment. He promised he would do better in school and obey his parents' rules at home. There was still an unresolved issue related to coming out as gay, but Danny insisted his father would never accept him if he was open about his sexual identity.

Although the staff acknowledged that Danny's progress was guarded at best and that he might require longer term residential treatment, they felt pressured to discharge him because the insurance company insisted they try outpatient therapy. It surprised nobody that he was soon readmitted to the unit after some dramatic displays of noncompliance with his program and once again was kicked out of school.

Danny was assigned to a different psychiatrist for his readmission. The doctor once again took a history and conducted his own examination, this time diagnosing the boy with a major depressive disorder exacerbated by polysubstance use. He prescribed antidepressants.

So, here's the question that frequently crops up when two different mental health professionals examine the same client and come up with completely different diagnoses and assessments of the condition. They both had access to the same background case file and viewed pretty much identical symptoms, and each followed basically the same standardized interview protocol. Of course, the details that were shared during each intake by Danny and his parents were probably not identical. Every time someone shares a story about anything there are slight shifts in emphases, with some things left out and others included. Danny probably felt different levels of trust and relational engagement with each of the examiners, perhaps more willing to share particular details while leaving others out.

In addition, each of the psychiatrists listened, heard, and focused on particular features of the narrative that most appealed to them. One psychiatrist felt that Danny was influenced by a negative peer group that reinforced and encouraged oppositional behaviors and drug use. The other psychiatrist was more in tune to Danny's shame and guilt, as well as his parents' denial of his sexual identity. It was believed that the boy desperately wanted to feel accepted in some way, even if that now came from a toxic peer group.

As is sometimes typical in mental health operations, the two psychiatrists never actually consulted with one another about the case to share their differences of opinion. The second psychiatrist decided not to even read the file until after he saw his patient, preferring first to form his own impressions. In addition, he never had any interest in comparing notes with his colleague who he believed was completely misguided.

A REMINDER ABOUT RELIABILITY AND VALIDITY

Of course, the case just described is hardly all that unusual. In one study of how mental health professionals were able to accurately and consistently diagnose their patients during a 40-year period, Vanheule et al. (2014) investigated their extent of agreement. They were interested in testing the actual usefulness of the *Diagnostic and Statistical Manual* (DSM) in daily practice, especially with regard to how much we can depend on the decisions that are made.

It may be helpful to review briefly how consistency and accuracy in diagnosis are actually determined. If you recall from your statistics courses, interrater reliability is determined using *kappa coefficients* (k) that measure the agreement between raters who are observing the same event, phenomenon, or, in this case, identical patient. If there is perfect agreement between the raters then a score of 1 is assigned; if there is no agreement between them whatsoever, then $k = 0$.

Vanheule et al. (2014) noted that in 1974, which used the second edition of the DSM (DSM-II), psychiatrists were determined to demonstrate the extent to which diagnosis was based on scientific principles. Basically, they wanted to know that when presented with a case during an intake interview, they could determine the extent of their agreement regarding clinical assessments. Surely this would be an absolutely critical thing to know if we are all going to rely on this system and make important decisions that will affect people's lives as long as they live.

Hoping to create greater flexibility and better outcomes, the researchers even set up broad ranges of categories to indicate to a greater likelihood of consensus. Imagine their disappointment when they discovered that, overwhelmingly, there was little agreement among the clinicians at almost *any* level. This really isn't all that surprising when you consider how a group of clinicians might very well talk to a client and come up with vastly different perceptions of the individual, focus on a variety of different issues as most salient, and recommend an assortment of alternative approaches to be of assistance.

In addition, diagnostic criteria often consists of a series of overlapping, recursive symptoms (Gola, 2017). It's also common that a client may be diagnosed with more than one disorder, especially by different practitioners. In addition, Gola (2017) noted this problem is not likely to improve since 15 new diagnoses were added to the fifth edition of the DSM (DSM-5), as well as revisions to prepare for many additional changes in the future. Ostensibly these additions are made to encourage public trust and increase the sophistication and accuracy of diagnosis. Unfortunately, the effect is probably quite opposite of what was intended.

Let's take the simplest example imaginable. During the intake interview a client complains of irritability, sleep disruption, restlessness, and difficulty concentrating. So, are we talking about depression or anxiety as the primary disorder?

If you hesitate to commit yourself or aren't quite sure, that's perfectly reasonable considering that these are overlapping symptoms of *both* conditions. Perhaps that's one reason why more than half of clients are diagnosed with more than one disorder. It's also one reason why the psychiatry profession has been so desperate to improve this situation. Each new edition of the DSM was intended to be more scientific, as demonstrated by greater consistency and accuracy. Massive and expensive studies were launched to measure this improvement over time. But alas, the level of agreement never got much better (Vanheule et al., 2014)!

This was a crushing disappointment, indeed. This led to Plan B. One way to improve the data on diagnostic reliability was just to change the standard required for agreement. This would be similar to an instructor who was disappointed in the performance of her students since nobody in the class attained an A on the exam. This did not reflect well on her at all, signifying she may have done a lousy job presenting the material. So one way to remedy the situation after the fact is simply to redefine and lower the standard of excellence. She could revise the grade distribution by lowering the standards to earn an excellent grade. This not only lets her off the hook but also makes the students happy and proud of themselves because their performance was evaluated at such a high level even though their mastery of the content was really quite inadequate.

Essentially the ability of experts to agree on diagnosis is a challenge that has been problematic since the mental health profession first attempted to standardize this process. The actual measures of agreement on diagnoses have not changed substantially over the years. Rather, the *standards* by which to judge agreement have been altered to demonstrate improvements that have never really existed (Vanheule et al., 2014).

You might think that a rationale for updating the diagnostic system used by psychiatrists and other mental health professionals would yield more consistency in diagnosis. Although it has been alleged that consistency in diagnosis has significantly improved over the years as the DSM has been repeatedly refined, updated, and improved, this has not actually been the case. The nature of the research on diagnosis tends to focus on accuracy and consistency of *specific* diagnoses, such as posttraumatic stress disorder among war veterans (Green et al., 2017), major depressive disorder (Mitchell, McGlinchey, Young, Chelminksi, & Zimmerman, 2009), substance use disorders (Rush, Castel, Brands, Toneatto, & Veldhulzen, 2013), and so forth. In a review of nearly 600 studies, the diagnostic accuracy among varied clients and symptoms was quite low or, in some cases, nonexistent. Most research on diagnostic accuracy relates to evaluating specific symptoms, identifying cognitive impairment (e.g., dementia, psychosis), and using diagnostic instruments.

The key question, then, is why our diagnostic impressions are so inconsistent? Is it really because our system, the DSM, is so limited and inadequate? Perhaps.

THE INHERENT UNRELIABILITY AND STIGMA OF DIAGNOSTIC LABELS

But what about the underlying process used to derive a diagnosis in the first place—the *intake interview*! That's why we are allocated more time to conduct the initial assessment, usually 90 minutes instead of the customary 50 minute hour. In a thorough review of the literature, we have not found a single study that directly links the accuracy of diagnosis and case conceptualization to the length of the first interview. It would make sense that, given more time, we could do a better job of figuring out what's going on and what to do about it, but this doesn't necessarily seem to be the case. Our best guess is that intake sessions are 90 minutes for schedule convenience and financial reasons—because that's what insurance companies have decided, even with no particular evidence that it is an optimal amount of time.

Another interesting consideration is that perhaps the diagnosis assigned to a client is not really based on the symptoms presented all all, but perhaps influenced by many other extraneous factors. For example, in inpatient treatment, once a patient diagnosed with a substance use disorder is no longer going through chemical withdrawal, insurance companies often will not pay for further inpatient treatment, as the patient is medically stable. However, a patient diagnosed with major depressive disorder might receive approval for additional treatment from the insurance company because the focus is on reducing mental health symptoms, not physiological symptoms of a chemical withdrawal that is often resolved within 24 to 48 hours. Given the choice between diagnosing a patient with a substance use disorder versus major depressive disorder, a physician might choose the option that allows for a more comprehensive treatment of the patient.

"I've always been concerned with the stigma associated with diagnoses that are accessible in clients' records," one therapist admitted. "I don't know if you could call it expediency, laziness, or maybe client advocacy, but I've been reluctant to label anyone with a diagnosis that might bite them in the ass in the future. There's all kinds of stigma and judgments that others make when someone is bestowed with a personality disorder or similar name that stays with them for life."

So, we asked, what *is* your system?

"Well," the therapist hesitated, seemingly a little embarrassed by his confession, "I really only use three diagnoses for almost everyone."

"Really?"

"Maybe not always. But let's say most of the time. My default diagnosis is adjustment reaction with anxious mood or depressed mood."

"What if you aren't sure which emotional response is more prevalent? Or what if there are both?"

"That's easy," he answered with a laugh. "Then I use adjustment reaction with mixed emotional features."

This therapist, of course, has decided to virtually abandon the traditional diagnostic system to supposedly "protect" his clients. Whether you agree that is ethical and professional or not, it highlights the kinds of diagnostic preferences that many clinicians favor. If you are overly vigilant looking for particular conditions or symptom configurations, then are you are far more likely to find evidence to support them.

We realize, of course, that the myth of DSM supremacy and intake interview reliability is based on justifying our decisions as scientifically based, but that is only true if we have a very low standard for compelling evidence. As preposterous and unnerving as this proposition might sound, there is actually some evidence to support that belief. Decades ago, Helstone and van Zuuren (1996) postulated that clinical decisions were based more on how the clinician *perceives* the client's presentation, foreshadowing constructivist and social constructionist theories that would eventually attain prominence. Nakash and Alegría also (2013) suggested that clinical judgments about clients were influenced by the clinicians' own prior experiences, the quality of the working alliance with the client, and various nonverbal cues, such as appearance, body language, tone, and facial expressions.

CULTURAL CONTEXT FOR DIAGNOSTIC IMPRESSIONS DURING (AND AFTER) INTAKE INTERVIEWS

In summary, the focus on client symptoms, which is supposed to be the core of assessment, does not appear to be the only factor that drives the diagnosis of a client. This helps explain why there is considerable disagreement with respect to diagnoses. Since intake interviews are primarily organized around the search for recognizable patterns that fit into one of the several hundred supposedly distinct diagnostic categories, we are limited by discrete, finite choices available. These relatively artificial templates are another example of a map that doesn't necessarily capture all the territory covered.

Danny's case turned out to be much more complex than either of the interviewers considered. With limited progress made in short-term hospitalization and documented outpatient failure, Danny was admitted into a long-term residential treatment program. His progress was limited at first, even when stabilized on medication and regular therapy sessions. It was clear that the current diagnosis and case conceptualization were not as comprehensive as necessary to settle on an effective treatment.

A new set of neuropsychological tests were ordered, including magnetic resonance imaging (MRI), which revealed some neurological problems. Medications were adjusted to reflect this new data. The treatment team then initiated some specific, targeted behavioral interventions. One area that seemed particularly important to address was related to Danny's confusion and distress over his sexual identity issues. He was thus provided with opportunities to fully express his feelings in both individual and group sessions. In both settings, he was met with considerable support and acceptance. He was also rewarded with desired privileges when he exhibited appropriate and compliant behavior on the unit instead of his usual acting out. His most appreciated reward was being allowed to wear red nail polish, which had important symbolic value to him during this process of coming out.

As his social skills improved, Danny verbalized how important it was to him that he felt heard and understood by the staff. Previously he said he felt like an insect that was being examined under a microscope by doctors who only seemed interested in assigning a label to him. He had felt dehumanized, as if he was simply an object that was processed through their system.

After his discharge, Danny made concerted efforts to abstain from drugs and alcohol. He was also grateful that the staff had looked more deeply into his case, identifying some of the neglected pieces of his complicated set of problems that had their origin in a host of different sources including neurological, psychological, social, and cultural influences.

Like so many other cases, diagnostic impressions of an individual are strongly shaped by prevailing cultural forces during the time. It is rare any more that we see cases of hysteria, neurasthenia ("American nervousness"), inadequate personality, dementia praecox ("atrophy of emotions"), or vapors (imbalance of bodily humors usually attributed to "women of an independent mind"). Or consider during the mid-19th-century doctors devised a diagnosis of *dysaesthesia aethiopica*, which was considered a disease that afflicted "lazy Negroes." The only cure for this condition was slavery to make certain they received exercise and obedience training.

This leads one to consider how misconceptions may still operate today in the ways that clients are diagnosed. There is a disproportionate number of extreme psychiatric labels assigned to those from lower socioeconomic status or minority cultures (South-Paul, 2015). If you happen to be wealthy, part of the majority culture, or in a position of power, you may be more likely to receive a more moderate and socially acceptable diagnosis. For example, minority adolescents are more likely to receive a disruptive behavior diagnosis (e.g., oppositional defiant disorder, conduct disorder) whereas mainstream clients were more likely to receive a mood disorder diagnosis (Liang et al., 2016). Research on adults and differential diagnosis with respect to ethnicity and socioeconomic status is limited to nonexistent. Among adults, ethnic minorities are far more likely to be diagnosed with a psychiatric disorder (McGuire & Miranda, 2008) That's why famous and rich people like Howard Hughes, Elon Musk, and Steve Jobs have been described as "eccentric" rather than "crazy."

Not only do intake interviewers view their prospective clients differently, depending on how they dress, talk, and present themselves, but also clients from different backgrounds describe their experiences and conditions in very different ways. For example, Guarnaccia, Canino, Rubio-Stipec, and Bravo (1993) studied anxiety in Puerto Rico after floods and mudslides devasted the territory in 1985. Referred to as *ataque de nervios*, symptoms included uncontrollable screaming, crying, trembling, fainting or seizure-like episodes, suicidal gestures, and verbal or physical aggression. Hsu and Holstein (1997) found that Asian clients were more likely to identify somatic symptoms such as dizziness and blurred vision and, only when asked later, admitted to emotional distress.

Yi disclosed during her first session that she was extremely agitated and upset because just before she falls asleep at night a disgruntled ancestor's spirit visits her. This disrupts her sleep to the point she is exhausted during the day. She also reported a number of distressing physical symptoms, especially in her abdomen and back. She had already been referred to medical specialists, but they had not been able to find any organic cause for this suffering.

It was only after more intensive questioning that the therapist learned that Yi, although born in the United States, had strong ties to her Hmong culture. At first, she denied feeling anything resembling what we ordinarily think of as depression, insisting that her troubles were caused by the angry spirits. Previous mental health professionals had recommended admission to a psychiatric facility to deal with her delusions and hallucinations, but Yi had refused until doctors first fixed her supposed medical problems.

Questioned further, Yi admitted that she was rather unhappy and nervous much of the time. Not only was she having trouble sleeping, but she had also lost her appetite. She had trouble concentrating on things for very long and reported she felt "sad" most of the time. This description is based on a case described by Chentsova-Dutton, Ryder, and Tsai (2014) in their discussion about the ways that depression is experienced, metabolized, and described by clients from different cultural backgrounds. As another example, a Vietnamese client complained to her primary care physician that her heart hurt. He naturally referred her to a cardiologist with a tentative diagnosis of congenital heart defect. After a thorough workup and electrocardiogram, they could find nothing amiss and so referred her to other specialists. It was only much later that it was finally recognized that in her culture and language, she was describing herself as depressed, lonely, and sad, having experienced a series of recent losses and disappointments.

In addition, how people from different cultural backgrounds experience and describe their conditions are strongly impacted by the prevailing values, rituals, media, and beliefs of the times. Consider the ways that certain popular conditions and disorders no longer exist while others seemingly emerge in epidemic proportions. During Freud's time, hysteria was a frequent diagnosis whereas a few decades ago attention-deficit disorder was the rage, fueled primarily by pharmaceutical companies that were promoting Adderall° and Ritalin°. At one time "inadequate personality disorder" and "gender identity disorder" were common diagnoses but then were eliminated once it was discovered the extent to which they reflected cultural biases. Then we saw a dramatic influx of Asperger's syndrome. Nowadays, opioid addiction, gaming disorder, disinhibited social engagement disorder, premenstrual dysphoric disorder, and Internet addiction have been added as options.

Perhaps one of the most dramatic examples of how culture affects and influences mental disorders and their diagnosis is in the case of Kevin Hall, an Olympic sailor and national champion. Hall believed his life was broadcast in real time in much the same way as the character from the movie *The Truman Show* (Gold & Gold, 2012; Kottler, 2019). Similar to the actor Jim Carrey in the film, Hall was convinced that his every action was being controlled by an unseen director and observed by the rest of the world. Sometimes the voice would order him to do strange or dangerous things, all to entertain the audience. It wasn't until Hall consulted with Joel Gold, a psychiatrist who specialized in the ways that culture shapes mental illness and its diagnoses (Gold & Gold, 2014), that he realized how he was being so strongly impacted by the popularity of reality television shows like *Survivor, Big Brother*, and *The Bachelor* in which viewers tune into live action as it unfolds. "The mind supplies the contours of delusions," observed Marantz (2013), but "culture fills in details." That helps explain, for instance, why delusions take such different forms in various parts of the world. In Taipei, people may report being visited by spirits that control their behavior whereas in Christian countries delusions take the form of feeling god-like. Given the pervasive influences of technology in today's world, it is no surprise that the particular manifestations of mental illness are evolving to include control by media.

AND WHAT ABOUT THE CLIENT'S AGENDA DURING A FIRST MEETING?

We sometimes forget that therapists aren't the only ones conducting an intake interview; clients have their own goals for the initial session and conduct their own assessment. They usually have particular questions in mind:

- "Do you know what the heck you are doing and are you qualified, expert, and experienced enough to help me?"
- "Do you like me?"
- "Are you someone I can trust who will not judge me harshly?"
- "Will you think I'm crazy or demented because of these weird problems I'm having?"
- "Will you tell me the truth about certain things that I may ask you?"
- "If the you think the 'truth' is more than I can handle, will you instead tell me nice things instead—in a convincing way so I believe they are really true?"

- "Will you believe what I tell you and agree with my view of the situation?"
- "Are you worth the time, inconvenience, and money I'm spending to come here?"
- "Will you fix me quickly, with a minimum of discomfort and pain?"
- "After I tell you how the terrible things in my life and you see me at my worst, will you *still* like me?"
- "Will you like me better than all your other clients?"

You will notice that a major concern, repeated several times, is the client's focus on impression management. A study of the tactics that clients often use during initial interviews to control and influence a therapist's perceptions and to solicit approval found several common approaches (Fruhauf, Figlioli, Oehler, & Caspar, 2015).

1. *Displaying a positive, upbeat mood.* Clients present themselves as amusing, interesting, and in a good mood, despite their troubles. When the therapist asks an intrusive, uncomfortable question, they may joke around or introduce a distraction in some way.

   THERAPIST: I see that you are trying to make the best of your situation, but you seem rather anxious to me.

   CLIENT: Well, you are observant, aren't you? My mother was like that at times, which drove me crazy. But hey, that's your job, isn't it? [Laughs]

2. *Offering complements.* Clients attempt to win approval and support by offering positive reactions, as much to reassure themselves as "seduce" the therapist.

   CLIENT: "Wow. That was really on target! I'd never really thought about things like that before. Thank you so much for pointing that out.

3. *Setting limits and rules.* As a way to give notice regarding what is off limits, clients issue warnings to control and influence the relationship.

   THERAPIST: It may very well be that part of your problems may be directly related to the amount of alcohol and weed you've been consuming to manage your stress.

   CLIENT: You know, I saw another therapist once before and she said something like that, which I thought was so rude and inappropriate. I never went back to her after that.

4. *Setting the agenda.* Clients may try to control the proceedings from the outset, dictating the content, structure, and chronology of the intake process.

   THERAPIST: I was wondering if you could tell me a bit more about the frequency and duration of those feelings of being out of control.

   CLIENT: Before we get into that I'd like to start from the beginning. If you don't mind I'd prefer to tell you about the way my parents always tried to control me.

5. *Complaining about external factors.* Clients often wish to introduce individuals and extraneous variables that can be blamed for the troubles. Once again this represents an attempt to shape the therapist's opinion in such a way that a more favorable impression is made. Ironically, clients don't understand this often has the opposite effect in that it triggers a belief that this will be a resistant, defensive case.

   THERAPIST: So what you have been saying is that this depression first began when you were dismissed from your previous job and . . ."

   CLIENT: Absolutely not! I'm sorry you got that impression. What I meant is that my boss was so manipulative, always taking credit for my work, that I had no choice other than to leave. Yes, I've been discouraged that I can't find another decent job, but the economy sucks right now. And besides, I told you I have to take care of my younger brother.

6. *Surrendering and supplication.* Presenting oneself as helpless and without the ability or power to control events. This is intended to win sympathy and recruit the therapist as a conspirator to support a position of laziness and inaction. In such cases, there is often a number of secondary gains the client enjoys related to avoiding responsibility, escaping dreaded tasks, gaining concessions, and controlling others to do one's bidding.

   CLIENT: Sure, I wish I could be more direct and assertive in these situations, but how can I? Nobody really lets me do what I want. People always seem to let me down. I've tried so many times, but it just doesn't work. I was hoping you might have some different ideas for me.

7. *Self-promotion.* This is the classic strategy of image management in any context in which an individual brags about accomplishments, achievements, importance, and social standing.

THERAPIST: From what you've told me so far, it would appear that these sudden panic episodes represent a complete loss of control at times.

CLIENT: Look, that's not really what it seems. I have a lot of responsibility at work. There are over a dozen people who report to me. The company depends on me to take care of our sales figures. I have over 8,000 followers on social media. So, yes, I may feel anxious a bit at times, but surely that's understandable given everything I have to deal with.

8. *Emotional avoidance.* We see this one all the time: Clients feel uncomfortable and display incongruence between what they seem to be feeling versus what they are showing on the outside.

THERAPIST: That must have been so incredibly disturbing to you, after everything else you've been through.

CLIENT: [Shrugs] Well, maybe at the time. [Laughs] But, hey, it's no big deal, right?

The researchers concluded their study of these various tactics employed by reminding therapists how important it is to observe and assess the client's impression management strategies and attempts to influence and control the interactions. This is what allows us to better structure and adapt a customized relationship that is ideally suited to a client's particular needs and style. This means that rather than trying to only accomplish our own agenda of collecting health and background information and conducting an assessment and diagnostic process, we should be equally concerned with allowing clients to feel actively empowered in pursuing their own checklist of concerns. While most of us would agree with this recommendation, it is far more challenging than we imagine because of the time constraints and pressures we feel to accomplish those tasks we believe are important to meet our own needs.

In a follow-up study to investigate how therapists actually respond to these various tactics, the researchers found that, naturally, some of them were more challenging than others (Fruhauf, Figlioli, & Casper, 2017). For instance, with respect to a client displaying a positive, upbeat mood, it's fairly standard that we might simply listen attentively and nod with an interested smile. However, when a client becomes overly critical, controlling, or argumentative during an initial meeting, it may be best in such circumstances to apologize and invite further elaboration.

There are clear differences between how beginners and more experienced therapists might handle these situations. It would make sense that those with less experience would be more deferential but also more defensive at times. Experts are more inclined to confront or challenge clients early in sessions but do so in a nondominant and cautious manner, paying close attention to the nuances within the interaction. By taking more risks, the authors also found that this led to the increased likelihood of clients feeling unappreciated but much depends on which tactics the clients used. The conclusion seemed to indicate that a neutral response to such provocations was most desired, resorting to a more direct challenge only with the most negative or critical verbalizations.

THE REAL AGENDA

There are some among us that view the whole intake process as focused exclusively on searching for what's "wrong" with people. Almost all the initial inquiries are directed at uncovering disturbing symptoms, unresolved problems, and evidence of psychopathology, small or large. We hone in on dysfunctions, toxic interactions, disabilities, weaknesses, deficits, limitations, disordered thinking, and self-defeating behavior. We search for illness and addictions. We assess for potential to harm oneself or others.

Although the illusion or myth of intake interviews is that they collect all the data and background necessary to settle on a diagnosis and treatment plan, such a definitive goal is virtually impossible. Of course, we recognize this most of the time, which is why we call it a "working diagnosis" or "tentative treatment plan," subject to amendments over time as we gather more information. In fact, the main purpose of this first meeting is to construct a working alliance built on mutual trust. Sometimes we are so overly focused on our own plans that we forget that our overriding goal is to connect with our clients.

Constructivist approaches and narrative therapy have been influential in reconceptualizing the intake interview as something much more than and different from assessment and diagnosis of a client. We must recognize and acknowledge how any first meeting, especially in a therapeutic context, has several important distinctive features. First, and most critically, it sets the stage and structure for most of what follows. A certain sequence of action unfolds in a particular way when two people meet for the first time, often creating a template that remains invariant over time. Second, the client in such a situation is in an extremely vulnerable and overreactive state. Besides, whatever is bothersome enough to lead the client to seek help in the first place, it is absolutely terrifying and bewildering to see a therapist for the first time. Anxiety is ramped through the roof and is often accompanied by a hefty dose of shame.

In an attempt to deconstruct the pathological emphasis within typical intake interviews, Timm (2015) views the process through a narrative lens that looks instead at the client's view of the story, as well as ways to increase hope for the future. The principal goals are not just to find problems but also to encourage the client to reflect and share the dominant story with a glimpse of what it might be like to reauthor a different version. In other words, while an assessment process is undertaken, a narrative intake balances identifying strengths and resources with identifying deficits. Attention is also paid to coping skills, examples of resilience in the past, external and cultural influences, relational connections, and so forth.

If you are wondering what a narrative intake might look and sound like compared to a traditional, mental model, DSM-driven version, Timm (2015) provides a list of potential questions (see Table 8.1). You will note how the inquiries are framed according to the more tentative, curious questioning style that is embedded in narrative approaches.

It's quite evident that there's a world of difference in the tone of the questions that Timm (2015) created compared to our usual procedure, which is more similar to an interrogation. It would perhaps not surprise you to learn that when the write-up and report is constructed, the client is invited to include his or her own descriptions of the problems, symptoms, and ideas, as well as an evaluation of what the session was like. Narrative therapists may routinely write summary letters to their clients after

---

Table 8.1 EXAMPLES OF ALTERNATIVE INTAKE QUESTIONS INFORMED BY A NARRATIVE APPROACH

---

1. What are you struggling with most right now? What would you call this problem? When you've sought help previously what have others named this problem? How has that label, diagnosis, or description affected you?
2. Tell me about the background and history with this problem.
3. Tell me about some times in the past when you were reasonably satisfied dealing with this difficulty, even if it wasn't completely successful.
4. Who in your life supports your decision to get help?
5. What strengths do you have that will be helpful to us in working through this difficulty?
6. What are some things related to your problem(s) that could possibly undermine or sabotage our sessions together?
7. What would you most like me to know about you that is especially important and significant to you?
8. What questions do you wish I had asked you? What questions do you have for me?

From M. Timm, 2015, Deconstructing pathology: A narrative view of the intake process. *Journal of Constructivist Psychology, 28*(4), 316–328.

every session, in the tradition of Michael White, one of the founders of the approach. Likewise, they may ask the clients to also write summary descriptions of their experience and perceptions. In a similar vein, the final report may contain direct quotes and excerpts from the client's own narrative.

There are lots of reasons and excuses why such a far more flexible and client-centered approach might not work well in certain settings, such as mandated court-ordered clients, incarcerated clients, military, employee assistance programs, and similar highly structured environments, but there are still ways that the intake process can be softened and expanded, even with time limitations. One main take-away from this description is that all of us could try to give more attention to client strengths, need for validation and approval, and personal agency.

It is another one of the myths and misconceptions of therapy that the ultimate purpose of the first session is solely for us to examine the client to assess and diagnose symptoms and plan for future treatment. The intake interview is most often viewed as simply the initial contact. Yet, Talmon (1993) wondered if in adopting this assumption we sell ourselves, and our clients, way short in terms of what may be possible. It has long been assumed that when a client never returns after the first session it must be because they were dissatisfied with the way they were treated; it is presumed this must be a failure. Working for a large health conglomerate, Talmon decided to investigate further and discovered, to his surprise, that 78% of those he contacted who never returned reported that they had already gotten what they needed. This was mind boggling, so much so that a colleague replicated the study and found even more compelling evidence since 88% of those surveyed reported they were pleased with the results they obtained after a single session. It turns out that these were not treatment failures at all but rather limited successes. This realization led to the dismissal of the previous belief that when clients don't return it is because they were disappointed. It also led to a very different set of expectations regarding what could be accomplished in a single meeting—if the therapist focuses on actually addressing the initial complaints rather than merely collecting data for a treatment plan (Hoyt & Talmon, 2014, Hoyt, Bobele, Slive, Young, & Talmon, 2018).

CHAPTER 9

༄

What's So Special About the 50-Minute Hour?

"So, I guess I should finally tell you what's been going on, what I've been holding back all these months. I know you've been wondering . . ."

"Oh, gee, I'm so sorry. But our time's up. We'll have to pick this up again next week."

There are all kinds of reasons why this potential confession was about to be disclosed at the end of the session. Maybe it was a kind of gamesmanship, a manipulative ploy to gain extra time, to find out how much the therapist really cared—enough to extend the session beyond the allotted time? It could have been an oversight; perhaps the client was simply not aware that the time had expired. It may also represent a magic moment of readiness in which the client felt sufficient trust to share what he had been holding back for quite some time. But regardless of the reason, the session was indeed over.

It's interesting to consider how this format became so universally standardized. Which definitive authority decided that therapy sessions should last exactly 50 minutes? How did that evolve into standard practice? Where's the evidence that 10 minutes short of an hour is, in fact, the optimal amount of time to get the most out of therapeutic treatment? Where's the research demonstrating this is the perfect "dosage" for every person who shows up, regardless of their symptoms and particular needs?

There is no other aspect of healthcare in which every single patient who walks in the door (or is delivered by ambulance) is given the identical

Myths, Misconceptions, and Invalid Assumptions of Counseling and Psychotherapy. Jeffrey A. Kottler and Richard S. Balkin, Oxford University Press (2020). © Oxford University Press.
DOI: 10.1093/oso/9780190090692.001.0001

treatment, medication, or procedure. The clinical decision depends on the person's age, weight, sex, frequency and severity of symptoms, family and medical history, insurance benefits, blood chemistry, health condition, kidney functioning, allergies, and probable compliance with instructions, to mention a few factors.

Individual treatment dosage—that is, how much and how often a drug should be taken or procedure repeated—is usually calculated according to empirically and mathematically derived formulae. Let's say, for example, a doctor orders 45 mg of a drug to be administered intravenously. The drug containers hold 20 mg per 5 mL of saline solution. The equation is solved at 11.25 mL of solution for the patient but then is adjusted according to other individual factors related to the particular case. So, then, how do we explain, much less defend, that we administer the identical dosage of psychotherapy to everyone, varying only the frequency and number of sessions?

Surely there must be some scientific and compelling evidence that this in the best interests of all our clients. Will (2018) provided a history of the 50-minute session until the present time, even though the reality is, as a matter of financial billing, it doesn't actually exist any longer. As noted by Muhlheim (2013), in an attempt to diversify billing practices (e.g., history and physical, medication management, psychotherapy), the American Medical Association and American Psychiatric Association lobbied the Center for Medicare and Medicaid Services to amend their procedural terminology, which is adopted by insurance companies. So, the 45- to 50-minute session, once billed as 90806, which allowed time for payment, appointments, and progress notes, was replaced by three other codes:

- 90832 – psychotherapy 30 minutes
- 90834 – psychotherapy 45 minutes
- 90837 – psychotherapy 60 minutes

Although these changes did allow for more flexibility by psychiatrists, the motive was primarily financially driven so that psychiatrists would have more options for scheduling their medication management and brief consultations related to side effects and to increase the likelihood of compliance. Nonmedical practitioners, however, still mostly stick to the "standard" time length that has become virtually universal across most settings, context, and time periods. There are a few notable exceptions for those who may work in school settings, conduct home visits, or otherwise serve clients who don't fit the usual mode.

DETERMINING AN OPTIMAL DOSAGE

In the good 'ol days of Sigmund Freud, a proper session was 50 minutes, even though he really did not watch the clock. But what's so magical about that amount of time? Why not, say, 25 minutes or 75 minutes?

The rationale behind the 50-minute hour was always for pragmatic reasons: It just fit nicely with one's work schedule to arrange appointments on the hour. However, in 1922, Max Etingon, working for a clinic in Germany, attempted to reduce session length to 30 minutes. It was an innovative idea, but alas, he concluded that this shortened session length was simply inadequate for the work he was doing.

Friedman (2013) wondered if two 30-minute sessions had the same potency as one meeting that lasts a full hour. He acknowledged that clients may save their best stuff for the very end since it is often assumed to have some manipulative component to it. But certainly it takes a client, especially someone with trust issues, to warm up a bit before they get to the most uncomfortable parts. The main issue, as he sees it, is that we really have little idea about the optimal "dose" effect in psychotherapy. This is all the more surprising when we consider that all the money allocated to research therapy outcomes represents less than 1% of what is invested in drugs. Psychiatrists know almost precisely how many milligrams of Prozac® to prescribe per day for a 3-week trial, but there is no equivalency for our work in sessions. We just shrug and assume it must be about 50 minutes, plus or minus a few.

There have been prominent figures who have tested this sacred cow, challenged the status quo, and experimented with alternatives that seemed to fit better with their client's needs or their preferences and workstyle. The French psychoanalyst Jacques Lacan experimented with all kinds of variations, depending on his mood or what the client presented. He refused to take appointments. Clients would just show up in his waiting room and become engaged in impromptu group sessions while waiting to be selected for a session. Then Lacan would appear at the door, scan the room, and point to someone. Once the session began, if he felt the client was wasting time, he might dismiss him or her after a few minutes and announce that the conversation was over. On the other hand, if there was serious work going on he might not interrupt the flow for hours.

To be truly transparent, it was generally agreed that Lacan was often impulsive and whimsical when dismissing a client. "The ending of the session, unexpected and unwanted, was like a rude awakening," one of his clients reported, "like being torn out of a dream by a loud alarm" (Schneiderman, 1984, p. 132). It was also suggested that the main reason he abbreviated his sessions was so that he could better fleece his clients out of their money, charging more for less.

At the other end of the spectrum, Albert Ellis felt that he could do his best work in 25-minute intervals, making it possible for him to see more clients during the day. And, of course, this brings up the underlying issue that the 50-minute hour (or 25-minute session or 90-minute intake interview) has always been structured this way for the convenience of the therapist, not because it is necessarily optimal for the work we do with clients. It makes scheduling easier on the hour. It allows us time to take bathroom breaks, reply to messages, and complete required documentation. Most of all, it creates a familiar structure for our days.

PROFESSION OR BUSINESS?

There has been very limited research on this topic and even less evidence to support the very idea of sessions lasting 50 minutes, as opposed to any other length of time. In one of the first such studies (Bierenbaum, Nichols, & Schwartz, 1976), there was absolutely no relationship between the amount of time spent in session and the eventual outcomes, although clients did report that they enjoyed having more time to talk things out. That's nice, but it didn't seem to have any effect on the reduction of presenting problems. Two decades later, another study (P. R. Turner, Valtierra, Talken, Miller, & DeAnda, 1996) once again found no difference in either client satisfaction or reduction in symptoms when sessions were 30 minutes or 50 minutes, perhaps supporting what Ellis had discovered. One interesting finding by Noble (2015) was that it might actually be best for clients to decide how long their sessions should last, based on their needs, schedule, and problems. Why should the clinician decide this alone, since not a single mainstream approach dictates a set number of sessions, nor does it prescribe the mandated length.

Grohol (2008) made the point that because psychotherapy is not just a profession but also a business, it must abide by certain rules and parameters that make the system run efficiently. Even though Grohol acknowledged that the standard 50-minute hour is for the therapist's convenience, not for any client benefit, he also challenged the belief that clinicians really need these breaks to get through their days with their composure still intact. Grohol cited as an example a colleague who actually uses a kitchen timer that ticks away through the hour, dinging when time is up, cutting a client off in mid-sentence.

The 50-minute hour is a convention that has become so accepted and standardized that we rarely question any longer whether this is the really the best option for our clients. We are not so much suggesting that we change the tradition as much as just examining the origins and reasoning behind the choice. There are all kinds of procedures and policies that are designed for the convenience of professionals so that we maximize our efficiency and comfort. There would be chaos if we decided that classes should be scheduled just as long as the professor and students feel like it or based on the amount of material on the agenda for that day. Airlines overbook flights to maximize their profits, not because it is better for their customers. Doctors schedule multiple patients during the same time slot so they can keep themselves most productive, regardless of how inconvenient or annoying this is to be those they serve. In each of these cases, professionals are in the business of selling space and time, limited commodities that demand we maximize their potential earning and productive power.

TIME MANAGEMENT

This brings up the whole issue of boundaries in sessions and how they are enforced. I (Jeffrey) learned to be very precise in my time management because I once had a supervisor who would knock on the door when 5 minutes were left in the session, and he demanded that we end after 50 minutes, plus or minus 60 seconds. If for some reason we ran 15 seconds over that time limit, he would open the door and stare at us. It was humiliating. And now I question my compulsive need to have so internalized this imperative that when I teach, give speeches, or do workshops I *still* end the experience within a minute of the assigned endpoint.

Yet the reality for many practitioners is something quite different from what Jeffrey describes. Some therapists routinely allow their sessions to run over the delegated time, especially if the client is in the middle of something gut-wrenching or especially significant. As with so many aspects of the profession, there is passionate disagreement and variations of style related to this issue. Some clinicians believe that because therapy is a "holding environment" (particularly for those who work with disturbed personality issues), it is absolutely critical to maintain time parameters. On the other hand, other professionals have a looser, more flexible view of session time, having no problem running over if there is nobody else waiting. So this becomes an issue that reflects what is going on in our own lives, how we view time as something stable and indelible, or whether we see it as a flowing experience that depends on the situation and context.

Let's also be honest about financial realities. We mentioned earlier how the coding procedures of insurance providers determine compensation for therapists. When new standards went into effect a few years ago, practitioners were informed they could bill for their services according to certain time increments. The standard 50-minute session was redefined in such a way that anything from 38 to 52 minutes would be paid at the 45-minute level; after 53 minutes, it could be billed as a 60-minute session. The intention of such changes was to allow for greater flexibility in care (for psychiatrists), but the result was increased confusion. And, once again, there is no real compelling evidence to support a decision about how long any session should last, whether it should be standardized or variable according to what is happening on any given day.

There are many times when it feels like everything has already been said in a given session. The client and therapist sit silently staring at one another, both glancing at the clock, wondering where things should go next. Supposedly these uneasy silences are productive in the sense that they push clients to dig deeper for material that had previously been buried or ignored. But another explanation is that this is just a good ending point. One can't help but wonder if it might be more useful to "bank" the left over 16 minutes and save them for another time when a more lengthy discussion is needed. We are not saying this is entirely practical, just asking the question why sessions are designed to be the length they are and whether that ought to be challenged in more meaningful ways.

VARIATIONS ON A THEME

Mountford (2005) was one professional who decided to challenge the myth that the 50-minute hour was the ideal standard, feeling quite strongly that one size can't possibly fit all. He decided to experiment with session lengths when one of his clients complained that she wasn't quite finished with her narrative and pleaded for a bit of extra time. He decided to extend the time for her, as well as with a few other clients, even though his colleagues vehemently criticized him for doing so. Noticing improved results in his work, he wondered what would happen if he experimented with allowing his clients to decide how long a given session should last, assuming this was feasible for his schedule. He even decided to market this to potential clients as "client-led" therapy.

Although you might imagine that clients would take advantage of this freedom of choice, Mountford found that most of his clients stayed within reasonable limits, most preferring longer sessions of 75 to 105 minutes and were charged accordingly. Almost nobody selected the standard 50-minute hour although some preferred briefer, more frequent sessions. It was his conclusion that therapy has a natural rather than an artificially derived ending and that we could take better advantage of that.

There are other advantages of variable-length sessions in that it empowers clients to control their own growth and recovery. It allows the material and issues to direct the structure, rather than the other way around. It maximizes flexibility. And yet, it also defers to clients that they really do know what is in their own best interests, which may be somewhat suspect.

There is also the matter of convenience and predictability in scheduling our days. Some practitioners have decided to standardize the length of their sessions but just in other increments than have been commonplace. We mentioned how Albert Ellis reduced his sessions to 25 minutes, but that was mostly so he could see more people during the day with a long waiting list. There are all kinds of other legitimate reasons for scheduling more abbreviated sessions for certain clients. Young children have shorter attention spans. Adults with attention deficit disorders would do better in briefer meetings. Then there are style differences in which some people do better when they can concentrate on more intensive, shorter, focused conversations.

CHALLENGING ORTHODOXY: ABBREVIATED AND EXTENDED SESSIONS

The more frequent variation on this theme is to conduct more extended rather than truncated sessions. One therapist, for example, sees a tremendous advantage for practitioners to design their sessions in such a way to best meet the needs of their clients and reflect their own style. "I can see a client for what I believe to be the optimum amount of time for concentrated focus. There's no 'time's up' when things are getting interesting" (Alman, 2015). She not only schedules 90-minute sessions but allows herself 30-minute breaks in between so that she can remain fresh and fully present.

Within the contemporary practice of psychoanalytic therapy, the 50-minute hour had been considered sacrosanct, even if the great master, Sigmund Freud, never bothered sticking with such rigid parameters. Friedman (2013) mentioned one example when Gustav Mahler consulted with Freud after the famous composer was immobilized by depression upon learning he had been diagnosed with heart problem and his wife was having an affair. Freud instructed Mahler to join him for a stroll, and they spent 4 hours walking through the streets of Vienna while discussing the problems.

Beginning at the turn of the century, scholars and clinicians began challenging this orthodoxy and experimenting with "double sessions" as an option for some clients who were likely to respond better to more intense, lengthy sessions. One review of this practice explored both the advantages and dangers of expanding the time frame for sessions (Shapiro, 2000). The author had discovered after an extensive literature review on variable length sessions that there had only been a single exploratory article (Cohen, 1980) during the preceding 20 years, at least with respect to psychoanalytic treatment. Even so, the focus of the discussion was primarily addressing the specific instances when such a structure was justified, framed in the vernacular of the model. Thus double sessions were indicated to accelerate the removal of defenses or work through transference issues.

The reality of such a practice, at least historically, is that longer sessions are scheduled as "makeup" when either the client or therapist has been on vacation, or else when an out-of-town person shows up with limited availability. Even in those circumstances, it was warned that this extended time frame may contribute to collusion since the therapist has obviously failed to deliver adequate service in the usual 50 minutes.

Although there are many such therapists (and their clients) who prefer extended sessions as their standard operating procedure, this is based mostly on first-person reports. There have been few systematic investigations actually comparing the relative efficacy of different lengths of sessions (30 or 60 minutes versus 90 or 120 minutes). In one of the few studies of the differential treatment effects of variable length sessions, P. R. Turner et al. (1996) divided three groups of clients at a university counseling center into 30-, 60-, and 120-minute sessions with each of the groups all receiving the same number of treatment hours. After first conducting intake interviews to rule out individuals with psychotic or personality disorders that would likely not respond well to any form of brief therapy, they compared the progress and satisfaction of the groups and found them to be basically similar. They concluded, "The ability of the therapist to be present and empathic with the client may be more influential than the length of the treatment hour" (p. 231). This, of course, is consistent with much of what we know and understand about the importance of the relationship as the single best predictor of success and satisfaction (Kottler & Balkin, 2017).

It should be pointed out that although the clients preferred and enjoyed the option of abbreviating or extending the length of their sessions, their therapists were much less satisfied. One of the realities of conducing 30-minute sessions is that sometimes they were forced to see two clients in a single hour without a break, increasing their burdens of stress. It would seem that systemic and organizational changes would need to be made to accommodate these more flexible formats.

FLEXIBLE FORMATS

As the practice of counseling and psychotherapy become more frequently associated with integrated medical care, it is important that clinicians are able to adapt their practice to fit the needs of patients in such a context (Lenz et al., 2018; Pomerantz, Corson, & Detzer, 2009). The therapist's role includes a variety of different responsibilities that might include health promotion, managing chronic pain, stress management, weight loss, ensuring compliance to medical recommendations, self-regulation, lifestyle adjustments, smoking cessation, and family consultations, each of which requires a different length of time to complete effectively.

This shift in professional roles requires being far more flexible in the ways we schedule and structure sessions in much the same way that physicians adapt their particular methods, resources, and time parameters to fit the particular complaints and needs of a case. Settings and organizations often dictate the amount of time that can be allocated. Whereas 5% of physicians spend less than 9 minutes with each patient, the vast majority average about 17 minutes (Statista, 2018). Of course, the amount of time would vary depending on specialty and the sorts of illnesses that are presented—which is exactly our point. Cardiologists, oncologists, and endocrinologists, who deal with more complex and life-threatening diseases, spend more time in consultations (20 minutes) while primary care physicians, who do mostly screening and more routine examinations, allocate about 15 minutes.

It's interesting to consider why we might demand that *all* our clients spend the exact same amount of time with us, regardless of their issues, complaints, preferences, resources, and needs, as if this one size fits everyone. Likewise, therapists who do hypnotic inductions for weight loss, eye movement desensitization and reprocessing for trauma, cognitive-behavioral therapy for stress inoculation, or psychodynamic exploration may similarly conduct standard 50-minute sessions.

It's also instructive how group therapists learned long ago to adapt their variable session lengths to fit the context of their clients and settings. I (Jeffrey) have led group sessions of 42 minutes in an elementary school, 65 minutes in a high school, 75 minutes in a university counseling center, 90 and 120 minutes in private practice, and 12 hours during intensive workshops and, while conducting home visits in rural Nepal, staying anywhere from 5 minutes to check on the welfare of a child to spending the whole night because it was impossible to return until transportation could be arranged. In each case, the time limit of the session was guided by the setting, context, population, goals, and institutional policies.

IN PRAISE OF THE 50-MINUTE HOUR?

Despite our passionate critique of the status quo and the myths associated with the standard practice, we've mentioned many of the valid reasons for this convention. Unlike medical practitioners we've highlighted, therapists are comparably limited in the options available to help clients with the "talking cure." We can't order (and charge) for a bunch of routine tests, nor can we rely on surgical or other medical procedures to address the presenting complaints. All we have to offer is our time, partitioned into appropriate segments. We are also in the business of communicating caring and respect, conditions that are hardly optimized when we keep people waiting for attention. That is why, unlike others in the healthcare professions, we scrupulously honor appointments at their agreed upon time. Whereas medical providers seem untroubled when they routinely make their patients wait for 10, 20, or even 30 minutes, so they can maximize their earning potential to take care of multiple patients simultaneously or deal with emergencies, therapists try as much as possible to see clients promptly and predictably. It is part of the treatment, so to speak—a boundary within the "holding environment." We mostly prefer the experience to be reliable and dependable, whether that is always advantageous or not. Our clients appreciate this consistency; they count on it. In a world of uncertainty and capriciousness, it's nice to know there's one place where their time is valued and respected.

Although concern for the client's experience is one important rationale for why we standardize our session times, another legitimate reason is so that we can maximize our own comfort and effectiveness. As we are all well aware, doing therapy is emotionally and physically exhausting, especially if our goal is to remain as much fully present as possible during sessions.

In the study mentioned earlier, for example, the researchers may have discovered that it doesn't seem to matter that much to clients whether their sessions were a half hour, 45 or 50 minutes, or 2 hours; however, it mattered a *lot* to the clinicians who felt increasingly burdened by shorter sessions that led to expectations of increased productivity. It's hard enough to keep track of 8 to 10 clients in a day, remembering all the details of their lives and specifics of their case; what about if we were expected to see 15 to 20 people in a day?

Our ability to be helpful to clients is directly related to the degree to which we can remain maximally attentive, focused, and present with them. Yet our concentration and energy are necessarily limited resources that must be carefully preserved and protected; they must be distributed wisely and judiciously so as to not waste our most precious commodities. That is why we arrange our days and the time available to allow us to function at our peak performance. To do so, we need opportunities for recovery, processing, reflection, and self-care. We need time to take a breath. We require time to complete administrative tasks and the voluminous amount of record keeping. It's also nice to be able to talk to colleagues about cases—and about our lives. It's important to keep in touch with friends and family during the work day, just as others do. It's lovely to be able to go for a stroll, top off our caffeine levels, and not just "grab a bite of lunch" but actually savor a meal to sustain us throughout the day. All of us this is predicated on a structure that includes periods of rest and recuperation, even if this is just a few minutes between sessions.

Each of us (hopefully) discovers and develops certain personal habits and an individualized style of practice that best reflect our signature strengths and preferences. Our intention in this discussion is not to suggest we discard the conventional 50-minute hour altogether but to challenge the myth that it is sacred and immutable. Each of us is different in a multitude of ways. Not only is our setting and client population quite varied but so is our therapeutic style and way of being in the world.

It has surprised us over the years how different practitioners are in the ways they operate throughout the day. Therapists furnish and arrange their offices in so many different styles. They develop or adopt such unique therapeutic methods. And they also seem to have such individualistic ways of structuring their time and metabolizing what they encounter. We have known colleagues who insist that the maximum number of clients they can see in a given day and remain at their optimal effectiveness is six to seven individuals. Actually we confess that is *our* limit. And yet we have known others who claim they can see 12 clients a day, 60 clients each week, without any negative effects either with themselves or reduced performance with their clients. Our only point is that each of us is different, and perhaps our practices should better reflect those unique variables.

It is freeing to consider alternative methods and structures that might better serve our clients, as well as to better suit our preferences and optimum effectiveness. At the very least, it would be interesting to have discussions with colleagues (and supervisors) about ways that we might become more productive and satisfied with our work. All of this begins with questioning sacred cows like the 50-minute hour, whether we decide to make adjustments or not.

CHAPTER 10

❧

Who Are the Most Exceptional Clinicians?

Who comes to mind when you think about the most accomplished, creative, and effective clinician you've ever encountered? Now that you've nominated this person, what is it about him or her that is absolutely extraordinary? According to what specific criteria have you determined that this professional far exceeds the norm?

It would appear that we all have a sense about who among us is better than the rest, either because their outcomes are consistently superior than others, or because they simply exude confidence and a sense of competence. It's interesting to consider the different ways that we identify excellence in our field, and there is by no means a consensus on this. Is it primarily about the outcomes that result, at least as reported by clients? Is it about the amount of effort and commitment devoted by the therapist? Or perhaps the degree of caring exhibited?

Perhaps the most valid means by which to assess excellent performance in any domain is to observe professionals in action, especially in difficult, high stress situations. In baseball, they used to rely on batting average as a measure of performance, that is, how many times a player managed to hit safely. But that didn't take into consideration a host of other factors, such as the ability to get on base through walks or to get a hit when others are in scoring position or when the game is on the line. Experts came up with other measures such as slugging percentage, weighted on-base average, or wins above replacement. In every other performance-oriented sport there are similar statistical measures to determine a "most valuable player." But how do we make such a definitive and valid evaluation in our field?

BETTER THAN THE REST

If clients sing the praises of a particular therapist, can that be a reasonable and valid declaration of excellence? Sure, this is a small sample but aren't the customers the best judge of their own services? Perhaps not.

Should we consider therapists who self-identify as among the best, perhaps based on the training they have completed, the prestige of their advanced degrees, or their fellow status within professional organizations? What about their senior position of responsibility within the organization? Doesn't that signal extraordinary clinical competence? Maybe not.

One thing we know for certain is that we are not the best judges of our own performance since we tend to overestimate our successes and minimize our mistakes and failures. Something like 85% of people consider themselves better than their peers in almost anything—driving skill, achievements, and yes, practicing therapy. And 86% of Frenchmen say they are better lovers than anyone else.

Do we rely on reputation in the community? If so, what shapes this image? Are those with a full practice and waiting list necessarily the best therapists? What about fame and notoriety, the standard most of us have used over the years? We assume that those who are well known because of their theoretical development, published writings, workshop or conference presentations, or self-promotion must be better than the rest of us; otherwise, how could they have achieved such recognition?

I'm (Jeffrey) not going to mention names, but one of my longtime heroes and one of the most influential thinkers and writers about therapy for the past generation generously offered to visit my campus to talk to my students. He was a celebrity for sure, charismatic, provocative, and somewhat eccentric. The students brought copies of his books to sign. They stood in line for his autograph, to take a photo, and/or to exchange a few words with this legendary guru who has had such a profound influence in the field.

We were not disappointed by his impassioned, interesting, and, at times, rather unusual talk about the state of the art. After so many years, his ideas were still somewhat, let's say, novel rather than necessarily mainstream. He had continued to evolve his thinking in many ways, not held back by any orthodoxy (his own or anyone else's). If anything, at he advanced in age, he had remained as much a maverick as ever.

You may be trying to guess who this luminary might be, but it doesn't matter. The point we wish to make is that just because someone is a good writer or presenter, an innovative thinker, or an effective self-promoter doesn't necessarily mean that he or she is (or ever was) all that great as a practitioner. Certainly, many famous therapists are (or were) indeed wizards in their craft, highly skilled models of perfection, able to demonstrate at the highest level precisely those strategies that they advocate for all the rest of us. However, just keep in mind that isn't necessarily the case with all of them.

The older, distinguished gentleman who was visiting us that day was asked by a few students if he would mind doing a demonstration of his approach to therapy. Ever the gracious guest, he readily agreed, asking for a volunteer to be his client. We all sat in eager anticipation of the drama that would soon unfold—and we were certainly not disappointed. It was dramatic indeed.

The interview that the theorist conducted with the student still remains one of the single most bizarre, incoherent, and confusing conversations masquerading as therapy, that I've ever seen. He peppered her with seemingly random questions that seemed to have nothing whatsoever to do with her initial concerns. He kept interrupting her before she could finish an answer, often abruptly and rudely. When the client protested that she didn't understand exactly what he wanted from her (she was trying *so* hard to be cooperative with the great man), he called her resistant, which brought her to the brink of tears. He didn't seem to notice or care much about that, because he kept pushing her harder and in directions none of us could figure out had any identifiable purpose. Finally, eventually, after an excruciating half hour in which everyone present was uncomfortable, and a few of us thought about ending the interview for the safety of those present, the theorist decided to offer his client a list of advice that he believed was good for everyone, but had no direct relevance to why she had volunteered in the first place. Not knowing what else to do, the woman thanked him for his help and then jumped off her chair and fled out of the room to regain her composure after surviving the experience with him. The theorist then folded his arms, took a little bow from his sitting position, and asked if there were any questions.

There was stunned silence. After a few uncomfortable moments, I had no choice but to thank him for his visit and then usher him out of the room and on his way home. It took weeks for me to undo the damage the students witnessed that day and try to explain what the theorist *might* have had in mind. It had occurred to me that he had actually lost a part of his mind.

We wish we could say this was just an outlier, a senile old guy who seemed to have compromised cognitive and memory functions. But alas, this is not the case.

PEEKING BEHIND THE CURTAIN

We put our theorists and writers on pedestals for worship. We deify them as godlings. We assume that they must not only be extraordinary thinkers but also the most able practitioners of their craft. We excuse their rudeness or insensitivity. We overlook their self-importance, believing on some level that because they are better than the rest of us, they deserve special treatment. We stand in line for their autographs or to take selfies with them, posting the images online, hoping to raise our own status through association with the great ones.

We are not just talking about "them," or "you," but *us*. Some of our most cherished possessions are books signed by the authors. We both take very seriously the role and responsibilities that come with being "known" in some way. We take great pains to be cordial and responsive to anyone who writes or talks to us. But that's not to say we don't sometimes appear to be inaccessible or insensitive. Because we do. Because we are.

Jeffrey spent more than 20 years interviewing famous theorists and therapists for a series of books, with his friend and colleague, Jon Carlson. They collected stories about their best and worst sessions, seminal or memorable cases, favorite or most creative interventions. In addition, they observed more than a hundred of them doing demonstrations of their approaches for several video series sponsored by the American Counseling Association, American Psychological Association, and a few publishers. They also moderated discussions between them at conferences in which they served as panelists.

There is little doubt that some of these famous therapists, maybe even most of them, are indeed truly exceptional in their clinical skills. Some of them just see and hear and can do things that mere mortals could never attempt. Because they developed their approach to better match their own personality, style, values, priorities, skills, and preferences, it shouldn't be surprising that they are among the best at applying these ideas in the world with clients. But it *is* astonishing how many theorists and famous therapists, known for particular models, actually aren't very good at using them with their own clients.

The magical demonstrations you often view in videos sometimes took multiple takes, several different clients, and careful editing to produce a version suitable for public release. Certain theorists needed to conduct three, four, or more different sessions to get one that was usable. The ones we eventually see usually seem perfectly graceful and effortless, quite unlike what our own experiences might be like when we are stuck in a room with a surly adolescent, severely depressed individual, or someone in the midst of a panic attack.

We also get the distinct impression that those on the workshop circuit are extraordinary practitioners of the theories and strategies they are selling. After impassioned speeches about the value of these ideas, they typically show videos demonstrating them in action. They always highlight miraculous cures in which the client, formerly a basket case, is somehow transformed after an hour or two into a high functioning being, forever grateful for the privilege of working with such a genius. Of course, we never see the client furiously resisting, much less walking out the door in a huff. If we searched long enough, any of us could extract such a perfect session from our own archives to show the world, one selected for its subtlety, complexity, and utter brilliance. What we need to see most in such demonstrations are the miserable failures when the strategy doesn't work at all and how the presenters recover and redeem themselves.

HOW DO WE REALLY KNOW WHO IS BETTER THAN THE REST?

So, if fame, notoriety, or being the founder of a theory doesn't necessarily predict clinical excellence, what does? We know, for instance, that such greatness is not related to which degrees you have, your discipline, choice of theoretical approach, or even years of experience (Kottler & Balkin, 2017). This would be important to know so you don't have to bother fighting for a position out of relative obscurity, nor do you have to become an author. Of course, there are different theories on what makes a therapist truly great, and they are divided into a few categories.

Wampold and Imel (2015) noted the importance of interpersonal skills of a therapist, which really emphasize what Carl Rogers (1957) discovered so many years ago related to the core conditions: communicating warmth, trust, empathy, and acceptance. But Wampold and Imel go a step further and note that effective therapists are quite expressive, both in their affect and verbal communication. The best therapists seem to have the ability, and willingness, to communicate expressively and adaptatively, depending on what is happening in the moment. This, naturally, better helps clients to feel like they've been understood (whether the therapist feels that way or not).

Lambert (2013) emphasized common factors for the best outcomes in therapy, including the therapist's ability to instill hope, utilize effective theory and techniques, but most important, to develop a strong, working therapeutic relationship with the client. Duncan (2014) followed a similar format but added the importance of feedback effects. Along with others (S. D. Miller, Hubble, Chow, & Seidel, 2015), he found that excellent therapists not only provide consistent input to their clients but also solicit feedback from them as to what is working best or not working at all. What seems especially important are specific assessments of the quality of the working alliance and how this is experienced by clients in the moment, while the session is going on.

These findings are useful because they are not confined to any one theoretical approach since all of them value the relational alliance and accurate feedback in some regard. Alfred Adler once broke with Freud because he wished for a more collaborative relationship with his clients, one that went beyond a transference encounter. Carl Rogers discussed this as core conditions while Judith Jordan (relational cultural therapy) calls it mutuality. These attributes are not likely to make you a famous therapist, but they are indeed the components of outstanding therapy in most cases.

PERSONAL CHARACTERISTICS OF EXCELLENCE

Whether we are talking about greatness as a politician, corporate or social movement leader, teacher, or therapist, there are trait theories that propose that certain personality attributes such as charisma, compassion, confidence, and moral fortitude are what drive ultimate power and effectiveness. It also seems important to be flexible and optimistic. While some characteristics of influential power may appear as positive, desirable traits, such as remaining calm in difficult situations or a willingness to share information, other traits might appear much less desirable such as rigidity, authoritarianism, and narcissism.

We've long been intrigued by the phenomenon that certain charismatic individuals seem to have little in common in terms of their values, priorities, abilities, and interpersonal styles. An autocratic, notoriously rude, volatile, and demanding micromanager like Steve Jobs was extraordinarily successful building and running Apple. Tim Cook, the current CEO, couldn't be more different than his predecessor, especially related to his interpersonal style, values, and priorities. He is responsible for building the single most valuable corporate entity in the history of the world and yet did so capitalizing on his own signature qualities. Cook is from a working class family in the Deep South and is the opposite from Jobs in every way imaginable. He likes the outdoors. He demonstrated courage as one of the first prominent corporate leaders to come out as gay. He is known by his employees as a good listener and demonstrates respect in his daily interactions.

Just as prominent corporate leaders like Jeff Bezos, Elon Musk, Jeff Zuckerberg, Warren Buffett, Richard Branson, Howard Schultz (yes, indeed, all white males!) are all successful in their own domains, they have little in common in terms of their personalities and interpersonal styles (except for the usual touch of narcissism). Likewise, in our own field, we've had prominent figures like Fritz Perls, Virginia Satir, Albert Ellis, Carl Whitaker, Carl Rogers, Milton Erickson, and so many others, who are so unlike one another they appear to come from different planets. Or at least it *appears* that way.

We've found it intriguing to consider that these supposed differences are just another myth. On the surface, they may seem to have radically different ideas about what leads to change and the best ways to facilitate that process. When we dig more deeply, however, we find that although they approach matters in their own unique ways, what they all have in common are much the same signature qualities connected to their persuasive influence and charisma. They may empower this spirit in various styles—either rather loud and bombastic or soft and understated—they each discovered a way to connect with others that best reflects their most powerful attributes.

Relational Skills

If it is the case that the most reliable predictor of a successful helping encounter is related to the *client's* perception of the strength and quality of the alliance, then exceptional clinicians must be really, really good at developing solid relationships that are customized to the needs of each individual.

In our studies of this effect, we've found it fascinating to distinguish between the ways that therapists and their clients might very well experience and view the relationship in quite different ways. It had usually been presumed that there was reasonable congruence between these perceptions. After all, how could any relational connection be truly solid if the participants are essentially in disagreement about the nature of that alliance?

Even though we might believe it's important how therapists perceive the quality of the relationship with their clients, this might not matter nearly as much as we think. It turns out that it is the *client's* view that makes all the difference (Cahill, Paley, & Hardy, 2013; Nissen et al., 2015; Thomas, 2006). Regardless of how tenuous and unsatisfactory we might experience a connection with a particular client, it is how they see things that determines the outcome. This means that exceptional practitioners might not always build and maintain the sorts of therapeutic alliances that fit their ideal or preferences, but rather they are expert at persuading their clients to feel connected to them. This may seem somewhat cynical and less than authentic, but it also dispels the myth that we actually have to like our clients for them to *feel* liked and respected.

Marvin just sits woodenly on the couch and scowls most of the time. His arms are crossed in an awkward position but he wants to make certain he is communicating his utter contempt for what has just transpired. This is his usual reaction to any comment or suggestion that doesn't meet with his approval, meaning that it implies he is somehow responsible for his troubles. He is constantly argumentative and critical. When he feels particularly ornery, he goes on the attack, questioning the therapist's essential competence. Sometimes when he feels pushed into a corner, he becomes threatening and even more aggressive.

Over time, the therapist has learned to be extremely cautious with this client. Marvin has mentioned several times how quickly and decisively he has fired a handful of other therapists who were supposedly even more clueless and ignorant than the present one. He has issued clear warnings that are impossible to avoid, given the extent of his behavior problems with others. Nobody else will tolerate him for very long, which is why he is in treatment in the first place.

The therapist doesn't care for Marvin very much and sometimes can't seem to hide his displeasure, nor avoid the inevitable dread at the prospect of his appearance. Yet, strangely, Marvin doesn't seem to notice his therapist's negative reactions. One reason might be that he is so used to people reacting to him in this way it hardly matters to him any longer. If anything, the therapist is far more polite and indulgent than anyone else he has encountered recently. That may be why he (mis)interprets the therapist's behavior toward him as supportive. In fact, he believes his therapist actually likes and respects him, and that's the only reason why he continues to show up each week.

Many of the people who come to us for help do so because others find them so annoying, frustrating, and difficult to deal with. They are often obstructive, resistant, and somewhat stubborn. Among those who say they are highly motivated, they may still display some pretty self-defeating behavior that makes it hard to earn their trust and affection. They may unconsciously or sometimes deliberately block our efforts to assist them because of their entrenched dysfunctional patterns. At times, they pout, lash out, and attempt to sabotage any progress that is made. Those with pathological personality styles are even more challenging to engage, much less "enjoy" spending time with them.

We've been told it isn't necessary to like our clients to help them, but sometimes it is difficult to even *pretend* to like them when they act out in spectacular ways. Nevertheless, it is reassuring to put aside the myth that we must appreciate and enjoy being with all our clients to truly help them. Surely that makes our job easier.

Knowledge and Wisdom

Supposedly great professionals know stuff, *lots* of stuff, that others miss. Yet, it isn't the breadth of knowledge or mastery of content related to one's specialty that counts most; rather, these individuals appear to have an inner wisdom that allows them to understand at a deep level what is happening and then know just what to do about it. They also have incredible *self*-awareness, that is, knowledge about their own limitations and strengths, as well as the ability and willingness to recognize their mistakes and misjudgments to correct them.

Knowledge and wisdom may be related, but they are quite different. Having knowledge means just that—access to information, ideas, and certain facts that may be relevant. True wisdom, however, involves an ability that is far more complex and discerning in that it critically evaluates particular values, accuracy, and rightness of any knowledge to determine ways it can be most useful. Merely competent practitioners, therefore, hold much valuable *knowledge* but the *wisest* clinicians are exceptional in their ability to discover deeper meanings in people's actions and adapt their knowledge in unique, customized, and personalized ways. In addition, they are passionately and diligently committed to gathering as much new information and feedback as possible regarding the impact and effects of their choices so that they continue to increase their effectiveness.

Some researchers on therapy outcomes (Duncan, 2014; S. D. Miller et al., 2015; Wampold & Imel, 2015) insist that almost anyone can become far better at what we do if only we would listen more carefully to our consumers, invite their input on a consistent basis, and then make continual adjustments to what we do to better serve them. This is one kind of knowledge about any current case or situation but there are many other sources that inform the best among us who look far beyond the boundaries of our own profession.

Before the days that mental health and treatment had its own accumulative body of work, the seminal thinkers read and studied widely beyond their own disciplines. Sigmund Freud was influenced as much in this thinking by the novels of Tolstoy and Dostoyevsky, evolutionary ideas of Charles Darwin, advances in physics proposed by Hermann von Helmholtz, the philosophies of Friedrich Nietzsche and Arthur Schopenhauer, the art of Michelangelo, and many contributions within the traditional study of medicine. Similarly, the existential writers like Rollo May, Erich Fromm, and Irvin Yalom relied heavily on the philosophers of Kierkegaard and Sartre to develop their conceptions of meaning-making as the core enterprise of human experience. Likewise, the early family therapy theorists relied on concepts of cybernetics to explain the nature of circular causality. Albert Ellis attributed a breakthrough in his ideas to the early works of Greek philosopher Epictetus, just as Carl Rogers, Milton Erickson, and so many others among the influential contributors found inspiration far beyond their own narrow fields. They all read widely and engaged in a continuous search for knowledge that transcended any singular discipline.

Whereas knowledge is often limited to a single domain, wisdom integrates what is known and understood, as well as what might be surmised from limited information available. Lao Tse once observed that wisdom is not simply an additive process but also a subtraction process, which is the key to reducing distractions, irrelevances, and extraneous variables that confound deeper understanding. It also represents the practical application of knowledge to real-life situations, a principle clearly embraced by popular culture in all kinds of ways. Writing about the important differences between wisdom and knowledge, Gutierrez (2017) shared his own epiphany while standing in line at a Thai takeout restaurant and noticed emblazoned on a woman's tee-shirt: "Knowledge is knowing that a tomato is a fruit. But wisdom is knowing not to put it in a fruit salad."

Well, there you go: Wisdom appears to be as much about actions informed by knowledge, having a sense about what to do when. There are so many instances when we know and understand what is best for others but still feel unable to communicate this insight in such a way that clients take the idea on board and run with it. Exceptional practitioners, somehow, have seemingly limitless ways that they are able to get through to others, and these are the classic stories that we still tell from one generation of therapists to the next. These have become the legends (or myths) of our profession in which Milton Erickson sat on a client and cured her, William

Glasser went on a run with his client and she was forever different, Fritz Perls asked his client to pretend he was an airplane and fly around the room, and Virginia Satir sculpted a family into a dysfunctional configuration to highlight their troubles. We celebrate these breakthrough stories as examples of deeper wisdom that transcended what had been done previously. It is precisely their novelty, creativity, and revolutionary features that encouraged others to move beyond orthodoxy.

Magic

Maybe we don't know and will never know what makes a therapist truly great. Maybe it isn't just one thing but a bunch of complex variables that all mesh together in a unique way. Perhaps the myth associated with what constitutes excellence is that it can be reduced to one thing, one skill or ability, when it is actually composed of many different factors.

This uncertainty and confusion related to identifying exceptional practitioners is reassuring in its own way in that many of the most accomplished and superior clinicians are not those you read about but rather some of you who are reading these words. What we've discovered, supported by research, is that the best therapists are often anonymous and obscure.

The reason why you've never heard of the most exceptional therapists is because the things they do that are most effective are precisely those that prevent them from becoming well known. They don't necessarily have the most experience, nor the most powerful and public positions that would bring them attention. They don't care to write books, achieve recognition, or conduct research studies to advance their academic careers. They live and work in the trenches, taking on the most challenging and difficult cases, all for the love of the action. They are passionately committed to helping those who need help the most, and they do so without complaint or the need for attention and validation. They don't advertise how wonderful they are, nor do they seek such acknowledgement; they are just too busy trying their best to make a difference.

It is this last quality of determinedly, even desperately, trying to be helpful that holds within it perhaps the most important, elusive, and magical characteristic of all—living what is taught to others. When a therapist is willing and able to apply the lessons taught to others to one's own life in a multitude of ways, there is a whole different level of persuasion and influence at work. It is far easier to be convincing when what we are advocating has also proven useful in our own lives and when clients can see clearly and unequivocally that we not only mean what we say, but what we actually do it on a daily basis. It is one thing to teach from books or spout ideas that we inherited from others and quite another to lead from the very front of the battlefield, so to speak.

There is all kinds of evidence about how important daily exercise is, not only to prolong life but to counteract the effects of depression, anxiety, and other emotional disorders. We know this from so much overwhelming research that it is one of the few activities that most consistently and reliably improves the quality of life. It is already well understood and accepted that vigorous physical activity has all kinds of health benefits such as reduced risk of cardiovascular disease, stroke, diabetes, and mortality. In one massive study of over 1 million Americans surveyed, it was found that some forms of exercise had better effects than others (cycling, team sports, aerobic and gym workouts) and that duration and intensity of the exercise mattered (45 minutes, 3–5 times per week). Nevertheless, *all* forms of exercise had some impact in lowering emotional burdens (Chekroud & colleagues, 2018). It is also often the case that the self-discipline involved in sticking with a regimen increases the resolve and pain tolerance in dealing with other problems in life. Learning to be more conscientiousness in one area of life can help people to generalize to other areas since this is the one trait that is most associated with safety and longevity. Conscientious people live longer because they follow medical advice, avoid smoking and fatty foods, take better care of themselves, and look both ways when they cross the street (O'Connor, Jones, McMillan, & Ferguson, 2009). They tend to be more successful because others prefer being with those who are dependable and do what they say they will do.

We can preach this standard advice as a means to reduce symptoms of insomnia, stress, depression, obesity, and lethargy, but we can be so much *more* convincing if this habit is part of our own lives. Although the two of us are very different in a variety of ways, each of us has chosen regular forms of exercise as part of our daily ritual. For me (Jeffrey), it was an attempt to save my own life when I was first informed in my 20s that my mother's death and father's heart disease and stroke destined me to an early death. I started running the next day, only managing to run a few blocks before I ran out of breath. I eventually worked up to a 10K race, half-marathon, and then marathon, before ramping up the challenges in high altitude mountain climbing. There was a period of 15 years in which I never once skipped a day on the road, whether I had the flu or it was −10 degrees during a Michigan winter. There was one time when I was rafting in the Grand Canyon that I ran up and down cliff faces so I could maintain my consecutive record. One might legitimately call this compulsive behavior but I prefer Glasser's term of a positive addiction to counteract stress, sleep disruption, and excessive energy. This lifelong commitment over 45 years (I still work out almost every day but now permit myself a rest day occasionally) is what empowers the passion with which I urge almost all my clients and students (and readers) to take better care of themselves through regular exercise.

For me (Rick), I first began martial arts when I was 8 years old. I was diagnosed with epilepsy at age 3 and was forced to take a lot of different medications to control seizures. The combination of being overmedicated, lacking coordination, and being small in stature contributed to a pretty tough childhood. I'm not going to tell you that I eventually became really excellent at martial arts. What I will say is that I became good to the point that I could compete at a high level. I would say that 90% of my success was consistency and just showing up. The hard work took care of the rest. The result is a life-long passion of martial arts training that I continue to this day.

A LIST OF SIGNIFICANT FACTORS

It's isn't precisely "magic" that magnifies the therapeutic influence of some therapists over others, as much as it is so-called nonspecific factors, those that are not so easily identified, much less described.

There are so many other traits, abilities, skills, and factors that you might nominate as distinguish features of an exceptional therapist. This is just a partial list of those you might consider:

- Ability and willingness to be fully present during sessions
- Strong, calibrated moral compass
- Demonstrating composure, optimism, and faith in the face of the most disturbing, upsetting, or traumatic stories, communicating, "No worries. We've got this."
- Ability to experience and express a sort of "transcendent" level of empathy toward others, a state that appears almost like a magical form of mind (and heart) reading
- Individualized and personal approach that best reflects one's unique strengths and resources
- Extraordinary sensitivity to nuances and subtleties that others may miss
- Intense curiosity about the mysterious, unknown, and less understood phenomena
- Honoring the complexity of each individual, issue, and circumstance rather than reducing cases to their most obvious and tangible features

- Unbridled passion, enthusiasm, and charisma that inspires hope, faith, and trust in the therapeutic experience
- Capacity for carrying one's own burdens without distraction, indulgence, or impairment
- Scrupulously aware of one's own emotional triggers, unresolved issues, countertransference reactions, and propensity to overreact to certain things that arise in sessions
- Willingness to challenge ones preferred beliefs and favorite assumptions in light of new experiences and additional information
- Expertise in negotiating and navigating different types of therapeutic alliances that may vary in structure, style, and support, depending on client problems, expectations, goals, and preferences
- Reluctance to ask clients to do things that they are either not yet ready or able to do, thereby preventing premature dropouts by ignoring optimal pace
- Propensity to set ambitious goals for self and others, those that facilitate higher standards, but also demonstrate forgiveness for falling short at times
- Willingness to take on extremely difficult cases that will test one's limits and push toward experimentation and new learning
- Demonstrating flexibility and inventive persistence, even when faced with seemingly intractable problems or so-called "impossible" cases
- Extensive catalogue of multiple options, varied strategies, and virtually endless resources that can be accessed, depending on the issues and client needs
- Exquisite sensitivity and responsiveness to the unique cultural and individual differences of each client, recognizing that everything we encounter and respond to has a particular context
- Refusal to blame the client when things don't proceed according to plan; willingness to accept responsibility for outcomes, regardless of client's alleged resistance, defensiveness, or obstructiveness
- Reluctance to even view certain clients as "difficult," preferring to see almost all impasses as an interactive, relational effect in which both (or all) participants play a contributing role
- Practicing forgiveness and inquisitive study when outcomes are less than satisfactory

Perhaps one of the more interesting findings on therapist effectiveness comes from Nissen-Lie and colleagues (Nissen-Lie, Monsen, & Rønnestad, 2010; Nissen-Lie, Monsen, Ulleberg, & Rønnestad, 2013; Nissen-Lie et al., 2017), who explored the relationship between therapist effectiveness and therapist self-doubt. In other words, research focused on how the self-doubts of therapists affected the client's perceptions of the therapist and the working alliance between them. Over the course of these studies, they found that client outcomes decreased when the therapist was experiencing interpersonal difficulties or struggles in practice. This was particularly true when the therapist had a negative personal reaction to the client. But when looking at contributions to positive perceptions of the therapist and improved client functioning, an important finding was noted. When the therapist had a healthy self-concept but endorsed professional self-doubts, the client noted less symptom distress and fewer interpersonal problems. Most important, it was the combination of positive self-concept and professional self-doubt that contributed to client outcomes. The conclusion of the research was to "love yourself as a person, doubt yourself as a therapist" (Nissen-Lie et al., 2015, p. 48).

We find it very interesting that it is precisely those therapists who brim with overwhelming self-confidence that have the most trouble with their clients. What is preferable is that when clinical problems become evident, collaborative and reflective conversation with the client generates the best outcomes. Albert Ellis (2001) noted that all humans are fallible, and naturally, therapists are no exception. But what is also pertinent is that our own fallibility makes for better therapy. So, when considering who is truly a great therapist, it is not the therapist with superior self-confidence, but rather those who admit to struggling with clients, who work with clients to find solutions and coping strategies, and who feel confident who themselves as a person.

FINDING YOUR OWN VOICE

As mentioned earlier, we often deify famous therapists, making them into mythological figures or gods in a sense in that we consider them superhuman. We are just as guilty as anyone else. During our early years in the field, we would dutifully attend the workshops of the most popular figures of the era, celebrities who commanded huge audiences of the devoted. As advertised, we would become spellbound by their extraordinary wisdom, ability, and skills applying their alleged foolproof model to the most hopeless cases. We were sold!

Once we returned to our own practices, however, more often than not, things didn't exactly unfold in the same way—no surprise really, considering we had little practice and perhaps even less understanding of the technique, strategy, or intervention we witnessed on stage or in the demonstration video. Nevertheless, we've found, again and again, that the more we tried to imitate our heroes and heroines, the more often we would lose ourselves in the process.

Each time we would become exposed to some new theorist, we would feel initially enamored by them, seduced as it were. We might try to imitate the cadence of their voice, perhaps even unconsciously mirror their gestures, all in an attempt to channel their magic. We felt unworthy or unqualified to form our own ideas, still merely apprentices in the guild, not permitted to go our own way. So we walked in the footsteps of the giants who came before us, doing our level best to imitate them in hopes we might achieve the same degree of effectiveness.

We would listen to stories about the "wild men" (and, of course, they were all men who would operate in this manner)—Carl Whitaker, Albert Ellis, Fritz Perls, and Milton Erickson, to mention a few—who would do such seeming crazy things in their sessions and yet we were unable to imagine ourselves doing anything remotely similar. After all, we were neither famous nor old dudes who could get away with stuff like that. Ellis would sometimes instruct clients to go to the local mall and pretend to walk a banana down the hall to overcome shame, or Whitaker might slap a client who said he doesn't feel alive, or Perls would scream at someone to elicit some reaction. And Erickson? He'd do almost anything! He'd sit on a woman to demonstrate dominance and instruct people to do things that made no sense whatsoever. These stories both inspired and appalled us. And it took many years for us to crawl out of the shadows of those we most admired to find our own way.

We wish to close this discussion by mentioning a student intern of our acquaintance. He was assigned a case consisting of an adolescent and both his parents who were upset with the boy's poor performance in school and unwillingness to follow directions. During the session, the boy became quite angry, leading to a heated conflict in the room. The kid was screaming at his parents who, in turn, were yelling back at him. Things had gotten out of control.

Without saying a word to anyone, the intern got up out of his chair and walked out of the room.

"May I ask exactly what you are doing?" the intern's supervisor asked. "Why are you standing outside here when I can hear your clients yelling at one another inside the room?"

The intern shrugged. "Everything got crazy in there so I walked out. I guess they'll just have to figure things out on their own." Then he grinned with satisfaction.

"May I ask where exactly you got this hare-brained idea to leave a volatile family alone in the middle of a session?"

The intern looked puzzled for a moment. "Why it was Carl!"

"Carl? What's Carl? Or rather who is Carl?"

"Carl Whitaker, of course!" the intern explained. "I read that he once did something like this. Isn't it great?"

The supervisor shook his head with worry. "You get back in there. Right now! And by the way, you are *not* Carl Whitaker!"

CHAPTER 11

◆◇◆

Why the Effects of Therapy Don't Often Last

It's always interesting when we compare what we do for a living with other kinds of professionals, say, for instance, a surgeon, a plumber, a car mechanic, or a software engineer. They actually fix things and are held accountable that the results will last after their service has been completed. Sometimes they even offer warranties or money-back guarantees.

On some level, it seems a little ridiculous that we actually expect to change long-standing, entrenched, chronic patterns of dysfunction, self-defeating actions, emotional disorders, or mental illness with a spirited conversation for a few minutes each week. We don't actually do anything other than talk to the sufferer. Try explaining *this* to healers in other cultures where they rely on an assortment of other methods to cure those who are afflicted with some noxious condition.

Throughout most of the world, healers command all kinds of resources to impact their clients in ways designed to change them forever (Keeney & Keeney, 2018; Kottler, Carlson, & Keeney, 2004). They call on the spirits of ancestors to offer assistance, as well as the support of divine intervention. They introduce rituals into the program. They include prayer, touching, dancing, singing, drumming, shaking in their treatments. They include the whole community in the healing ceremonies. They assign difficult trials, ordeals, and tasks to complete. They prescribe hallucinogenic substances to access the content and meaning of the symptoms. They combine methods that access not just the mind and heart, but also the body and soul. There are places in Africa where the healer actually moves into

Myths, Misconceptions, and Invalid Assumptions of Counseling and Psychotherapy. Jeffrey Kottler and Richard S. Balkin, Oxford University Press (2020). © Oxford University Press.
DOI: 10.1093/oso/9780190090692.001.0001

the home of the client so as to better observe, monitor, and control the proceedings. Alternatively, sometimes the client is required to live with the healer until significant, permanent improvement takes places. Among all of these strategies and methods, the one thing healers around the world almost *never* do is expect the client to talk about problems. One indigenous healer among the Bushmen of the Kalahari in Southern Africa once remarked, after hearing about how psychotherapy works in our culture, "Have you ever helped anyone just talking to them like that?"

Good question.

WHAT REALLY MAKES A DIFFERENCE IN THERAPY?

It's worthwhile to review once again what it is about the therapy experience that leads to decisive change. Keep in mind, however, that such discussions often do not include the qualifier, "permanent, enduring change." All we seem to care about is that when the client leaves our care the symptoms are (at least temporarily) reduced, if not eradicated altogether. Of course, we are supposed to do follow-ups to check on clients months afterwards, but the reality is that this rarely occurs except in controlled research experiments.

For the most part, therapy is effective, at least in the short-term, but the positive results are not necessarily long-lasting (Knekt, Lindfors, Sares-Jäske, Virtala, & Härkänen, 2013). Of course, it is difficult to truly know the real effects once treatment is over. Studies tend to focus on a single treatment site or a specific diagnosis. The types of analyses used tend to require large sample sizes, but clinicians generally see individuals and small groups, which provides a serious limitation to conducting research and publishing results. When looking at two of the most common diagnoses, depression and substance use, the findings are not that encouraging. In studying long-term effects of therapy for depression, Steinert, Hofmann, Kruse, and Leichsenring (2014) discovered a publication bias, meaning that results are difficult to generalize because a lot that is studied is not published. The authors were only able to locate 11 studies.

Moreover, they found that most clients diagnosed and treated for depression relapse to once again experience their disturbing symptoms. After 2 years, posttreatment relapse results were relatively high (53.1%) but much less than those who had received care with no psychotherapy (71.1%). Similarly, therapy effects when working with substance use problems may also stagnate. In examining outcomes of clients up to 7 years posttreatment, substance use did decline over time, but individuals continued to struggle with unemployment, unstable house, poverty, and other issues (Karriker-Jaffe, Witbrodt, Subbaraman, & Kaskutas, 2018).

The relapse rate for many emotional disorders is astronomical, as we mentioned previously. Certainly, our treatments for adjustment reactions and "uncomplicated" trauma and loss are quite impressive, and the results are known to last once clients have internalized the skills for counteracting disruptive thoughts and negative feelings. But those who consult us for addictions, chronic drug abuse, bipolar disorder, and other severe affective and impulse disorders are known to experience many ups and downs throughout their lives, regardless of how successful the initial treatments might have been.

As we've mentioned before, in cases of successful outcomes there is significant disagreement between therapists and clients about what was most helpful. Keep in mind how rare it is that consumers and the professionals they hire would be so at odds regarding what was reported as most useful. A homeowner who contracts with a plumber or roofer about a leak would consider the only possible successful outcome is if the problem is fixed, not just for a day or week but at least for the next 20 years. The service person would similarly agree to this outcome. All parties would also be on board with whatever solution eventually took care of the problem.

Yet, this is not at all what happens in our domain in which there very well could be a significant difference of opinion about what happened and why. As we've mentioned, whereas therapists attribute positive outcomes primarily to their chosen interventions and strategies, clients are more inclined to say they felt heard and understood, gained a renewed sense of faith and hope, and felt a strong connection to their therapist.

We wish to be clear that we are not referring to "little" or relatively minor alterations in someone's behavior but rather what has been called "quantum changes" (W. R. Miller, 2004). These are considered major personality or behavioral shifts, usually quite vivid and intense, accompanied by strong emotional arousal and followed by long-lasting, positive effects that can be readily observed and experienced. These are often described as the sorts of insights and greater awareness that leads to the transformation of ordinary or dysfunctional lives (Bien, 2004; Kottler, 2001; Skalski & Hardy, 2013; Wood, 2006).

In the modern age of psychotherapy, quantum change may be rare. Bien (2004) noted that meaningful change is often a slow, gradual process, which may not be conducive to the practice of the brief psychotherapy emphasized and rewarded by third-party payors. Quantum change is not something that can be promoted by a given approach but rather occurs as a result of the therapeutic environment in which sustained attention is offered to the client's issues. Fosha (2006) noted that instances of so-called "big" changes appear to relate to the therapists' emotional engagement, as well as the use of experiential techniques and clients' reflections on therapeutic change. A strong working alliance, which takes a certain amount of time to develop, is needed for the sort of deep, experiential work that elicits strong emotional responses.

What's interesting about this research on the dramatic epiphanies and quantum changes that sometimes take place—in therapy or in daily life—is that they almost all take place in a highly emotional arousal state in which the person is disoriented, even lost and desperate. Hardly anyone ever chooses to change their life, much less go to therapy, until they've exhausted other alternatives. Change is messy and inconvenient. It involves a major investment of time, commitment, energy, and resources. It's unpleasant most of the time and certainly uncomfortable. That's why people work so hard to avoid changing if they can get away with it.

Clients offer many excuses and reasons why they relapsed and couldn't seem to maintain momentum over time. They say it's too much work and effort. They complain they didn't receive enough support. Sometimes, they say they just forgot to stick with it. But often they were just unprepared to deal with inevitable setbacks or crises or lacked appropriate coping skills for dealing with critical situations. In some cases, they simply enjoy too many benefits for being stuck, capitalizing on all the excuses for avoiding responsibility, blaming others, and remaining helpless. They still get a lot of attention and sympathy from others. They have a ready excuse for behaving badly ("I can't help it; I have this problem"). And they are able to avoid the unknown, as well as distract themselves (and others) from other problems they prefer not to examine or acknowledge.

WHY CHANGES STICK

We speculate about why some of the progress that clients make stabilizes over time or even continues to grow, while in other situations there is an eventual return to the previous state of dysfunction. It is a peculiar, if not mysterious, phenomenon that some changes last and others do not. To some degree, it is certainly a matter of motivation and commitment since desire is a critical feature of sustained action. That helps explain why only 8% of individuals ever follow through on their New Year's resolutions, and the average number of times they make the same promise is 10 (Willett, 2015).

Basically, people make serious changes in their lives for two reasons. First, because they are required to do so or they will lose something important to them, such as their sanity, job, partner, or illusions. They are forced to make adjustments to accommodate others or because the consequence of not doing so would result in catastrophe. The second reason is voluntary in that they desire changes to gain something important to them, such as equanimity, resolution of conflict, growth, or some prize.

Whether change is forced or voluntary, a common motivational factor is to move away from discomfort. From an innate, physiological viewpoint, even a shift in a chair or stretching before getting up in the morning is based on avoiding pain or discomfort. So, when considering changes that stick, it usually has something to do with the search for relief. Consider a client who struggles with substance use and addiction. Before the client attempts any change in behavior, there usually is a set of rather negative consequences. People in the addiction field often refer to it as "hitting rock bottom." Perhaps family members are angry and hurt, health and legal consequences are evident, interpersonal relationships are severely strained, and/or financial problems are evident. The amount of discomfort has superseded the pleasure gained from drug use, so the individual struggling with addiction becomes convinced to make necessary changes. But if this is the case, why is it so difficult to make lasting change? In part, it is because of the physiological and psychological dependence. But when discomfort seems more remote, lasting change can be difficult to achieve.

This theory that we are motivated by discomfort has been proposed in many different forms and applied to a variety of psychosocial problems. For example, Prochaska and DiClimente (2005) developed a seminal model outlining the stages of change, in which people move from denial and unawareness of a problem (precontemplation) toward identification (contemplation), preparation to change (preparation), engagement in the process of change (action), and maintaining progress (maintenance). For many people, emotional and psychological discomfort become the motivating factor to seek help and elicit change.

We've always found it helpful to look at quantum or transformative changes that occur in daily life as potentially instructive for what may happen in therapy as well. Among all the contexts for such growth and learning, one of the most fertile areas has to do with travel experiences. When asked to identify and describe some life-altering experience that persists to this day, people often mention a particular travel experience that was important to them (Kottler, 1977). It's intriguing to examine the particular features of these seminal events as a way to reveal those that most often lead to relatively permanent and enduring changes.

Although during times of crisis or transition in our lives, each of us has sought counsel from therapists, supervisors, and mentors, with satisfactory results. And yet, if the goal is to truly transform our way of being, to make radical and lasting changes in our lives, nothing has quite touched the power of a travel experience that tested us in ways we could never have imagined. At various times in his life Jeffrey has been trapped in a blizzard for 3 days on a glacier with no hope of rescue, survived earthquakes near the epicenter, been lost in a jungle, climbed 6,000 meter summits, and been stuck in a crowded bus for 12 hours on a treacherous road. As traumatic as each of these experiences was, each of them taught a critical life lesson related to patience, resilience, and making the best of a bad situation.

In its own way, a therapy session is similar to a trip abroad in that it has many of the same elements: (a) temporary insulation from other influences while in a novel environment; (b) an enriched environment in which you are permitted, if not encouraged, to experiment with new behaviors and skills; (c) high emotional arousal; (d) a heightened awareness of self and the environment characterized by an altered state of consciousness; and (e) teachable moments and opportunities to consider alternative ways of solving problems and getting needs met. While sessions often contain pieces of these factors, what is unique and even more powerful is the opportunity to both make meaning from the experiences and to discuss ways to transfer the learning to other situations and encounters.

It is precisely the intensity of these sorts of encounters that make them so powerful and enduring. Although people tend to romanticize their travel adventures, minimizing the discomforts and trials along the way, they are often quite traumatic experiences at the time. They usually involve stories of being (or feeling) lost, missing luggage, delayed flights, or inexplicable annoyances, all of which made the experience somewhat miserable but makes for an amusing anecdote to share: "The bus left without us and we had no idea what to do next. We couldn't speak their language, and we didn't know how to get back to the hotel. But finally, after walking around for a few hours, we persuaded someone using sign language to helps us find our way by riding on the back of his scooter. It was hilarious."

Actually, it was terrifying. But it is so impactful to have such an experience and to live to tell others. People learn so much, and tend to remember what they learned, when they survive a posttraumatic growth encounter like this. It also helps explain why certain conditions associated with a deep religious or spiritual conversion takes place—once again the kind of change that sticks over time. Such experiences usually take place when someone is desperate and hit bottom. There is a loss of power and control, accompanied by an acknowledgment of personal inadequacy. This leads to a search for something else, something more, or at least different. Mystical visions, fasting or meditation, pilgrimages, surrender of false pride, oneness with Nature, and aesthetic awareness of the divine all so-lidify this new way of being.

Surely we can recognize some similarities between transformative travel or spiritual conversions and what happens in therapy. For that matter, these are the same sorts of things that lead to any big change in someone's life, regardless of the setting.

FACTORS THAT LEAD TO CHANGE—INSIDE AND OUTSIDE THERAPY

If you were going to make a list of all the things you can think of that lead to lasting change in someone's life, what would you include on this inventory? You'd probably begin by mentioning some dissatisfaction with life, whether in the form of general unhappiness or some set of specific symptoms like depression, anxiety, boredom, or lack of meaning. Next, we discuss some other common factors.

External Influences

Circumstances coalesce at times to make it untenable to continue in the same way. Economic downturn, war, natural disasaster physical illness, and change in job responsibilities all require some new way of adapting, whether you like it or not. There is no choice in the matter and so no way to avoid the needed changes. Clients often seek our help when they are faced with situations that surprised, confused, or destabilized them, leaving them no choice other than to develop alternative coping skills.

External factors can present a significant obstacle for therapists. On one hand, external factors are often the primary contributing factor to counseling outcomes and success (Duncan, 2014; Lambert, 2013). Lambert estimated approximately 40% of client outcomes are attributed to external factors—elements that therapists have no control over whatso-ever. Client history, past trauma, failures, and relationships are just some common examples of what clients bring to therapy that have an impact on outcomes. With likely no influence on external factors, therapists focus on the elements that can be more easily controlled within the therapeutic pro-cess, such as the relationship, quality of feedback to clients, instillation of hope, and the interventions that might be beneficial to client progress. Yet, when these other elements come in to play, taken together they can have far more impact than anything that we try to do in sessions.

Epiphanies and Insights

Either gradually or suddenly, people realize that things aren't the way they have seemed or the way they convinced themselves. They acknowledge that a relationship is not only over but has been for some time. They understand they don't have to accept the status quo but have within their power to behave differently. They become aware of a new strength or resources that had previously been unknown. This new awareness leads to all kinds of previously inaccessible options. And there is no turning back.

As a qualifier, it isn't necessary to know and understand why something happened that made all the difference. "Had Ove been the sort of man who contemplated how and when one became the sort of man one was," writes Fredrik Bachman (2012), "he might have said this was the day he learned that right has to be right" (p. 44). But Ove wasn't the sort of person who dwelled on such matters, or ever reflected much about the meaning of his actions. Nevertheless, this moment was instrumental in forging his sense of morality, even if he didn't care to think about that.

Facing a Truth

This is among the most powerful of all insights, the moment when defenses crumble, self-deceptions collapse, and one must see, with perfect clarity, the things that have been avoided, denied, and disowned. This is a coming to terms with oneself, often initiated by a realization that things are not what they seem. Although such an awareness can occur at any time and place in life, therapy is the optimal setting for facing a truth that has been previously avoided because of the very nature of the encounter designed to challenge and confront avoidances.

Mike was a delivery driver, who primarily served convenience stores. He had been doing this for well over 20 years and was in his early 50s. Recently, he got called into his supervisor's office who wanted to know why money picked up from various locations was coming up short. Mike admitted that he was buying lottery tickets, and when he did not win he just assumed the company would dock his pay. But now they were withholding his pay to the point it was actually exceeding his total salary. His supervisor, therefore, expressed some concern, "Mike you have been with this company for over 20 years and have been a good employee. You need to get a handle on this. Get some help, or we are going to have to let you go."

Mike accepted a referral his company's human resources office and went to see a counselor. In his initial session, he admitted to his gambling problem and knowing that the money was not his. He talked about not being very capable at school but his father instilling good values in him. He mentioned that his father had been respected among the farmers in the community and that he missed him. His father had dued within the previous year, and he wanted to carry on his father's name with the love and respect of the community. He cried during the session, and his therapist mostly just listened to the sad story. Mike was able to get his composure together at the end of the session and indicated he would return the following week. He appeared considerably more calm during the next visit: "You know doc, I haven't gambled since the last time I saw you. I know the money is not mine. I have not even felt like buying any lottery tickets. I had beer with my friends this past weekend and I told them about you and that this therapy stuff works, and they need to do it too."

Mike's therapist did not pursue a history or even initiate processing grief issues. The client initiated the dialogue and reconciled the truth of missing his father. Questions of why the client engaged in a behavior were never asked but were nonetheless discovered quickly in the process. Once the client discovered and processed his own grief, he was on the way for more permanent, positive change.

Trauma

Survivors of trauma, assault, neglect, illness, or death of a loved one respond in different ways. Some remain crippled for life while others recover quite quickly and resume their previous level of functioning. Even more interesting is that some people (estimated to be as high as one third of trauma survivors) report incredible growth and transformation as a result of what they experienced. They report being more psychologically sophisticated, more appreciative of their intimate relationships, more willing to recognize and embrace uncertainties, having greater resilience and hardiness, and more willing to accept responsibility for their own reactions (Renden, 2015). Some of these effects are noticed by many therapists who experience significant positive effects vicariously while working with their clients' trauma (Bartoskova, 2017).

One of the more elusive areas of mental health research and trauma is resilience, the ability to adapt to stress and adversity. Although there is plenty of research on resilience, there is no universally agreed upon measure or particular strategy that has taught resilience. Wu et al. (2013) noted that resilience is influenced by genetic and biological factors that make it difficult to influence. Adverse childhood experiences also play a role in the development of resilience. Hence, attempts to influence resilience through psychoeducation and guidance may continue to evoke limited results.

Hitting Bottom

As previously mentioned, this is a scenario common among those with addictions in that they first have to lose (almost) everything important to them before they realize they have no other choice but to make some changes. It is sometimes life or death: Either they accept that they have a problem they can't fix on their own, or they spiral into increased self-destruction. They have nothing else to lose.

Of course, there is no universal experience of hitting bottom. It is different for everyone and is tied to resilience and toleration of discomfort, which varies according to pain tolerance, context, mood, and context. Many clients exaggerate the extent of their misery while others minimize their discomfort, finding excuses to maintain the status quo.

Life Transitions

We know from developmental stage theories that there are certain age-related crises, or at least opportunities, when people undertake honest self-assessments that lead to changes in their lifestyles or choices. This could occur when experiencing a major life event (pregnancy, divorce, graduation), hitting particularly significant ages (18, 21, 30, 40, 65), or simply confronting the age process that sparks existential crises related to the prospect of disease, deterioration, or death. These are the sorts of adjustment reaction cases that lend themselves to relatively swift progress in therapy because the change efforts have already begun and often require some tweaks and continuity. The changes that are made become long-lasting because it isn't possible to return to the previous condition.

Mortality

Mortality is the ultimate life transition that surely gets people's attention in ways that nothing else can. It sparks a series of existential questions related to the meaning of life, the nature of personal responsibility, and the legacy one wishes to leave behind. Those who have had a close brush with death, lost a dear loved one, or faced the impending prospect of limited time are strongly motivated to ramp up whatever feels unfinished or unfulfilled.

While the focus on this chapter is on what makes change permanent, it is important to note that not all such change is desirable. Freud (1922) discussed the death drive, also referred to as *Thanatos*, with respect to individuals moving toward negative coping, including harmful activities, self-harm, and death. Freud noticed this behavior when working with soldiers returning from World War I, finding that his patients often re-enacted or repressed traumatic experiences, resulting in unhealthy relationships or self-destructive behaviors.

In the mid-1990s I (Rick) worked with an adolescent client, Mark, who was hospitalized for drug addiction and suicidal ideation. Mark was diagnosed with AIDS, which was contracted as a result of a blood transfusion. Mark did well in treatment and was even considered a leader on the unit, providing excellent feedback to other patients in the hospital during group therapy and addressing his own issues with courage and devotion. But as he moved toward discharge, the futility in his voice came out. Previously, he would talk about staying sober but as discharge neared, he was asking, "What is the point?" As he left the hospital with a referral to continue outpatient treatment I was not so sure he would live a clean and sober life or even continue in therapy.

Of course, awareness of one's mortality can provide impetus for positive change. When faced with a major life transition or event, people will work toward lasting, meaningful changes. An individual who suffers a heart attack may choose to exercise more, eat healthier, and spend more time with family. Therapists encounter clients with existential crises quite often and help them work through these crises. Awareness of one's mortality provides a strong motivation that may positively impact client hopefulness, motivation, and the working alliance (Kottler & Balkin, 2017).

Keystone Behaviors

Keystone behaviors are the seemingly small, but significant, actions that lead to bigger things later on. After all, change is actually an incremental process, one that begins with unnoticeable shifts that may only be recognized afterwards. Duhigg (2016), an expert on industrial productivity, supplied an example of a keystone behavior, a seemingly tiny, irrelevant action, that set in motion a cascade of other undesirable effects. He was frustrated that his family seemed unable to coordinate their schedules so that they could eat dinner together during the evening. He borrowed a method employed by Toyota quality control staff in which he sought to uncover the roots of their difficulty in following through on what they all said was important. Nevertheless, any attempt to stick with their commitment ended in only temporary results.

Duhigg determined that one reason for their problem was that the family was always running late in the morning because the kids took so long to pick out their wardrobe and get dressed. Once they started selecting and laying out the clothes the day before, there was no longer any disputes, procrastination, or wasted time in the mornings, allowing everyone to depart for school and work on time. This, in turn, kept things calmer, better organized, and composed, such that they were all able to get their work done in a timely manner and return home earlier—in time for dinner.

Many brief therapists have also harnessed this notion of keystone behaviors by helping their clients who feel daunted by the prospect of making dramatic changes to just begin with something small and seemingly insignificant. Instead of asking someone to do something that is beyond their capability, say, approach an attractive stranger, the idea is to begin with something symbolic and a small step in the ultimate desired direction. The client is urged to practice smiling more at strangers to note what impact that has, without any pressure to do anything more challenging.

Validation and Affirmation

Sometimes all someone needs is a little support or permission to do what is needed. Period.

Empowering Story

Whether from assigned reading, media, television, movie, or conversation, it is remarkable how people can identify with the narrative in such a way that it shifts their own personal identity. Actress, comedian, and commentator Whoopi Goldberg remembers as a child seeing a new show on television that featured an African American character (Uhura from *Star Trek*) who wasn't a housekeeper or slave, and she attributes that awareness to offering her the awareness that she, too, could someday become an actress, even on *Star Trek* (which she eventually did as Guinan). People often mention that a story they heard or a film or show they watched changed everything for them in terms of what they imagined was possible. Within therapy, as well, we are constantly telling stories to our clients, those that are designed to show them alternative ways of viewing their predicament, as well as to inspire them to take decisive actions (Kottler, 2015a).

Lifestyle Adjustments

People engage in all kinds of unhealthy habits related to their diet, sleep, spending patterns, lack of exercise, and similar daily habits. For reasons that are often inexplicable, sometimes people wake up and consciously decide to change what they've been doing because they no longer like the consequences of this behavior. Someone with high blood pressure and a propensity toward obesity leaves a doctor's visit with test results that push him over the edge to the point he is now determined to alter his diet. A girl's boyfriend breaks up with her because he's tired of her texting on the phone all the day, rarely fully present during their time together. A couple is forced to declare bankruptcy because their credit card debt is so out of control. They vow not to spend money on anything they can't afford to pay for with cash—and they follow through on this commitment because it feels like they don't have a choice. In each instance, circumstances of their lives made it feel untenable to continue with the same behavior.

Solitude Versus Group Support

Sometimes it is isolation from others and an unfamiliar environment that leads to deep reflection and new choices. The opposite can also be important when people feel the encouragement and backing from others to undertake difficult tasks. While these settings of being isolated from others' influence or in the middle of a supportive group are powerful forces to inspire change, unfortunately, the changes don't often last very long.

People make all kinds of promises and commitments while communing with Nature, on a silent meditative retreat, or during reflective thought, but don't follow through for very long. Almost every single morning, someone awakes and declares to herself this will be the day that she finally takes charge of her life, which is spinning out of control. But then she gets so busy and distracted, she "forgets."

Group support can be just as short-acting in that participants initially feel all kinds of enthusiasm for making needed changes, that is, until the group ends and, with it, the encouragement it provided. That's why weight loss groups aren't very effective over the long haul and why support groups work only as long as people continue to attend regular meetings. There are all kinds of different support groups for various maladies, and most are helpful in providing some level of encouragement, a sense of belonging, and structure for continuing recovery or coping with addictions, chronic illnesses, co-dependencies, and similar conditions. Indeed, alcohol abusers who attend regular meetings of Alcoholics Anonymous (AA) are twice as likely to maintain sobriety (Kaskutas, 2009; Kelly & Yeterian, 2011). Although we cite a few studies, we would be remiss if we didn't mention that data on success of 12-step programs are all over the map. AA claims that three fourths of their members remain abstinent, although they admit that one fourth of them end up relapsing at some point before they resume sobriety.

However—and you knew this was coming— support and therapeutic groups are also notorious for their high relapse rates once the program ends, sometimes as high as 60% to 70% of participants falling back into old patterns (Bertrand & Boulze-Launay, 2018). We'd expect there'd be a qualitative difference between self-help and professionally led groups since in the latter there would likely be more attention to relapse prevention strategies, but the results are still rather disappointing.

This isn't particularly surprising when we consider our own experiences when we attend workshops and seminars. We might leave a program all fired up, handouts stockpiled and notes carefully filed away, but a few weeks (or days) later after we have re-entered the crushing and frantic world that has become our lives, it all seems but a dream, and we have reverted back to our old and familiar patterns.

Our discussion has been centered not just on what leads to change in people's lives but why these changes endure over time. More relevant to our purposes, we are interested in dispelling the myth that just because our clients leave our sessions reporting positive outcomes and success doesn't mean that these changes continue once treatment has ended and we likely no longer receive regular reports. It is convenient and optimistic for us to just assume that things are going well or otherwise clients would contact us again. But this is hardly the case when we consider all the reasons why they might be reluctant to do so. Clients are ashamed of their disappointments and blame themselves for the failures. Once they return to previous dysfunction, they may lose faith and confidence that returning sessions would do much good. They relocate or run out of time and money. They just don't want to face what they imagine would be their therapist's disappointment in them.

PREPARING CLIENTS FOR LASTING CHANGE

Lasting change remains elusive as a fundamental outcome in our work even though we rarely take the time and opportunity to assess it. For those who work in community mental health, tracking long-term outcomes is particularly fraught with obstacles, including low return rates, high drop-out rates, and the transient nature of the population being served (Balkin & Juhnke, 2018). Most clinicians do not utilize outcome measures or devote the time to engage in follow-up after treatment. Research on long-term change remains limited. Yet, the research on quantum change and contributions to lasting change in therapy remain compelling.

W. R. Miller and Rollnick (1991) developed motivational interviewing to address issues of lasting change. They combined concepts of the transtheoretical model stages of change (Prochaska & DiClimente, 2005) and Rogerian strategies to elicit client change. But perhaps more important, change was not elicited through persuasion or confrontation. Rather, the client has the responsibility to initiate change, process and reconcile ambivalence, and collaborate with the therapist to evoke a constructivie process of maintenance once the desired change is achieved. Although external factors, as mentioned before, are outside the influence of the therapist, developing trust, demonstrating respect, initiating a collaborative relationship, and engaging in a directive but supportive nonconfrontational approach are qualities of motivational interviewing that are universal to a variety of theoretical approaches and appear influential in lasting change for clients.

In the beginning of the chapter, the challenges of how therapy leads to lasting change were highlighted. The reality is that when clients come into counseling, there is so much that is outside of the influence and control of the therapist. Yet, there are a number of factors that lead to lasting change, which may be considered collaboratively with the client or incorporated by the therapist.

CHAPTER 12

ᴄⱽɔ

Scolding Therapists About Social Justice and Advocacy

L et's talk about a secret about that we almost never talk about, except in whispers to a close friend. How tired are you of having sanctimonious, self-satisfied (and self-congratulatory) people stand up on stage (or in an article) and scold you for not being more actively involved in social justice and advocacy issues? We get that this is absolutely one of the most important issues of our time, especially during this era when political figures exhibit such rampant racism and complete disregard for the plight of refugees, immigrants, minorities, and the underclass. This is a period in our history that has been marked by a rise in homophobia, Nazism, violence against people of color, discrimination against those how are already marginalized, and even a discrediting of media. And yet, 40% of Americans don't bother to vote in elections, all the while they complain about injustice, post their protests on social media, and perhaps even show up for a parade.

It is part of the ethical codes of every helping profession that we are not only encouraged but required to advocate on behalf of marginalized and dispossessed people. The American Psychological Association (2017) included in the preamble of their Code of Conduct, "Psychologists respect and protect civil and human rights and the central importance of freedom of inquiry and expression." The National Association of Social Workers (2017) included advocacy as their central mission and urges their members to become active politically and legislatively to address issues of voter suppression, immigrant and refugee displacement, criminal justice reform,

Myths, Misconceptions, and Invalid Assumptions of Counseling and Psychotherapy. Jeffrey A. Kottler and Richard S. Balkin, Oxford University Press (2020). © Oxford University Press.
DOI: 10.1093/oso/9780190090692.001.0001

and economic justice for all. The American Association for Marriage and Family Therapy (2015) stated in their code, "The areas of service, advocacy, and public participation are recognized as responsibilities to the profession equal in importance to all other aspects." The American Counseling Association (2014) stated even more clearly in their Code of Ethics that a "core professional value of the profession" is to "promote social justice" for the purposes of "promoting equity for all people and groups for the purposes of ending oppression and injustice." Wow, that's quite a responsibility indeed.

Most conferences nowadays have social justice as a theme and require all program submissions to clearly indicate how they will address some salient issue of our times. Leaders within the profession and editorials in the flagship journals, scold, cajole, and shame practitioners to take a more active stand on behalf of the neglected or oppressed.

We don't know about you, but it often strikes us, despite the most honorable intentions, that leaders in positions of power, who are often themselves not inclined to invest much time in advocacy beyond their own self-promotion, are among those who are most vocal in scolding others to become more actively involved. This leads to the question of whether social justice and advocacy are really the priority that we make it out to be? There's a lot of talk but precious little *sustained* action. Yet this is not another one of those pie in the sky admonishments.

REALITIES OF ADVOCACY EFFORTS THAT ARE IGNORED

I've (Jeffrey) spent the better part of the past 20 years working primarily outside of a clinical office to launch and maintain advocacy projects abroad. I've been working in a half dozen different projects with colleagues and students to address issues of human trafficking, exploitation of children, educational inequities, refugee trauma, and extreme poverty. These efforts have taken place in Africa, South Asia, and indigenous communities both on the North American continent and abroad. I'm often applauded for these efforts, but my confession is that this was never an intentional choice nor an effort that was primarily motivated by some desire to change the world. Rather, the first time I became involved, it was an impulsive action that had far-reaching consequences from which I couldn't escape. I had no choice in the matter. And neither would most anyone else if you imagine yourself in situations in which you are the only person standing in the way of a girl being forced into sex slavery or a newly arrived refugee who is struggling with trauma from having watched his family tortured and murdered.

In our experience, advocacy and social justice efforts are often overromanticized. The reality is that they are usually extremely uncomfortable and sometimes terrifying and dangerous. When working abroad or in socioeconomically deprived environments, you are operating in rather basic conditions in which contagious diseases, physical restraints, and safety issues are present. There is a price to be paid in terms of health, physical and emotional exhaustion, compassion fatigue, vicarious trauma, and contagious despair.

The environments, at least those in which we are most familiar, are chaotic and confusing. You can be working in another culture or country for decades and yet still feel bewildered most of the time by the customs, language, and behavior. It is imperative to rely on local experts to help navigate the complex dynamics, but there is always something lost in translation.

When working in many Third World countries, there is a certain amount of resistance and obstructiveness to be encountered. There may be resentment toward some privileged professional who shows up, allegedly to "save these poor people from themselves." Even when one's presence is gratefully appreciated and honored, there is still a degree of sabotage, fraud, deception, and manipulation that may be operating behind the scenes.

All in all, if the intention is not just some token symbolic effort to make oneself feel good but a genuine commitment to begin a project that will be maintained, grown, and supported over time, then the time and energy commitments are massive, interfering with other life, work, and family priorities. Sometimes you are away from home for months at a time, living in the most miserable circumstances, isolated, frightened, fatigued, disoriented, and usually pretty frustrated at times when things hardly ever go as expected. You become sleep deprived, often physically depleted, and sometimes despairing at what seems like utter futility given the scope of the problems.

ADVOCACY EFFORTS CAN BE COMPLICATED

Advocacy efforts are sometimes criticized across the political spectrum. A therapist can advocate and work with women who have had an abortion but also adopt a child from a Third-World country. When encountering criticisms about not honoring the sanctity of life, the therapist responded, "I adopted a child. What have *you* done lately?" Advocating for honoring spirituality, religious, and indigenous customs can conflict with advocacy for women or LGBTQ+ populations, and these conflicts play out within the various mental health professions. Someone's advocacy can be another's oppression.

The most unrealistic aspect of the social justice mandate for mental health professionals is related to the crushing responsibilities of our lives. Some of us have the time and space for these endeavors because we may be in a position developmentally, financially, emotionally, and professionally that we can afford to take time off for months at a time to live and work in one of the most remote, inhospitable, and challenging places in the world.

For the majority of practitioners, however, there is already plenty to do with never enough time and resources to keep up with all the responsibilities and workload. First, there is the current caseload to keep up with, serving all the clients clamoring for attention. Then there is all the case files and paperwork that must be maintained during the brief intervals between sessions. One of the most trying aspects of the job has nothing to do with serving clients but rather navigating the complex interpersonal dynamics and office politics with colleagues. Plus, there must be time for supporting loved ones, nourishing all those neglected friendships, and just trying to take care of oneself. It's altogether overwhelming. And the prospect of adding one more thing feels like it's just not on the radar, as much as one might like to do something.

We are not trying to make excuses, let anyone off the hook, or undermine the advocacy mission that is so much a part of our profession. We are just trying to be realistic about the timing, place, and context for such efforts, since most of them don't appear to last very long.

This is a time when people often describe advocacy as symbolic gestures in which they might "like" a cause on social media, wear a ribbon or wrist band proclaiming their support for an issue, or perhaps even join a march or protest against some injustice. *Slacktivism* is a pejorative term for a seemingly virtuous action that is actually insignificant and self-aggrandizing and designed to make one feel good about oneself. It involves minimal effort or risk, as well as low investment of time, effort, resources, and money. It represents a token gesture that shows one cares (or pretends to care) about some issue. A subcategory, *clicktivism*, involves the rather convenient option of simply posting or liking an article or comment online. It's quick and easy and can be accomplished with one hand while drinking coffee with the other hand.

With that said, the lines are sometimes blurry between what is true activism and what is slacktivism. After all, the Arab Spring Movement of 2011 started and was sustained as a result of overwhelming responsiveness on social media. Nevertheless, there is some evidence that token gestures may ultimately have a detrimental effect on advocacy and social movements. When people just sign online petitions, "like" something on Facebook or Instagram, share an article on social media, or wear a ribbon, there's evidence that it actually derails the likelihood they will become more actively involved in some meaningful and sustained action. Sometimes the primary reason for such minimal efforts is to feel a sense of belonging in a group with minimum investment (Schumann & Klein, 2015). Whereas it is often surmised that such initial behaviors are stepping stones to greater involvement, they can actually function as substitutes for more meaningful actions.

Taking things a step further, people may volunteer to feed the homeless or conduct trauma assessments on depression awareness day. These efforts are certainly worthwhile and admirable—to an extent. But what our communities and the world needs more than anything are those willing to begin a project and then to stick with it to make sure it is self-sustaining and flourishing over time.

THE RECIPROCAL GIFTS OF ALTRUISM, ADVOCACY, AND SERVICE

Becoming involved in advocacy and social justice is not just about saving the world, but also saving ourselves to some extent. By definition, it involves some risk and self-sacrifice on the part of an individual, often accompanied by some cost, which explains why evolutionary processes reward those who work on behalf of the greater good so that others may survive and the species will flourish (Kennedy, Higginson, Radford, & Sumner, 2018; Marsh, 2016).

There is some pretty impressive research that highlights the benefits bestowed on those who are actively involved in altruistic service, that is, without any tangible financial compensation (Arnstein, Vidal, Wells-Federman, Morgan, & Caudill, 2002; Kottler, 2000; Kottler & Marriner, 2009; Post, 2007, 2011; Walsh, 2011). Chief among them is enhanced levels of empathy, but there are other more curious advantages; for example, men who are inclined to be generous, giving, and altruistic toward others enjoy greater mating success. This can be explained, in part, because they are viewed as more trustworthy, reliable, and supportive (Arnocky, Piche, Albert, Ouellette, & Barclay, 2017). In Table 12.1 we list some of the other benefits that may be accrued.

"The best way to find yourself," Mahatma Gandhi once observed, "is to lose yourself in the service\ of others." There is indeed incredible joy, if not

---

Table 12.1 BENEFITS THAT ACCRUE TO SELFLESS, ALTRUISTIC INDIVIDUALS

Greater sense of well-being and life satisfaction	Increased appreciation of one's own life situation
Expanded world view of self and others	Sense of meaning and purpose to life's mission
Feelings of affiliation and belongingness	Increased intimacy and collaboration with others
Immunity to disease, colds, and flu	Reduced chronic pain
Receive reciprocal generosity from others	Status, trust, respect within community
Elevated oxytocin and vasopressin ("helper's high")	Increased flexibility and creativity
Renewed faith	Spiritual transcendence
Leaving a meaningful legacy	Expressing and receiving love and compassion
Release of guilt by paying something back	Feelings of redemption in using own pain and losses
"Ticket" to heaven or divine validation	Increased lifespan

---

spiritual transcendence, when one is a witness to—or, better yet, a companion to or instigator of—another's growth and development. Of course, we experience this every day in our work with clients, but there is another, special kind of reward when the actions are truly selfless and aimed at those who would otherwise never be able to receive any assistance.

In a series of interviews, therapists who have been passionately involved in service projects were asked to talk about what they learned along the way that was most valuable to them (Kottler & Safari, 2019). Evian, who volunteered to work with at-risk children in remote villages, commented on the enduring effects of her experience: "The first school visit will be a memory that forever is imprinted in my heart like a tattoo to my soul." Although it has been 5 years since her visit abroad, she believes that it is what is primarily responsible for helping "put [her] life in perspective." It clarified a path for her to follow, one that is devoted to serving others.

Alyssa, who described herself as somewhat shy with a propensity to withdraw in groups, found that her experiences working on a project helped her to come out of her shell and, in one sense, reinvent herself. "The entire trip consisted of engaging with complete strangers in an extremely intimate way. I felt that this was something I had to do for myself, and I knew that if I didn't do whatever it took to go on the trip, I would regret it for the rest of my life."

The whole experience was so emotional and moving for Alyssa, not just in the joys she experienced feeling like she was making a difference, but also the burdens and difficulties she suffered. Once she returned home, it felt like her whole world had been turned upside down with a new appreciation for life and what it can offer.

If you have worked abroad or in marginalized communities, then it is likely that these disclosures resonate with you, as do some of the reasons listed next that people offered why they become involved in social justice projects.

- They feel like their lives are redeemed. They are doing something that seems like it matters.
- They are giving their lives greater meaning. Many have left high-paying jobs because they felt empty.
- They are paying back what others have given to them. They have been wounded or hurt earlier in life and recovered sufficiently to want to ease others' suffering.
- They are following a spiritual path, one that is self-serving to earn God's validation or following divine inspiration.
- They are developing new areas of expertise and gaining valuable experience. This can range from beefing up one's resume to developing skills that will be useful in the future.
- They are hiding from things they wish to avoid. Helping others is a good way to distract from dealing with issues that may be painful or to avoid problems that feel overwhelming.
- They can feel like a martyr, making sacrifices and suffering deprivations, all for the greater good.
- They are feeling useful. Their sense of self-worth and importance can be directly related to the impact they believe they're having on others.

For those of us stuck in our offices wielding our therapeutic magic wands, it is often frustrating that it seems to take so long for people to make needed changes. Clients sometimes argue with us and resist our best efforts to help them. We only see them for a few minutes each week, and any progress made can easily unravel once they return home and to their peer groups. In addition, if you work with the "worried well," at times you can seriously question the value of your life's work and wonder whether you could so easily be replaced by someone else. Perhaps one of the most satisfying motives of all for advocacy work is feeling like you are truly making a measurable difference, within a relatively short period of time, with a population that is not only desperate but also eager and grateful for your efforts. Rather than just smoothing adjustment to a rocky relationship, frustrating job, or life disappointment, you are literally saving lives.

Advocacy does not have to be a special project. It can be the day-to-day work of a therapist. Rick worked with twin girls, 13-years-old, who were placed in psychiatric hospitalization for oppositional behavior and running away. Both twins had been living with their grandmother after child protective services (CPS) was called due to allegations of abuse by the children's father. The girls disclosed during a session that they ran away from their grandmother's house because their father lived directly across the street. He had come over and dragged one of the girls across the street with the other twin fighting back. When he released the other twin, the girls ran off, and the police were called. Rick called the CPS caseworker to find out why the girls were placed out of the home in such a dangerous situation. The caseworker said, "We have not taken custody, and we do not believe we need to take custody." Fearing for the girls safety, Rick found the number for the director of human services in the governor's office to file a complaint and received a call back from the regional director for CPS in the county. The county director and Rick met with caseworkers, and they opted to take custody and place the kids in a safe environment. Ultimately, the challenging of the system, even on a case-by-case basis, can be important advocacy with sustained results.

INVOLVEMENT IN SOCIAL JUSTICE PROJECTS

One of the major obstacles for devotion to a cause is finding a suitable match and opportunity that fits with one's abilities, interests, time constraints, and budget. And yes, time *is* money, especially for therapists who are just struggling to make ends meet and pay off debts.

One of the most daunting challenges related to undertaking some advocacy project is that it is often framed as an all-or-nothing effort or it represents someone else's idea that doesn't quite fit one's needs. There is also the myth that it has to be something big, rather than a modest beginning. Jeffrey's serendipitous project in Nepal started by impulsively offering a small sum of money to support the education of one girl who was in danger of being trafficked into sex slavery. Full disclosure is that this seemingly small gesture occurred in a place that is one of the most alluring destinations in the world for a mountaineer, which is one of the real reasons he was working there in the first place. That is another myth associated with noble efforts—that is, they are supposedly only for the greater good and do not also serve to disguise an intensely personal motive.

Among all the reasons to become involved in a charitable cause, perhaps the most important is that it reflects one's true interests in such a way that it feels like a gift and privilege to become involved. In this sense, it is no longer another obligation or work responsibility, one more burden added onto everything else, but rather a relief from the usual daily pressures.

For those who return from service projects after an intense, extended visit, the most difficult part is adjusting to some of the realities back home. One therapist confessed that she felt "ruined" after resuming her clinical practice: "Compared to the problems of the people I was seeing, just functioning on a survival level, it was hard for me to listen to some of the clients in my office. They would complain about stuff that now seemed so petty. They'd whine about how difficult their lives were because they couldn't buy some luxury they craved or that they weren't appreciated as much as they deserved. I'm ashamed to admit that I kept hearing this voice inside my head screaming at them to wake up and realize how lucky they were." She admits that her levels of patience and compassion were compromised because of the severity and depth of despair she witnessed in the weeks prior to her return.

As we've mentioned, people get involved in this type of work for all kinds of reasons that are quite personal and selfish. That is not only normal but probably desirable, dispelling the myth that you must be a heroic martyr. There are also so many different kinds of projects that can be undertaken in small doses, until such time that there is space and opportunity for greater commitment.

1. *Challenging* systemic inequities within an organization or community. This involves first *recognizing* that some individuals or groups are marginalized in some way and then *doing something* to change the status quo.
2. *Transforming* social institutions. Once inequities are identified, steps are taken to change the ways that schools, agencies, government departments, and other organizations operate.
3. *Inviting* fuller access to resources and full participation on the part of excluded people. Again, this involves constructive *action* (rather than mere talk) to advocate on behalf of those without equal rights because of their race, age, religion, gender, disability, sexual orientation, education, socioeconomic status, or group membership.
4. *Bringing attention* to issues of oppression, prejudice, and social inequities within an organization or community.
5. *Combating* racism, prejudice, homophobia, ageism, and sexism as it is witnessed. Speaking out and taking action in the face of injustices and oppression.
6. *Advocating* on behalf of human rights, especially among those who have minority status or who have been historically denied privileges afforded to those of the majority. For example, this could refer to Native

Americans, African Americans, and other minorities within the United States or those of the "untouchable" caste in India, the Kurds of Iraq, or the hill tribes of Cambodia, Palestinians in the Middle East, and so on.

7. *Empowering* those who have historically been without a voice. This may involve personal self-sacrifice, as well as surrendering some of your own privileges and advantages.

8. *Volunteering time and devoting personal resources* to make a difference among those most in need. Whether this is with the homeless in your own community or with those most at-risk across the nation or abroad, you develop and implement strategies to make a difference.

CHANGING PEOPLE'S LIVES WHILE TRANSFORMING YOUR OWN

We've discussed how clients in therapy become our greatest teachers and supervisors in so many ways. They inform us about what is most and least helpful to them, but far more than that, their complaints trigger our own issues, urging, if not forcing, us to address unresolved difficulties. If this sort of reciprocal influence and impact takes place within the structured and circumscribed confines of therapy, imagine how much more powerful the effects are when surrendering control in a novel environment. Traditional boundaries are gone. The sheer intensity and drama of daily life is overwhelming to take on board. Vicarious trauma is the norm when witnessing such unusual and tragic scenarios.

"We spent a weekend working and staying in a homeless shelter downtown," a therapist intern reveals.

> At night we'd go up on the roof and look down at the streets below. These were some of the same people we'd see during the day to assist them with basic needs or talk to them about their lives. But late at night, it was like the most profane, disturbing, and inhumane behavior would be on full display. We'd see both men and women giving blowjobs on the street for the price of a small nugget of meth worth about $5. I remember seeing one guy shooting heroin and, with the needle still sticking out of his arm, he collapsed on the sidewalk. Perhaps dead. It didn't matter. Other people stepped over him and just continued on their way.

Experiences like this will never, can never, be forgotten. They penetrate our psyche in ways that the typical narratives of clients can't touch. They are powerfully memorable and impactful precisely because they are beyond our prior experiences. As we reviewed earlier, this sort of work leads to a number of personal and professional consequences, some of which may be expected while others are unanticipated.

We may not consciously become involved in volunteer service for personal reasons, but there's little doubt that those motives are operating beyond awareness. On the positive side of the ledger, we are able to use our own suffering from the past to make a difference in others' lives. We have access to a secret world that is beyond view except to those who make the journey. We improve our knowledge and deeper understanding of the world. We enjoy exciting new adventures that test our limits. Most important, we experience a parallel process of growth that could not occur any other way.

We've also highlighted the price paid for this work. The despair and hopelessness we encounter is contagious at times. We may gain a greater sense of faith, but also lose confidence in prized convictions. It is impossible to turn away from some of the realities that are encountered, especially those that reveal such cruelty, neglect, oppression, and abuse of others who are helpless to fend for themselves.

If the goal is to take the risks that may lead to personal transformation and professional maturity, there are certain steps that can be taken that increase the odds that something remarkable will take place. This involves taking on new challenges that are beyond one's comfort level. It means pushing oneself into new territory. If the sorts of therapeutic (and travel) experiences that most lead to enduring change are those that are novel, then it is crucial to get outside of our offices into neglected parts of the world where little help is available.

As we are certainly more aware than most, experiences that have enduring effects are those in which people choose to reflect on their meaning and significance. For those eager, open, and searching for such growth, the process begins by looking for the smallest indicators of new learning. It's important to talk about these insights, if not revelations, with colleagues, friends, and family so they understand better what this might mean for the future. It's not unusual after an intense service experience—just like after a particularly evocative therapy session—that we need time and opportunities to make sense of what happened and integrate the new awareness into future choices and behavior. It's also important to share the stories of what happened to honor the work and involve others. This is similar to what we tell clients when we say that although they may be the designated person from their family to seek help, it's likely the whole system will be irrevocably altered as a result of the changes an individual makes.

PRACTICING LEADERSHIP IN EVERYDAY LIFE

If we reframe social justice and advocacy as less daunting, it doesn't necessarily mean disrupting one's life in a significant way but just demonstrating leadership in our daily lives. We talk a good game about how we stand for principles of advocacy, activism, and healing, but the real question is how we live those ideas in our everyday interactions. Leadership is not just something we practice on the job or when in a designated position of authority and power; rather, it is part of who we are. It is the manifestation of, or our internal sense of, morality, compassion, and caring for others.

We close our discussion of the myths and misconceptions about what it means to become involved in advocacy and social justice by summarizing some basic principles by which all of us could be more congruent, authentic models of what we say is so important for others.

1. *Believe and practice leadership in all aspects of life, not just when on stage or in session.* This means taking a more proactive stand to advocate on behalf of issues, concerns, and problems that we claim are important to us, not just by "liking" or posting something on social media, but through taking direct action and following through on this commitment.

2. *Practice healthy, measured daily habits, focusing on the positive.* We spend a good part of our day advising, recommending, persuading, and convincing others to take better care of themselves through their eating, sleeping, and exercise habits. We would do well to listen to our own advice.

3. *Do less, not more.* We realize this is a paradoxical recommendation considering we've just spent the bulk of this chapter saying that we all have a responsibility to do more to help the disenfranchised. But we also hope we've been clear that there is a time and place for this in each person's life. When it feels like another obligation, such service can have deleterious effects on both us and others. Practice self-care, balancing work with leisure, friendships, and family.

4. *Lead others in pursuing a meaningful life, seeking well-being instead of the unattainable goal of so-called happiness.* Part of the wisdom we accrue over time in this field is the realization that people work so hard trying to attain some ultimate ideal of life satisfaction that they are eternally frustrated and disappointment when things fall short.

5. *Acknowledge our mistakes, miscalculations, and failures as opportunities for reflection, humility, and to learn and grow.* Proudly share examples of lapses (when appropriate) to make it easier for others to disclose their own.

The supreme irony of our profession, as well as an ongoing myth that is perpetuated, is that we really aren't the perfectly selfless, endlessly patient, absolutely brilliant people that clients encounter in their sessions with us. Alas, our clients get the best of us when we give (or sell) them our undivided attention without distractions or intrusions. They experience us as confident, yet humble, respectful but hardly deferential. We are almost always polite and considerate. It would certainly be congruent, if not desirable, if we were able to demonstrate an equivalent amount of such compassion and hovering attention to everyone else in our world, especially colleagues, friends, family, and loved ones.

CHAPTER 13

❧

Mythology and Ethics

It used to be that there were absolute moral authorities that dictated what was acceptable and what was sinful or against the rules. The Ten Commandments, Five Pillars of Islam, Code of Hammurabi, and the Bible all proclaimed that thievery, murder, or other behaviors were forbidden. Likewise, adultery, homosexuality, eating pork, consuming meat that was not ritually slaughtered were also prohibited. Priests, rabbis, ministers, imams, and the pope were the arbiters of what was considered proper actions.

If someone was having an affair, stole property, or cheated a neighbor, such behavior would be condemned and the person was required to seek forgiveness and be punished for the transgressions. Nowadays, it sometimes appears as if therapists are the ones sought out when there are questions of conscience or feelings of guilt. Rather than judging behavior critically, we are far more inclined to invite the "sinner" to explore feelings and consequences of these actions so as to determine a personalized course of action. We typically don't take a stand as to whether premarital or extramarital sex is "wrong" and instead invite clients to talk about feelings associated with the choices.

There are exceptions, of course, to this principled stand of neutrality since the ethical codes of all the mental health professions prescribe that we fight against injustice, racism, homophobia, and other forms of oppression and marginalization. When clients do espouse hateful, vicious attacks against others, we are fully expected to challenge this behavior in an appropriate, "therapeutic" manner.

Myths, Misconceptions, and Invalid Assumptions of Counseling and Psychotherapy. Jeffrey Kottler and Richard S. Balkin, Oxford University Press (2020). © Oxford University Press.
DOI: 10.1093/oso/9780190090692.001.0001

COUNTERTRANSFERENCE: EMOTIONAL VERSUS VALUE-BASED CONFLICTS

Historically, we are supposed to be morally neutral (relatively speaking) unless someone is a danger to themselves or others or perhaps engaged in fairly obvious self-destructive behavior. And yet, a significant amount of literature in the mental health disciplines (e.g., counseling, marriage and family therapy, psychology, psychiatry, social work) is focused on the impossibility of this position. Specifically, Freud's (1953, 1910) concept of countertransference flies in the face of the neutral, objective therapist since we may become unconsciously and emotionally enmeshed with our clients, personally triggered in such a way that we can't help but have rather strong feelings toward something a client says or does.

Dennis was a 19-year old male who lived at home with his mother, a situation neither of them was happy about. He was in a gang, sold and used drugs, and had a history of considerable violent behavior, including drive-by shootings and physical altercations. He admitted to robbing gas stations and convenience stores but had never been adjudicated. In addition, he regularly used an assortment of drugs and alcohol with methamphetamine as his drug of choice.

Dennis had an 11-year old brother also living at home. At this mother's urging, and feeling guilty over his negative influence on his brother, Dennis agreed to check himself into treatment. After 48-hours in detox, he attended group therapy sessions and Alcoholics Anonymous meetings and had his first family session, after which he informed his mother and therapist that he was going to check himself out of the hospital. The therapist was adamantly against this decision, believing Dennis was going to continue to use drugs as soon as he returned to the streets. After some rather heated arguments, he eventually agreed to attend a day treatment program as an alternative.

Throughout the next week of his sessions, Dennis was both somewhat belligerent and uncooperative, arguing that, first, drugs really aren't that bad, and second, he didn't really have a problem with them. Needless to say, this was less than helpful to other patients in the group who were struggling with their own ambivalence about their treatment. Clearly, Dennis appeared to be a disruptive force and a danger to the recovery process of other patients.

During a meeting with the physician who had released Dennis from his original treatment program, Dennis's therapist expressed his frustration with the current situation. Their conversation went something like this:

THERAPIST: "I told you not to discharge him! I am sitting there with his mother, watching him cry, and I knew he was being manipulative. I told both him and his mother this was not going to work. He just smiled at me!"

PHYSICIAN: "He got to you."

THERAPIST: "And then you went ahead and discharged him!"

PHYSICIAN: "I cannot hold him against his will. This is just what addicts do."

THERAPIST: "But now he is sabotaging others in the group. It's one thing that he doesn't care about his own recovery, but it's just not acceptable that he compromises the progress that others are making. He's a toxic influence!"

PHYSICIAN: "You are angry with me, and you are angry with the patient."

THERAPIST: "I am indeed."

PHYSICIAN: "I really think this is just part of your own countertransference reactions to him, which is fine, as long as you acknowledge it."

After this last comment, the therapist took a deep breath and tried not to react defensively. After the pause, he nodded his head and agreed there was some emotional entanglement with Dennis and that these feelings were affecting his ability to provide quality care.

In cases like this, there are a number of ethical issues that may influence clinical decisions and interventions. The therapist wondered if he was obligated to refer Dennis to someone else on staff, perhaps someone who was not so bothered by the ways his behavior was hurting others in the unit. Seeking additional supervision was also an option considered. Yet, in both of these choices, the options were somewhat limited because of staffing shortages and budget considerations.

Cases of countertransference like this are not limited to just the emotional responses to clients' behavior. Religious beliefs also may impact the willingness and competence of therapists to work with certain clients who may have diametrically opposite values. In such cases, countertransference may deviate from the classical definition of emotional enmeshment (although one could argue that religious convictions are tied to emotions, along with sincerely held cultural beliefs). Balkin, Schlosser, and Levitt (2009) studied the relationship between religious identity of professional counselors and counseling psychologists and their propensity toward multicultural competence, sexism, and homophobia toward clients. It turns out that religious identity was not related to multicultural competence, but clinicians who endorsed strong religious identities that were found to be less accepting, authoritarian, and inclined to be more sexist and homophobic. In other words, therapists across a variety of religious identities agree about the need to be open and accommodating toward ethnic and racial cultures, but sexist and homophobic beliefs still permeate the professions.

Despite ethical codes and mental health organizations that explicitly oppose conversion therapy, the practice still remains. Many jurisdictions have outright banned conversion therapy, but some courts are not necessarily supportive or in agreement, creating conflicts between religious beliefs and professional ethics. In one such case, a therapist refused to treat a client who wanted to explore a same-sex attraction and insisted on referring the person elsewhere (Oppenheimer, 2012). The controversy related to this landmark case that ended up in the courts highlighted the conflicts between a therapist's strong moral and religious convictions and professional conduct.

Legal decisions and ethical codes may sometimes be at odds, but the unspoken issues of ethical practice in conducting therapy is the emotional state of the therapist. The mental health professions attempt to delineate differences between referrals based on competency and those based on personal values of the therapist. Although these two issues are different, the emotional state of the therapist is at the core of each of them.

In the first scenario with Dennis, the therapist was dealing with emotional entanglement—the client's manipulative behavior and the therapist's frustration in working with the client. In the latter case, the therapist reacted to being forced to work with a client on issues that conflicted with her religious beliefs. While there are numerous ethical decision-making models that relate to training and supervision, the emotional enmeshment of the therapist requires additional consideration.

BRACKETING AND COUNTERTRANSFERENCE

Ethical "bracketing" is the process by which therapists deliberately separate their own personal values from their professional responsibilities to provide more responsive treatment of client unique needs (Kocet & Herlihy, 2014). This, of course, is predicated on the idea that we are actually aware of how our values are impinging on the therapeutic relationship, a difficult prospect no matter how much supervision or personal therapy we have under our belts.

A therapist, for example, may become frustrated dealing with a client's persistent denial of problems and manipulative behavior. Despite acknowledging the difficulties, the therapist still keeps a certain distance and self-protection in place, demonstrating significantly less warmth, affection, and engagement than might ordinarily be present. The therapist may blame the client for obstructiveness and resistance, but there is also likely an interactive effect as a result of the therapist becoming more withholding.

In the professional literature and various ethical codes, values-based conflicts are considered separate and distinct from emotional or personal conflicts the clinician might face with a client. However, countertransference affects each of these in distinct ways.

We May Not Be Able to Change Who We Are

Mental health training programs are popular among both public and private institutions. Religious institutions often provide accredited training along with education for providing spiritual support to clients—a need among many clients seeking counseling services (Balkin et al., 2009). But some accredited programs occur at institutions that use nonaffirming language (e.g., discouraging same-sex relationships) with respect to student expectations. L. C. Smith and Okech (2016) identified 15 private, religious-based institutions with nonaffirming language that are accredited and train mental health providers. Given that therapists from a variety of sociopolitical persuasions will continue to be trained as mental health providers, value-based conflicts among providers are unlikely to disappear.

There Is a Research Base Supporting the Concept of Countertransference

Kächele, Erhardt, Seybert, and Buchholz (2015) reviewed quantitative and qualitative studies and measures related to countertransference, which date back to the early 1950s. The presence of these personal reactions is beyond any single conceptual framework and appears as an established construct through both quantitative and qualitative findings. Kächele et al. noted an absence of randomized clinical trials, noting that such designs would be difficult to construct to study countertransference; however, true experimental designs were noted in the review and supported the presence of countertransference.

There Is No Research Support for the Existence of Ethical Bracketing

Kocet and Herlihy (2014) noted that ethical bracketing was a borrowed concept from qualitative research. In qualitative research, bracketing refers to the researchers' self-examination of their perceived experiences and biases prior to data collection, such as conducting interviews and observations or evaluating data through coding and identification of themes (Marshall & Rossman, 2011). Bracketing, therefore, allows the qualitative researcher to identify potential personal factors that could impact the quality of interpretation; provide transparency to the research and findings by noting any potential biases; and consciously put such biases aside to provide a more objective overview of the results. Extending the concept of bracketing to ethical issues was a novel approach to address values-based conflicts. However, in contrast to countertransference, there are no research studies about ethical bracketing. This does not mean that the phenomenon does not exist; rather, a research base is needed along with how the conflicts between ethical bracketing and countertransference can be managed.

Ethical Bracketing May Not Be Possible

Presently, ethical bracketing remains an idea—a theoretical construct with little, if any, empirical support beyond case reports. Moreover, given the validation in the literature of countertransference, the willingness and ability for therapists to engage in ethical bracketing is questionable. By definition, countertransference refers to the therapist's *unconscious* and *unaware* issues and perceptions projected onto the client, which makes it rather difficult to identify when it occurs. Even when therapists are aware of personal biases and projections, there is no evidence that they can be held in check to the extent that there will be no effect on the working alliance between the therapist and client.

On the other hand, therapists should be held to a higher standard of ethical conduct than the general population. It is the nature of our training, preparation, and experience that we are always working toward a greater state of clarity, internal stability, and accuracy of perceptual acuity. We will never be perfect, or even close to where we'd ideally like to be, but we are usually more objective than most others. The idea that therapists can keep values-based conflicts in check is admirable but also incredibly challenging. Although the extent to which therapists unconsciously project emotions and conflicts onto clients has been debated for decades, the majority of therapy proceeds productively and ethically.

There is a responsibility, first, to do no harm and, second, to be helpful. Professional bodies across mental health disciplines all struggle with the nature of competence, training, and values-based conflicts. It's preposterous to believe that all therapists can serve everyone adequately. Furthermore, those who teach, train, and supervise others have the professional responsibility to monitor who receives the education and training to become a clinician in compliance with the ethical codes of the professional body. Often, clients seek therapy to find answers, and they turn to therapists as a source for those answers. Not only can perceived biases hamper the therapists' abilities to facilitate the client's journey, but sometimes just the lack of understanding about what the client is experiencing can affect therapeutic progress. Whereas ethical codes provide a basis for clinician behaviors, which are often aspirational, the reality is that clients are likely to present with concerns for which therapists, along with their clients, struggle to find answers.

LITTLE LIES

CLIENT: "I've kind of always had this problem being so fearful of crossing bridges. It's weird because I'm not afraid at all of heights or anything. And I have no trouble going through tunnels."

THERAPIST: "That *is* interesting."

CLIENT: "So, what do you think it says?"

THERAPIST: [Stalling] "What do you mean?"

CLIENT: "You know, like how should I interpret this? What does it have to do with my problem?"

THERAPIST: [Thinking, thinking, thinking . . .] "Well, it could be a lot of things."

CLIENT: "Like what?"

THERAPIST: "Well, for instance it could have something to do with the reluctance you said you feel whenever you encounter a new challenge?"

CLIENT: [Shaking head]

THERAPIST: "It could also relate to loss of control. When you are in the middle of the bridge you have no way out . . ."

CLIENT: "Then why don't tunnels bother me even more?"

THERAPIST: "Okay, then, how about the connection to some of your early history when you talked about those difficulties you had with all the frequent moving to new locations. Maybe . . ."

CLIENT: [Again shakes head]

THERAPIST: "Okay, how about this? Another possibility is that this 'bridge thing' doesn't have anything at all to do with your problem. It could be something completely unrelated."

CLIENT: "How do you mean?"

THERAPIST: "Well, let's explore this more together and see where it leads."

This means, naturally, that the therapist really has no idea where this leads, nor does he have much of an idea of exactly what the fear of crossing bridges means. Oh, he's got some hypotheses. Some guesses too. But it's not like he has a limited choice of four possibilities from which to choose the one, and only one, right answer. And even if he did manage to find a suitable interpretation, one the client accepts as accurate, there's never any way to know for sure whether that was just a convenient explanation that has no relationship to "the truth."

On one hand, there is the expectation that therapists operate within their own scope of competence, but on the other hand, therapists are expected to adapt, understand, and serve clients from a variety of backgrounds with a broad range of problems or issues. Consider the newly minted graduate who works in a community mental health center or hospital setting. Such sites are always a great way to start clinical practice because there is no telling who is going to walk in to the office and what issue will need to be addressed. Novice clinicians get exposed to a variety of mental health issues to which they likely had no previous experience addressing in their coursework. The idea that therapists, especially those early in their career, have no say in whom they work with or an opportunity to address some niche or specialty area often is quite a surprise to beginners as they leave the sheltered, structured confines of their education and training. Oh, there will still be multiple choice exams to complete as required continuing education credits. Sometimes even to renew licensing requirements. But otherwise, the real world welcomes us with the most ambiguous, uncertain arms.

The client operates under the assumption that some truth might be discovered over being fearful of crossing bridges. The therapist appears open to exploring but never admits to having no idea about the client's fear, or even that some absolute truth may not be available. At some level, the therapist lacks transparency. But does this little lie unethical constitute a breach in ethics?

Most codes of ethics (e.g., social work, psychology, counseling) address the need to practice honestly and responsibly. However, none of the codes of ethics in the aforementioned professions address when it is okay to lie or deceive clients. The only time deception is mentioned is in reference to conducting research. In terms of research, extant literature on therapist deception in counseling is extremely limited. Solovey and Duncan (1992) noted that consciously deceiving a client is unethical and, if caught, would not only undermine the working alliance but could also be detrimental to the client's view of therapy. However, they also admit that absolutely prohibiting client deception is not that simple. A therapist may manipulate the client or family system to create change in creative ways.

THERAPIST: "It sounds like you are having difficulty regaining the trust from your wife after your affair."

CLIENT: "Yeah. Anytime I say I am going out or working late, she thinks I am cheating on her."

THERAPIST: "What about when you and your wife had a trusting relationship? What was that like?"

CLIENT: "It was great. Even if I worked late, she was okay with it. We talked more when I got home. We were both more affectionate with each other."

THERAPIST: "You should do that. Act as if you had a trusting relationship. See what happens. Maybe you will get a different response."

CLIENT: "I don't know that she wants that. I don't know that I feel that. It seems dishonest."

THERAPIST: "Sometimes you have to take risks and do something different to create change."

Is this scenario a conscious deception? The client admits that such actions would not be heartfelt but rather a response to what the therapist is asking the client to do. Yet, these types of interactions are quite common. "Acting as if" is a common Adlerian strategy discussed in a multitude of general textbooks on theory and practice. As therapists we sometimes practice forms of manipulation as a mechanism for eliciting client change, even though it appears objectionable.

Conscious deception is sometimes even part of standard care. When working with clients who are diagnosed with dementia, lying and deception (or at least shading the truth) are common practice. James, Wood-Mitchell, Waterworth, Mackenzie, and Cunningham (2006) found that 96% of staff on a dementia care unit used lying and deception as a normal part of patient care. Common examples were lies such as saying to a patient who calls for her deceased mother, "She's not here right now," or telling another patient, "Your children are coming to visit you," as a way to motivate him to get dressed and out of bed. Or the most frequent lie of all: "You will get to see the doctor soon" (Elvish, James, & Milne, 2010).

Lying and deception are also regularly used with clients to prevent self-harm, encourage compliance, or decrease stress (Elvish et al., 2010). There are four common types of deceptions used with clients:

1. *Avoiding arguments and conflict,* such as not challenging delusions or hallucinations by simply going along with the patient's perceived reality.
2. *Omission of facts* to prevent the client from becoming more distressed.
3. *Lies,* such as statements of things that will not happen but encourage a patient to adopt a behavior. For example, a client refuses to get out of bed so he is told that visitors are coming.
4. *Tricks,* which include conscious deception to encourage a behavior. For example, a prized pocket knife is removed from the room so the client is not at risk of self-harm, and the client believes it was simply misplaced.

Elvish et al. (2010) found that clinical professionals believed lying is most acceptable when keeping a client from engaging in self-harm. However, lying became less acceptable when it was geared toward manipulation—getting someone to engage in a more desirable behavior. Often, however, therapists engage in both of these scenarios. Even when lies are used to keep a client safe, the danger is that such behaviors will lead to mistrust in the therapeutic relationship. When clients believe that therapists are inclined to lie, engaging the client in future therapeutic processes can be a challenge.

Ann was a 14 year-old adolescent female. As is typical of initial sessions, her therapist told her, "What comes in here stays in here, but I will break confidentiality if you tell me that you are a danger to yourself, going to hurt someone else, or have been physically or sexually abused.

CLIENT: "So I can tell you *anything* and you won't tell my parents?"
THERAPIST: "That's correct, as long as what you tell me is not a danger to yourself, someone else, or that you have been abused or abused someone else."
CLIENT: "Okay, then, I've been having sex."
THERAPIST: "Uh huh."
CLIENT: "Well, kind of a lot."
THERAPIST: "Kind of lot, what?"
CLIENT: "With a lot of people. Probably more than 50 different partners. Both guys and girls. I've been keeping a list."

So, now what do you do? Is this a safety issue that justifies breaching confidentiality and perhaps destroying trust in the relationship. This therapist believed so because he felt compelled to notify the parents of what he considered extremely risky and dangerous behavior on her part, especially given her age as a minor.

Perhaps this wasn't exactly a tough call, given the sheer extremity of her behavior that was clearly a form of acting out. The interesting question is, where and how we draw the line as to when something becomes dangerous. What if the girl had "only" five partners? Or only one?

We'd guess that there could be some variations as to when telling parents is necessary. If the client was 16-years old, does the decision of the therapist to break confidentiality change? Making the decision of what is in the best interest of the client or even if the client is no longer safe can be quite subjective, and ethical codes fall far short in helping therapists make these decisions. Moreover, the choice of the therapist to break confidentiality in this scenario is likely tied to the therapist's countertransference—the therapist's perceived value in abstinence. Hence, the values of the therapist, which are supposed to be kept separate from the therapeutic process, could become a guiding rationale for therapeutic decisions.

COMMON LIES WE TELL OUR CLIENTS

As noted in the previous scenario, the most common practice of disclosing boundaries of confidentiality ended up as a questionable practice, as the client felt betrayed by the therapist's decision to break confidentiality and identify her sexual activity as a threat to self. In addition, there is not a clear indicator as to when the client's sexual activity would not be perceived by the therapist as a threat to self. The role of confidentiality is central to competent care. Yet, lies to clients may also be just as central. Here are a few other times when we might be inclined to fudge the truth, if not outright lie.

You Don't Have to Be Here

Sure, this is true. But the fact is that the client is present and, in many cases, is paying for the time with the therapist. There is a pressure to use that time. There is even a punishment if the client does not use the time, namely, being billed for a session that was not used. So, whether self-inflicted or part of the therapeutic process and environment, there is pressure to be in therapy and make the most of the time.

How I Feel About You as a Client Does Not Matter

We know it *does* matter. We know that clients are easiest to work with when they are YAVIS clients—young, attractive, verbal, intellectual, and social (Hollingsworth, 1985). Furthermore, responding honestly could be detrimental to the therapeutic process by either appearing seductive or being extremely unaccepting toward the client.

I Know I Can Help You

We actually do not know if therapy will be helpful or if, in fact, the specific therapeutic relationship will be successful. Most experienced therapists have considered other colleagues who might be more helpful to the client. But there is perceived value in appearing optimistic. In addition, therapists will often rely on their experience, even if experience has little predictive evidence of therapeutic outcomes (Kottler & Balkin, 2017). What is predictive of positive client outcomes is client hopefulness (Duncan, 2014; Lambert, 2013), and the desire to instill hope in the therapeutic process might actually be a small, deceptive practice from the therapist.

Ultimately, client deception can have honorable goals. When interventions are used to change a client's behavior and the client is doing better, there is a positive outcome to the deception.

CLIENT: "I took your advice and tried to engage more with my wife when our relationship was in a better place."
THERAPIST: "What did you do?"
CLIENT: "I tried to engage her more when I got home. Instead of laying on the couch and getting on my iPad, I put it down and just made conversation. She seemed to really like that, and I think we are talking more and some trust is coming back."
THERAPIST: "That's great. So you are reaching out more, and she is reciprocating. Nice work."
CLIENT: Yeah, I think so too."

The practice of deception may seem inherently unethical due to the power differential between the client and therapist. Balancing client control versus positive encouragement is likely key to making sure that client well-being is central to the goal of any deceptive practice. When positive outcomes occur, the client is less likely to perceive being deceived.

Published data on ethical misconduct is very limited, but estimates in North America and Canada range from 4% to 8%, and reports tend to focus on more serious misconduct, such as sexual misconduct with clients (Grenyer & Lewis, 2012). Elvish et al. (2010) indicated that clinicians are likely to draw hard, polarized lines between what is ethical versus unethical, but training can be helpful to broaden the perspective of therapists. Kagle (1998) indicated that client deception is far more commonplace as part of interactions with clients and that a much broader view of ethics is warranted.

THE CHALLENGE OF ETHICAL PRACTICE

When interviewing for a job as a therapist, the applicant was asked, "Have you ever experienced any challenges adhering to your profession's code of ethics?" The applicant did not even pause to think but confidently responded, "My personal ethics go far beyond any ethical codes set by a professional organization." The interviewer smiled, not wanting to indicate that the applicant missed the mark completely with that answer.

It is nice to believe that ethical care is easy. However, this is a misnomer. Emotional conflicts, values-based conflicts, countertransference, and even the tendency to compromise honesty represent common ethical dilemma. The work of therapists can be extremely rewarding, but the stress and challenges we experience working with clients and being true to ourselves can lead therapists to feelings of despair and burnout. We will take a look at some of the myths associated with these issues in the next chapter.

CHAPTER 14

∽

Balancing Hope and Despair and the Real Reasons for Burnout

Angie was depressed. Not just ordinary, run-of-the-mill a little bit sad, but profoundly, disturbingly, chronically, hopelessly depressed. This was the kind of depression that you could see at a glance, that you could hear in an instant, that you could feel seeping into your pores. It was depression that represented utter despair.

Angie had already seen a half dozen other therapists. She had tried a number of medications without improvement, the side effects only making her worse. She had been referred to a neurologist and a host of other specialists looking for an organic origin but again without success. By the time she showed up for an intake, she was beyond caring. In fact, the only thing the therapist got out of her in the first session is that her parents made her come, but she didn't see the point. Angie was 15 and felt her life was over.

During the first few sessions, the therapist tried to sound as upbeat as he could, suggesting that the two of them really could make a difference if they put their heads together. The therapist couldn't tell how well this went over because Angie hid behind a cascade of hair falling forward over her face. She sat hunched over on the couch, grasping her knees, sobbing wordlessly throughout the whole session. Sometimes there might be a slight nod of her head, acknowledging some question that is asked or comment that is offered, but that may have just been wishful thinking. About one thing the therapist was totally certain: He had caught her client's despair.

Myths, Misconceptions, and Invalid Assumptions of Counseling and Psychotherapy. Jeffrey A. Kottler and Richard S. Balkin, Oxford University Press (2020). © Oxford University Press.
DOI: 10.1093/oso/9780190090692.001.0001

Over the course of the next 18 months that that they spent together, meeting once a week, sometimes more often, Angie spent virtually all of the time in session crying. She spoke in a language of tears. The therapist, in turn, felt helpless, impotent, and worthless because he could do nothing to help her and could not even get her to verbalize the most basic feelings. Angie would just sit on the couch and sob behind her curtain of hair. The therapist would watch her shoulders rise and fall in synchrony with her sobs, waiting for a sign that she was ready to talk.

During this period of time, the therapist went on a pilgrimage to a dozen workshops hoping to discover a secret elixir that might work with his most resistant client. Each time he would return to the next scheduled session with renewed hope that he might finally break through Angie's despair. He must have tried at least a dozen different strategies during their extended time together. After exhausting his usual repertoire, the therapist experimented with hypnosis, then psychodrama (with him playing all the roles since Angie wouldn't speak). He sought consultation with different supervisors and twice as many colleagues, asking for advice, feedback, and support. Most of all, he kept the frustrations and feelings of ineptitude to himself. It was one of his most deeply guarded secrets that he had begun to lose hope in his ability to heal. This therapist was fairly experienced and hardly new to the field, yet he was finally being forced to acknowledge one of the most pervasive myths and secrets of our profession—that we know and understand what's going on most of the time and we are totally in control of the process. We are eternally optimistic and hopeful about the future, the prognosis, and the outcome—except when we are not.

CARING A LITTLE TOO MUCH

We became therapists in the first place because of our own sense of worthlessness. We believed that by devoting a life to helping others we might somehow redeem lives that, until then, had felt wasted. We lived for the validation we felt knowing that we made some kind of difference in others' lives. It gave some meaning and purpose to the suffering that we encountered earlier in life. But it also left us vulnerable to those times when we felt like failures. We are skilled practitioners with lots of experience and yet there are still times when we feel like frauds, especially when clients like Angie don't improve. This was actually Jeffrey's case, and it sent him into a tailspin.

Like many others I (Jeffrey) entered the profession to help work through my own sense of despondency. I was beginning to question whether I still belonged in this profession. I continued questioning whether I had *ever* known what I was doing. The therapist I consulted, who was perhaps more direct and less than compassionate than I would have preferred, called me lazy. Truthfully, I think what I was going through struck a chord with him as well.

I often wished Angie would just go away, that her parents would give up and take her to someone else who specialized in lost causes. I was supposedly an expert on hard-to-treat cases, having done research and a book on difficult clients so it was nothing new for me to work with such challenges. But there was something about *this* case—no, not the case but Angie as a person—that struck terror in my heart and soul. By this time I cared so deeply for her that I convinced myself I could save her, that I could do what nobody else had done before me.

We had settled into a routine after so much time together. Angie would come in, take her accustomed seat (on the right side of the couch next to the Kleenex box on the table), nod at me once, and then lean forward so that she could slip behind a curtain of hair.

"How are you doing?" I'd begin.

Angie nodded, at least I *think* there was a slight head movement, but otherwise silence.

I'd wait her out for as long as I could—2, 3, 5, sometimes 10 agonizing minutes with her sitting as still as a statue.

"So," I'd try again, "what would you like to talk about today?"

Then I'd see a slight tremor, the hair waving just a bit, before the tears would start falling. I'd see them falling, little droplets that were so weightless they'd settle on top of the delicate hairs of her arm. I'd watch them evaporate as I tried to keep myself occupied during these interminable silences.

"I know this is agonizing for you," I'd reflect after a while, "coming in here week after week, letting yourself feel the full brunt of your pain, but nothing really changes." I wasn't sure if I was speaking to myself or to Angie.

And so it would go for close to an hour, Angie crying, sometimes sobbing, sometimes so still she seemed frozen solid. I would stare out the window and wait. I'd offer deep interpretations or empathic reflections of feelings. I'd share my own feelings of helplessness or talk about times in my life when I felt out of control and misunderstood. I told her stories. I created metaphors. I'd say out loud (even if I didn't believe it) that it was perfectly fine for her to do whatever she was doing.

On some level, I knew that this was the one place in her life where she felt safe to cry and let herself go—a number of colleagues and supervisors had already pointed out that this, in itself, was invaluable help. After all, she *was* still functioning in school and performing in ballet recitals, doing quite well in both arenas. And she hadn't yet killed herself, nor even made a serious effort to follow through on threats. So maybe I was doing something right.

CROSSING A BOUNDARY

During one of the rare times when Angie was willing to throw me a few bones (I know she felt sorry for me, being stuck with her as a client), she told me about an upcoming ballet recital in which she would be dancing a lead role. Without consciously thinking about it, I made a mental note of the time and place that coming weekend. I showed up at the auditorium, mostly out of curiosity. The only time I had ever seen Angie was when she was in the throes of despair. I wondered what she looked like in the "other" world. I told myself this was a research venture, but I knew all along that I was crossing a boundary. My only defense was desperation—not only to save my client, but myself.

In the darkness of the auditorium I found a seat toward the back, at the end of a row so I could make a fast getaway if I needed to. When the curtain came up, and the performance began, I completely forgot everything else except Angie's incredible grace and beauty on stage. She danced like an angel, like someone with passion and *life*. I had never seen anything so beautiful, and I was dumbfounded by how much this meant to me. I was crying out of control, trying to contain myself so I didn't make a scene. This was an Angie I had never known existed, and it was moving beyond anything I could possibly explain.

It was at that moment that Angie met my eyes. It seems improbable that she could actually see me in that darkened room, one among hundreds in the audience, but she saw me, and she knew that I saw her recognition. There were times throughout the rest of the performance that I saw her glancing in my direction as if to reassure herself that I wasn't an illusion. I slipped out before the lights went on.

When Angie visited for her next session, neither of us said a word about the performance and my presence there. It was like it had never happened. But there was something different from that time onward. There had been some kind of breakthrough—for both of us.

Stories like this are often told as if there was a transformation that occurred all at once; this was far more gradual. For the first time, Angie began to speak to me with words, giving voice to what her tears had been saying all that time. If this sounds like this is all it took, I assure it was not.

In some ways, things were even worse for a little while because now she was actually *talking* about how awful she felt most of the time (except when she was on stage). If it had been difficult to "hold" her despair before, now it was even more challenging in some ways. I still felt her helplessness and hopelessness.

Eventually, Angie did grow out of her despair. From ages 15 to 17 that I was privileged to know her (and it did seem like a privilege by the end), Angie blossomed into a mature young woman. She would most likely struggle with depression in some form most of her life, but it seems that she did learn a thing or two from our work together.

Since this is a story about the therapist's own despair, and our reluctance to own and talk about it, the ending of the story is less relevant to the theme we are exploring. I actually heard from Angie recently who tracked me down on the Internet after more than 20 years since I had last seen her. She has a family now, works in the helping profession, and seems to be quite successful. I didn't ask her how she was doing with her despair: I didn't want to know.

HOPE AND DESPAIR

If there is one thing that therapists must confront on a daily basis, it is the sense of hopelessness that clients bring to sessions. Doing therapy can crush the spirit, if not the psyche, of its practitioners. Although there has been some investigations of burnout related to our profession (e.g., Maslach, 2015; Norcross & VandenBos, 2018; Simionato & Simpson, 2018; Skovholt, 2010), more generalized, accumulative despair has not been raised often with the exception of a few studies (Chessick, 1978; Fine, 1980; Gee & Loewenthal, 2013; Rabu, Moltu, Binder, & McLeod, 2016; Sussman, 1995). It is perhaps not that surprising, then, that one fourth of practitioners don't much enjoy their work, being classified as either "disengaged" from their clients or outright "distressed" (Orlinsky & Ronnestad, 2005).

Whether depressed, anxious, lost, or frustrated, people come to us in the first place because they can't find a way out of their struggles. Furthermore, they don't honestly believe that anyone else can help them either. Therapy often represents a last desperate chance before all hope is surrendered.

It is a paradox that while despair springs from an absence of hope, it is also the consequence of reaching for expectations that are beyond one's grasp. The British novelist Graham Greene claimed that despair is the price we all pay for setting grandiose goals. It is, he writes, "the unforgivable sin," but one that could never be practiced by someone who is corrupt or evil; such individuals always embrace hope. "He never reaches the freezing point of knowing absolute failure. Only the man of good will carries always in his heart this capacity for damnation."

Hope and despair are a therapist's constant companions. The price we pay for our optimism, our hope for the future, and our belief in our own powers to help others is that we must also live with the limits, disappointment, and failures of our best efforts. We must maintain optimism even as we recognize the depths of our own discouragement with some clients who don't improve no matter how hard we work.

Therapists are virtually required to keep a smile on our faces. We are in the business of selling hope. Everything we understand about the way therapy works is that if we can convince clients that what we have to offer them is useful and we believe this, then they will more likely respond to our interventions. The placebo effect is all about capitalizing on these positive expectations.

Yet in the privacy of our own minds and hearts reside an assortment of doubts. Do we *really* make a difference in anyone's life? Do the effects really last? What sort of impact can we really have on people who are wracked with such intractable, chronic problems? And what can we do for those who will never really recover from traumas, illness, or disorders from which they suffer?

One answer is that we believe our own myths and illusions that we present to others. We deny our own sense of despair, disown our failures, and pretend as if we have everything fully under control. We believe our lies when we tell clients that everything will be fine, that we have the answers, that we can cure their suffering or relieve their pain. Oh, we reassure our colleagues and supervisors that we understand our limits and acknowledge our failings. But deep down inside we really do want to save people; on a good day we actually believe this is possible.

And what of our personal despair, that which emanates from our own disappointments and failures? Apart from anything depressing that our clients bring us, we each have our own demons. Some of us suffer from chronic depression and all of us from the kind of existential angst that comes with being alive. Let's face it, as therapists, there is no place to hide.

Every day, we must square off against precisely those same issues that terrify us the most—the fears of mediocrity, failure, loneliness, meaninglessness, losing control, and being responsible. Countertransference doesn't begin to cover the territory: We must live not only with our despair but also shoulder the burdens of all those who come to us for help.

A client confesses to her therapist that she has no reason to live, and a part of the therapist agrees with her. He wonders if she will ever experience anything resembling happiness or even numbness. Another client suffers from a chronic disease for which there is no cure, and the therapist believes he is only applying psychological compresses to ease a bit of the pressure. Another client has been so traumatized by a host of early experiences that he has serious doubts about whether he can put a dent in what is needed. Still another pilgrim crawls into the office seeking an end to pain, only to display a bewildering array of chronic addictions, mood disorders, and florid personality disorders.

Then there are those who come for the most pedestrian of reasons—to lose a few pounds, quit smoking, find another job, make a life decision, recover from a lost love, stop drinking so much. Sure, the success rate in our work seems pretty high, approaching 80% or even 80% among those who seek our services. But during moments of our own despair, we wonder whether these changes really matter much to the person, much less to the rest of the world.

How can one *not* feel despair when looking at the poverty, the starving, the dispossessed, and the indigent in the world? How can one ever feel satisfied with the small efforts we make when confronting how much there is to do? How can we avoid despair when spending our working days with people who are miserable, conflicted, dissatisfied, depressed, despondent, addicted, suicidal, and sometimes even actively hallucinating?

MYTHS REGARDING BURNOUT

Burnout has been described as a state of emotional and physical depletion that occurs as a result of excess work demands, or at least as they are metabolized by an individual. The high prevalence of burnout among mental health professionals is surmised to seriously compromise both professional effectiveness and well-being (Johnson et al., 2018). It has been alleged that advances in technology, increases in the hours of the standard work week, the continuous presence of mobile devices, and sleep disruptions are the reasons for this predicament, but it turns out that people have been complaining about mental exhaustion throughout the ages. They have blamed the corrosive mental state on bad humors, black bile, melancholia, polluted spirit, sin, astrological sign, weak nerves, capitalism, among others.

Freudenberger (1974) was the first mental health professional to coin the term to describe the kind of mental exhaustion and depletion that was typical among those trying to help chronic drug addicts. Supposedly this was a rare affliction that only struck the most achievement-oriented among us or those who work under the most stressful, unrelenting conditions. In reality, this condition has supposedly been so commonplace that an estimated 50% of American workers admit to feeling this way at times (Puniewksa, 2016). It would appear that the term is used indiscriminately whenever anyone is just sick of their job or tired because of accumulated life responsibilities.

But we actually know quite a bit about what contributes to burnout and even some information on protective factors related to this condition. For example, one aspect of care that appears to influence burnout but may be difficult to control is the extent to which therapists deal with ethical dilemmas. Therapists who specialize with populations such as child welfare and abuse might experience higher stress and burnout due to the higher rate of ethical dilemmas encountered with clients (Mullen, Morris, & Lord, 2017). Increased attention to moral issues tend to impact therapists' perceived stress. The presence of ethical dilemmas may not be considered as typical and part of the professional work but rather viewed as an extraordinary, high-risk encounters that impact client welfare or the therapists' practice.

Organizational factors, such as client load and hours worked, appear to be the strongest predictors of burnout (Kim et al., 2018; Steel, Macdonald, Schröder, & Mellor-Clark, 2015; Thompson, Amatea, & Thompson, 2014). Thompson et al. (2014) also explored how that nature of client problems affected burnout and found that the severity of clients' problems may not impact burnout, especially compared to the influence of caseload and hours worked. In fact, therapists in private practice may actually experience *less* burnout due to having greater autonomy and more control over organizational factors.

It seems increasingly clear that "burnout" is the wrong description to capture the experience we are describing. Burnout implies that a professional one day (or in a single moment) sputters, misfires, and then is unceremoniously extinguished. The reality is that we are far more likely to "rust out," an insidious, gradual process that escapes our notice until it is far too late. Burnout is almost never the result of a single mishap or realization but signals the accumulation of months, if not years, of self-neglect, poor morale, and a sense of helplessness to alter the situation.

A therapist doesn't just awaken one morning and decide, "That's it! I don't like what I'm doing very much anymore." Far more likely, there has been a series of disappointments and disappointing incidents, or just plain boredom, inertia, and fatigue, each of which have sucked the passion out of therapeutic work. Whether it is labeled compassion fatigue, vicarious trauma, secondary trauma, or a more serious form of impairment, these symptoms did not suddenly erupt in dramatic flame-out but rather festered and then infected one's spirit over time.

Like so many phenomena that we witness, one's attitude and personal traits predispose certain professionals with the propensity to develop symptoms. Most notably, burnout victims feel a disconnection from others to the point that their clients are depersonalized and their work begins to feel meaningless. They tend to be younger, less experienced practitioners who become excessively involved in their clients' problems. The researchers describe other factors that contribute to the problem that afflicts half of all therapists at some time:

1. Inexperience is one of the most frequent reasons that explain feeling overwhelmed and overworked since there is a marked lack of resources and coping skills for managing workload and processing difficult assignments.
2. Certain personality traits are associated with high prevalence of burnout. Those who are overly rigid and unbending, perfectionistic, competitive, shy and introverted, are at greater risk.
3. Lack of social and collegial support is also a contributing factor. Or rather the *perception* of such support is what matters most rather than its actual presence.
4. Coping skills to deal with negative emotions helps prevent depletion in a number of ways. Some clinicians overpersonalize their disappointments or dwell too much on things they can't control. Those who are in therapy or intensive supervision are protected in ways that those without such resources are not.
5. Women appear to be more vulnerable than men to burnout, and married women with children in particular since they were at higher risk because of their added responsibilities for household and childcare responsibilities.

What all this leads to is dispelling the myth that burnout is the result of overwork when, in fact, it is far more likely to be an attitudinal problem in which a professional feels (and acts) as a martyr. It is not the result of a single influence but rather encompasses a range of possibilities that include mental and physical exhaustion that result from lifestyle choices, chronic fatigue, feelings of helplessness and being trapped, tedium and boredom from repetition of tasks, and work-related restraints and limitations. This suggests that we can and should challenge the myth that burnout is simply the result of overwork when it is more likely perpetuated by one's chosen approach to work. It is not simply the emotional response to working long hours in an overly challenging job since those in caregiving professions like therapy are much more prone to this condition. It seems that it is the work environment that most contributes to developing stress problems, especially those in which there is a mismatch between an individual and the demands of the job, feelings of control over outcomes, and a sense of fairness in terms of how employees are treated (Maslach & Leiter, 2015). It isn't a lack of commitment and passion that are the problem but rather, according to physician Richard Gunderman, "the accumulation of hundreds or thousands of tiny disappointments, each one hardly noticeable on its own" (Michel, 2016).

"It was the constant repetition that got to me," one therapist explained. "All my clients started to sound the same to me. They seemed to present problems that just seemed so petty and inconsequential, whining, complaining, blaming everyone else for what's wrong. See? There I go again.

"I thought maybe going to workshops and seminars would rescue me, fortify me, maybe make things fresh again. But whatever thinking that I brought into sessions I also brought into these trainings, which seemed like it was the same old crap in a slightly different package.

"Someone, maybe it was a friend or something, asked me when I became so discouraged about my work and I just stared at him without any coherent answer. The reason is because I could no longer remember when I didn't feel this way. Surely once upon a time I must have been eager and enthused about my job, but I can't seem to remember very well."

There are similar myths related to what can likely fix the problem. Therapists may resort to the usual coping methods of the general population, that is, thinking that taking a vacation, going to a spa or resort, or buying oneself a treat will somehow alleviate the pressure when, in fact, things often become worse when nothing changes except an inflated credit card balance. People also commonly believe that to reduce the suffering it is necessary to make radical shifts in life, even quit one's job. But, of course, we take our cognitive habits with us wherever we go, so nothing much changes. It is actual small adjustments in the ways we work and the ways we organize and think about what we do that provide relief.

Although burnout is often linked to compassion fatigue, it also turns out that one of the strongest predictors inversely related to burnout is compassion satisfaction—the accomplishment we feel in working with clients (Thompson et al., 2014). In other words, reflecting on our clients successes, as opposed to our challenges and failures, is important for professional resiliency. In addition, peer support, collegiality, supervision, and humor are also protective factors related to burnout.

Humor is somewhat of a mixed coping mechanism with respect to burnout. On one hand, using humor effectively with our clients and peer support/supervisors is a protective factor from burnout, but on the other hand, humor can take on a darker tone, especially with colleagues. When humor comes across more cynically toward therapeutic work with challenging clients, the clients become depersonalized and burnout is exacerbated (Steel et al., 2015). Cynical depictions of clients can be a symptom of later stages of burnout and likely preceded by emotional exhaustion (Steel et al., 2015). The combined effects of longer hours, high client workload, and the ever-present pressures of addressing ethical issues with vulnerable populations appear to be contributors to the physical exhaustion and emotional despair therapists identify in burnout.

Burnout actually measurably changes the structure of the brain, as do all other forms of chronic stress (Liston, McEwen, & Casey, 2009). Memory, mood, morale, and learning become impaired, just as corrosive effects of cortisol and other stress hormones wreak havoc in the body and mind. There are disruptive connections between neurons in the brain, leading to reduced performance and, just as important, compromised enjoyment of work and activities. In their study of how medical students experienced and recovered from burnout in their studies, the researchers found it took more than a month to heal and recover from the neurological damage. The good news, however, is that small adjustments in scheduling, work structure, and expectations were effective in repairing the problems.

It may very well be that it is the misconceptions and myths that surround burnout, and conceptualize it as a form of compromised empathy, are actually responsible for its growing prevalence. Sometimes it isn't a lack of empathy, but rather its excess, that creates the most difficulties. When therapists are given—or take—the responsibility to manage their own workload, better clarify their priorities, release burdens over which they have little control, and engage in emotional self-regulation, they are able to counteract negative effects (Villacieros, Olmos, & Bermejo, 2017).

It is also clear that one size does not fit all, since generalizations about burnout, compassion fatigue, and related conditions occur for so many reasons unique to the individual and setting. For instance, symptoms may vary depending on whether they primarily feature emotional depletion, physical exhaustion, depersonalization and cynicism, reduced productivity, or a combination of these factors. When interventions are designed to address specific and unique problems, whether through additional job training, lifestyle adjustments, personal therapy, supervision, or change in role, they are more likely to alter the pattern and improve functioning (Dreison et al., 2018).

REKINDLING HOPE

The despair associated with burnout has been such a neglected, taboo subject in our field. Certainly, there is plenty written about depression and burnout, but almost nothing about the more amorphous, pervasive, intangible misery. Despair, writes English novelist George Eliot, is "the painful eagerness of unfed hope." There can be no despair without yearning, without thoughts for the future. This point is only too obvious when attending any conference or gathering of therapists. In any staff room or meeting, you hear tales of discouragement and disillusionment, of desperate searches for the latest therapeutic technique or magic cure.

Therapists complain that managed care has taken the pleasure out of their work, or at the very least, robbed them of choices. There is too much paperwork and too little control. More and more clients want instant cures, if not from our efforts then from medications. "They just don't want to take responsibility for their own change," one therapist complains. "We are working with a generation of whining narcissists."

Yet hope and optimism can only be rekindled if therapists are given permission to admit the despair they experience on a daily level. In some ways, despair is our friend, our asset, that heightens our empathic attunement and our ability to truly understand a client's experience. It also means that we live with such uncertainty and ambiguity about the nature of our work and its actual impact. The reality is that many of the people who seek our services will struggle with their problems for the rest of our lives, no matter what we do, no matter what anyone can do.

"This woman came to me for help and she was just about the most kind, considerate, lovely person that you could ever meet," a therapist mentions in the context of his own rising discouragement. "I remember thinking to myself after shaking her hand and seeing the most amazing, hopeful smile on her face, that *this* is someone I'm going to save for sure. I rubbed my hands together and concentrated with all my heart on hearing her story with as much compassion and focus as I possibly could.

"Then her story leaked out, in a reluctant tone, as if apologizing for being subjected to so much suffering. She'd quite literally said she was sorry for burdening me with what she lived through. First, there was the forced displacement of her family from their home and then their nation. Her mother died because she couldn't deal with the disruption. Then she spent so much time in refugee camps that she became separated from her siblings. So began a 2-year journey, being moved from place to place, all without her consent or input. Then she was diagnosed with a chronic health issue, probably one that resulted from the mistreatment, poor diet, and deprivations she had suffered. Now she was stuck in a place in which she didn't understand the language or customs, had no visible means of support, and most recently was told she was no longer eligible for services. Then she just shrugged and smiled at me and asked what she should do.

"What could I tell her? What could I say to her? What would really make any kind of difference to her? I just wanted to scream. I wanted to quit. But all I really did is nod my head and try to reassure her that we'd try to tackle this together. But I know then, and I know now, I was just kidding her, and kidding myself."

It seems peculiar that anyone who needs to feel validated and useful would ever choose a profession in which we are often unsure whether we helped anyone. Our clients lie. At times even they aren't sure what is real and what is imagined. Those who appear to deteriorate the worst in sessions may actually be making great strides outside the sessions; likewise, those who respond spectacularly well to every intervention may not be changing a single thing in their lives. Even more confusing is that lack of ongoing feedback after they leave: Do the changes they *appear* to make really last?

There are times when therapists feel such despair at what it is they do, even if it is rarely acknowledged, much less spoken aloud. Some of the people we attempt to help have problems that are so long-standing, so chronic and unremitting, and so severe that whatever we do seems like nothing but a token gesture. The kids leave the session and return to their gangs or abusive homes. Those with impulse disorders, hallucinations, personality disturbances, chronic drug abuse, major depression—the list goes on and on—sometimes seem impervious to the most powerful interventions. When some of our most challenging cases do show definite signs of progress, we are left to wonder how much of these changes will persist over time, especially with toxic families, limited resources, dysfunctional environments, addictions, medical conditions, abject poverty, and/or crime-filled neighborhoods.

Each of us is forced to confront our own sense of powerlessness, perhaps the same motive that led us on this path in the first place, yearning to make a difference in the world, wanting to help people who are suffering, and craving to feel a sense of potency.

It starts with despair.

And ends with hope.

CHAPTER 15

༒

Last Chapter, But Not the End

I t's really, really hard to change anyone's mind about hardly anything. We know that more than most people given how often we encounter clients who stubbornly insist on holding onto ludicrous ideas and self-destructive beliefs that are clearly harmful. Change is often threatening, or at least uncomfortable, on some level. This is true not only for clients but for us as well: It's pretty difficult to dispel entrenched beliefs and myths.

It feels good to believe strongly in something, especially when others share those notions. The brain rewards any immunity against cognitive dissonance. Gorman and Gorman (2017) explain how the brain defends itself against the "threat" of changing one's mind. Once an idea becomes fixed, the ventral striatum and nucleus accumbens become activated. Any additional information that challenges this idea triggers a fear response in the anterior insula: Danger! DANGER!

Reason kicks in next via the dorsolateral prefrontal cortex, attempting to override the primitive brain via logic, rational argument, and reflective decision-making. But this is a relatively slow process that requires time, energy, and commitment, plus the motivation to do so. It is hard work, and it's much easier to just stick with what we think we already know and understand. It is the reason the authors say "changing our minds is among the most unnatural actions known to the human species" (Gorman & Gorman, 2017, p. 252).

It takes a tremendous amount of effort to challenge our own beliefs. One example cited is the supposed connection between vaccinations and autism. There was one article that appeared several years ago that alleged that the government was covering up the secret that vaccinating African

Myths, Misconceptions, and Invalid Assumptions of Counseling and Psychotherapy. Jeffrey Kottler and Richard S. Balkin, Oxford University Press (2020). © Oxford University Press.
DOI: 10.1093/oso/9780190090692.001.0001

American children was causing them to develop autism. The authors did an experiment in which they simply googled the two words, *autism* and *vaccinations*, and scrolled through over 100 results before they found a single scientific article by a legitimate scientist. Meanwhile, there were blogs, opinions, rantings, and unsubstantiated claims by conspiracy theorists, all of them supporting this belief. Who has the patience to wade through all this garbage before arriving at any clear evidence?

WHAT WILL THE FUTURE BRING?

One thing for certain, just as human beings continue to develop in myriad of ways shaped by the environment, genetics, culture, and desire, so too must therapy evolve. For tens of thousands of years *Homo erectus*, our Neanderthal ancestors, were only able to produce shaped flint as their greatest technological breakthrough to create knifes, spearheads, and fire. As our species evolved into *Homo sapiens*, we were able to invent internal combustion engines, computers the size of a watch, and vehicles that could travel to distant galaxies. But evolution is hardly done with us. With increasing innovations related to driverless vehicles, virtual reality, bioengineering, chemical substances, nanotechnology, artificial neural networks, quantum batteries, genome targeting, Internet of Things, ingestible robots, bionic body parts, artificial intelligence, and wearable and implanted devices, one thing is clear: the human body and mind will be altogether different entities in the future. We will be able to upgrade ourselves with the latest performance innovations just like a software enhancement.

Consider that in a single generation, lifespan doubled from 40 to 70 years of age. With an increasingly aging population (there are more diapers sold in Japan for the elderly than for infants), there is a corresponding shift in values, priorities, needs, and interests. What will people do with all their discretionary time after retirement since this stage of life may now last three or four decades or longer?

It's clear that the human mind is no longer what it once was. Changes in nutrition, environment, culture, experience, and habits have led to parallel adaptations. Consider what has happened just in the last few decades alone in which mobile devices, computers, and social media command our attention in such a way that the brain is shifting to deal with the assortment of multitasking activities that are part of daily lives.

We really do not know how changes in the way we perceive and process information will impact psychotherapy in the future. But just as new information on neuroscience continues to inform changes in learning and human behavior, it is reasonable to consider that the way we practice therapy is going to continue to evolve in ways that challenge our traditional conceptualizations of helping our clients. For example, as psychopharmacology advances to target specific neurotransmitters, might there even come a time when the "talking cure" is considered a quaint artifact for the bored or curious? Will there eventually be cures for schizophrenia, bipolar disorder, and even personality disorders through medical interventions? If these are essentially all controlled by neurological structures, then why couldn't they be reshaped into more functional processes?

Experiences of trauma, for example, are known to change the plasticity of the brain and short-circuit neural functioning. Ingesting certain chemical substances likewise alters the brain's micro-cellular structure. Will customized drugs, genetic engineering, and neurological tweaks neutralize unpleasant emotional responses, erase traumatic memories, and improve feelings of well-being? There is even experimental research implanting electrodes in the brain to allow depressed patients to send and control electrical impulses to the cerebral cortex to change their mood (Rao et al., 2018). For those who might object to having something actually installed in their brains, there are also transcranial direct-current stimulators that do much the same thing. Other innovations along the horizon include intravenous infusions of ketamine or MDMA that are alleged to produce a full remission of major depression or bipolar disorder in just a single hour and are considered the new "wonder drugs" (Lyford, 2019; Mathai, Meyer, Storch, & Kosten (2020); Sessa, Higbed, & Nutt, 2019; Zarate et al., 2006). Clinical trials and experimental treatments are also gaining ground that employ mobile apps to disrupt disturbing thoughts and wearable devices that prevent addiction relapses or signal impending stress responses (Utley, 2016). More and more often, it would appear that anxiety, phobias, and posttraumatic stress will be treated not through therapy but via virtual reality that introduces in vivo exposure to one's fears. Recent research has found this to be more cost effective and effective than traditional exposure therapy or cognitive therapy (Carl et al., 2018). There's also little doubt that this new technology will eventually be employed in the training of future therapists, although this prediction was also made over 15 years ago (Beutler & Harwood, 2004) and has yet to catch on.

Will this mean that psychotherapists in the future are relegated solely to the mission of meaning-making conversations or operating remote devices? Even that could be a bit sketchy when you consider that soon in the future even drones and military technology will run automatically with a minimum of human control. Will prospective clients just ask Siri,

Google, or Alexa for counsel or advice? Will their watches carefully monitor bodily functions and automatically balance hormonal, synaptic biochemistry, and blood levels? There's even some question whether most doctors and pharmacists will eventually be replaced with artificially intelligent algorithms that can draw on data instantly from all over the world to make far more accurate diagnoses and then begin robotic or chemical treatments.

We have long assumed that therapists could never really be replaced by some automaton, avatar or algorithm because we have the capacity and training to truly *know* our clients intimately and hold their secrets. But how are we to compete someday with artificial intelligence managed by Google or some other platform that knows *everything* about us? Quite literally. There may be nano-robot and biometric implants that collect ongoing measures of blood pressure, hemoglobin levels, stress responses, emotional reactions, and other physiological measures. Facial micro-gesture recognition sensors will provide instant feedback on internal emotional responses. This leads to a prediction that sessions will be considerably abbreviated, improving efficiency, decreasing costs, and reaching far more people in need of help (Nemko, 2019).

This entity (system, program, device, or object) would have known us from birth; read (and remembered, or at least archived) everything we've ever written or said aloud; is perfectly familiar with every book, film, or show we've ever consumed; and understands the dynamics of every relationship, rejection, disappointment, triumph, or love we've ever experienced. In addition, this "thing" also holds precise data on every facet of our being including DNA composition, biometric studies, physiological scans, and every imaginable physiological test that has yet to be devised. It would also know when we are lying, exaggerating, and telling the truth. Based on all this voluminous data, this technological "therapist" could make predictions with perfect accuracy, recommend decisions with precise levels of confidence, and suggest courses of action with corresponding figures of probability (Dormehl, 2014).

At an extreme other end of the continuum, some therapists are beginning to experiment with structures and strategies that push the boundaries of a traditional office visit for a conversation. Instead, some clinicians are inviting their clients to go for walks outside, conduct sessions within more natural environments, or in other outside settings that severely limit any technology intrusions (Dockett, 2019).

With all this said, we are pretty certain that therapists will hardly become obsolete any time in the near future. If anything, people will become even more driven to find greater purpose and meaning in their lives. There will be even greater longing for insight, intimacy, understanding, and self-improvement precisely because we will have so much discretionary time on our hands to reflect on our lives.

Yes, there will be innovations in treatment that make our jobs easier in some ways in the same way that telehealth uses distance technologies (e.g., phone, video-conferencing, web portals, etc.) to provide mental health services (J. Turner, Brown & Carpenter, 2018). A distinct advantage to using these technologies is that mental healthcare is even more readily available to populations in which access was previously limited (J. Turner et al., 2018). As the prevalence of these services increases, the conceptualization of therapy is evolving, if not becoming transformed.

Clearly there are benefits to alternative mediums of therapy, but the quality and impact of these alternatives remain in question. Something might be better than nothing, but the extent to which these services detrimentally affect outcomes in favor of traditional modes of therapy still needs to be evaluated comprehensively and critically. Typically, what we see is a set of clients who receive traditional therapy compared to clients who receive therapy through some type of technology (e.g., Saeed & Pastis, 2018; Stewart, Orengo-Aguayo, Cohen, Mannarino, & de Arellano, 2017; J. Turner et al., 2018). These studies often are poorly constructed and lack the conditions that help to produce meaningful results. For example, the studies lack random assignment. There are some participants who travel long distances to their sessions, creating additional hardships and challenges for them and influencing their assessments. Also, many therapists are somewhat skeptical of the value of alternative therapeutic delivery modalities compared to face-to-face sessions (J. Turner et al., 2018). One reason for this is that some practices have been taken to an extreme, offering Web-based subscription services that charge by the word that therapists write in response to client inquiries. We are certain that silence is not valued very much as an intervention to allow for client reflection.

THE WORLD IS CHANGING AND SO IS OUR PROFESSION

Consider all the jobs likely to become obsolete in the next few decades: Taxi drivers, bank tellers, travel agents, mail carriers, publishers, fast food cooks, agricultural workers, assembly workers, cashiers, telemarketers, sailors, waitpersons, insurance underwriters. Even pilots, soldiers, and farmers are being replaced by technological substitutes! It's been predicted that half of all jobs in the Western world will become extinct in the next 15 years (Frey & Osborne, 2017).

It is absolutely stunning to consider what psychotherapy has become, compared to what it used to be. Consider that a generation ago our method basically consisted of having someone lay on a couch and spontaneously spout aloud whatever came to mind, with the professional occasionally offering an interpretation or two. Given all that we have learned in the past century, all the research and innovations that have taken place, all the breakthroughs in a deeper understanding of how the therapeutic process operates, it is even more mind boggling to anticipate what might come next and whether it will be recognizable to those of us practicing today.

There were ideas we thought were improbable, if not ridiculous, when they first came upon the scene. Eye movement desensitization and reprocessing and equine-assisted therapy are just two options that are currently popular even though they didn't exist a few decades ago. MDMA (ecstasy) therapy has recently been used to treat posttraumatic stress disorder with an "astounding 76% success rate" (Hardy, 2018; also see Thal & Lommen, 2018).

As the world changes and the brain tries to adapt and catch up, the nature of our work will also evolve. People will have more idle times on their hands. Their lives will become even more complex and technology driven. They do more things remotely, automatically, habitually without having to make choices: Devices may know us better than we know ourselves. In addition, face-to-face human intimacy is becoming more rare, replaced by messaging, video-conferencing, and social media. Attention span is declining; impatience for instant results is already the norm. Clients bring new and different expectations to the therapeutic encounter, some legitimate and others wildly unrealistic.

DISPELLING CLIENT MYTHS

One of our main jobs in life involves dispelling myths. We suppose it's possible to say that this is what we do for a living. People come to us with beliefs about themselves, others, and the world at large that are extremely distorted, exaggerated, irrational, or only tangentially based in reality. They attribute their suffering to bad genes, bad breaks, or bad luck. They spout theories to explain their predicaments that absolve themselves of any responsibility and blame others. They also bring some interesting, but seriously misguided notions to us as their default positions that are hard to budge. As we've emphasized throughout our discussion, it's really, really challenging to change anyone's mind about hardly anything.

We also may play a role in perpetuating myths as it appears to take a long time before certain assumptions and beliefs are actually challenged rigorously and critically. We can recall our first introduction to Freud who was certainly someone we greatly admired, as much for his courage as anything else. A professor was elucidating on Freud's theory of personality, discussing the id, ego, and superego, and then explained with perfect confidence that unconscious psychic energy determines which aspect of the triad is dominant. It was at this point that a question might reasonably come to mind.

"Let me get this straight," you might have questioned the instructor. "The id, ego, and superego represent three parts of our personality?"

"Yes," the professor agreed.

"And what determines which part is dominant is psychic energy?"

Again, the professor nodded appreciatively.

"And people believe this?"

The professor went on to explain Freud's seminal contributions. He described how Freud identified defense mechanisms, transference, and countertransference and provided a way to address mental health that was accepted by scientists. He ended with the conclusion, "He may not have gotten everything right, but I give him an A, perhaps 95%."

Nowadays, over 100 years later, some of the explanations and interpretations of behavior certainly seem outdated, oversexualized, or downright bizarre. The idea that people smoke cigarettes due to an oral fixation emanating from unresolved issues during the oral stage of development may seem both far-fetched and out of touch, given what we now know about nicotine addiction. If beliefs about psychic energy were once accepted, consider today's ideas about tapping into meridians to alleviate psychological distress, which have become mainstream practices despite the lack of evidence to support them. Not only can the public be fooled by placebo effects, but so can the therapists facilitating them.

Although some myths may be perpetuated by the various mental health professions, therapists are also at the forefront of dispelling myths. One of the roles and responsibilities of mental health professionals is to serve as expert witnesses in cases of child abuse, trauma, and violence. We are asked to clarify and explain to judges or juries the nature and meaning of behavior and its consequences. One striking example was described by Gemberling and Cramer (2014) in cases of rape that are fraught with mythical misunderstandings. Some of the more common misconceptions involve blaming the victim for somehow inviting the assault or absolving the perpetrator with excuses and faulty explanations that are completely unsupported:

1. "She asked for it wearing that outfit."
2. "He didn't mean it. This was just a misunderstanding."
3. "It wasn't really rape, just some spirited lovemaking—and she seemed to enjoy it."
4. "This never happened the way she remembers it."

We've seen this dynamic played out in so many ways in which the survivor is discredited in some way with the assumption that "Boys will be boys" and they can't help it. Therapists are, therefore, called upon to explain the true nature of sexual assault and challenge some of the myths that have become common. We are also asked to present the actual evidence based on what is known, for instance, that rape survivors are five times more likely to experience depression and anxiety (Choudhary, Smith, & Bossarte, 2012).

There are so many other myths we are asked to challenge (see Table 15.1). Many of them are introduced not just by clients, but also by their families, significant others, and uninformed critics who undermine our efforts to be helpful.

Many of these myths represent what Lambert (2013) referred to as external factors, which represent the largest common factor that influences therapeutic outcomes. These myths, in part, represent the history and influential factors that therapists can't control but represent some of the most important obstacles clients face when attempting to change their behavior. The emphasis on establishing a working alliance, utilizing theory and techniques, and instilling hope are mechanisms of the therapeutic process we exert some control over to circumvent the external factors that often inhibit client progress. If one of our most important roles is to help

---

Table 15.1 SAMPLE OF MYTHS

---

1. Depression is something you can get over if you just decide to stop feeling sorry for yourself and just snap out of it.
2. Medication will fix the problem.
3. Addictions represent just a lack of commitment and will power.
4. Being gay or transgender is a lifestyle choice.
5. People with emotional problems are just weak.
6. Once you have a mental illness or emotional disorder, it can never be cured.
7. You don't really need therapy; positive thinking and prayer will fix it.
8. Time heals all wounds.
9. Therapy takes a long time.
10. Therapy is just like talking to a friend.

---

people to critically examine their beliefs and assumptions, then understanding myths and misconceptions, as well as how to challenge them effectively, is a neglected but crucial skillset.

DISPELLING OUR OWN SELF-MYTHOLOGY

We define ourselves by our cultural identity, tribal affiliation, or unique characteristics. But, in the end, we are essentially a bag of water and bacteria. There are more bacterial cells in the human body than all the rest put together—by a factor of 10! In addition, at least 60% of our composition consists of H_2O. That's why novelist Tom Robbins once observed that water invented humans as a way to transport itself from one place to another.

Yet it is our minds, our consciousness, our drive to find and create meaning in our lives that distinguishes us from all other creatures, microscopic or gargantuan. We are not just driven to feed, rest, survive, and reproduce, but also to understand our position in this world and our ultimate purpose.

Previously, we shed light on the advances in technology and the threats that could make traditional therapy obsolete. But in all likelihood, psychotherapy will remain an important outlet and service even if its structure and form might change. Psychotherapy and counseling have been, and perhaps always will be (at least in the near future), the primary vehicles for meaning-making and maintaining or restoring stability. It is, after all, homeostasis that is the ultimate commanding force of all life forms.

Positive psychology, wellness, self-care, and life balance are terms used to identify and express the need for homeostasis. Whether a biological drive or humanistic endeavor, people tend to seek ways to make their lives "healthful, meaningful, and sustainable" (Matuska & Christiansen, 2008, p. 11). Davis, Balkin, and Juhnke (2014) provided empirical support for 10 life balance domains that may be positively impacted by therapy:

- Positive orientation, a sense of happiness and optimism toward the present and future
- Stress/anxiety, dealing with coping, the impact of stress, and feelings of loneliness
- Substance use, referring to the use and abuse of drugs and alcohol
- Spiritual support, indicating to the comfort and support derived from spiritual beliefs
- Friendship, covering the ability to make and sustain meaningful relationships
- Sleep disturbance, describing the amount of rest and sleep patterns

- Career, describing the quality of success and satisfaction one perceives
- Sex and intimacy, addressing satisfaction with sexual experiences and intimacy
- Global health, including both physical and mental perceptions of health
- Quality of relationships, referring to the satisfaction with significant relationships/life-partners.

It is really not a surprise that 4 of the 10 domains deal with relationships with others and that emotional and physiological health are crucial to life balance. The experience and expression of feelings represent the "mental expression" of this striving for balance (Damasio, 2018). We experience shivers, fevers, aches, pains, disorientation, and lightheadedness when narrow physiological limits are breached, whether blood pressure, heart rate, or other metabolic functioning. We feel anxious, upset, angry, confused, frustrated, when something doesn't quite feel right, or at least to our preference.

THE MYTH OF CERTAINTY

Recall that in the very beginning of our training we were warned to expect that we would have to live with a certain amount of ambiguity, as well as accept a degree of confusion as part of the journey. Consider that as confident as we may feel about our theory, skills, and practice of psychotherapy, researchers in psychotherapy often focus on what is not known or even what is addressed inadequately. For example, despite having 60-hour programs to prepare master's students to be clinicians or requiring a doctoral degree for practice, a large amount of research is conducted, not on client care and outcomes, but on the quality of training and supervision. Entire academic journals are devoted to addressing competencies, training, and supervision. Common issues include addressing the inadequate or limited training related to ethnically diverse clients, LGBTQ+ clients, religious and spiritual issues, ethical conflicts, and working with specialized presenting complaints. If stakeholders were to review the content of research, they might conclude that we have little faith in what we are doing or that we are extremely selfish in our preference to conduct research on ourselves as opposed to the clients we serve.

Here is a typical warning offered to beginners who are studying the essential conceptual frameworks of psychotherapy for the first time:

For every explanation you hear that makes sense, there will be a dozen other ones that directly contradict it. For every possible course of action you could take with a particular client, afterward there will occur to you several others that seem more advantageous. Once you get input from colleagues and supervisors, you will feel the burden of even more alternatives. (Kottler & Montgomery, 2019, p. 47–48)

This is followed by a reminder about how much disagreement will be encountered among professionals, even for the most basic ideas such as what the therapist's primary role is or who should be primarily in charge of the proceedings. Some would say the client determines what happens while others insist that therapists are the ones in control. Some therapists see their role is as an expert and authority; others view it more as a teacher, coach, consultant, confidante, advocate, parental figure, authority, or doctor. In Table 15.2, we consider all the ways we differ with one another in our beliefs, values, and philosophies, much less preferred ideas and signature skills or interventions.

What are we to make of these discrepant theoretical underpinnings? Theory is supposed to provide direction and yet many of the therapeutic conceptual foundations at least appear highly contradictory. In fact, many of these discrepancies can be understood when recognizing that healing can come in different forms and may be achieved across a wide variety of pathways.

For therapists who had the opportunity to meet or even train under the modern, seminal therapists from the humanistic, cognitive-behavioral, and postmodern movements, such as Albert Ellis, Virginia Satir, William Glasser, Irving Yalom, Fritz Perls, Carl Rogers, Steve de Shazer, and so forth, the one element they all share in common is being forceful personalities. The same could be said going back to the days of psychodynamic psychotherapy of Freud, Jung, and Adler. As each of these theorists built a movement within psychotherapy, they worked to convince other clinicians that

Table 15.2 VARIATIONS IN THERAPIST BELIEFS AND PHILOSOPHIES

People are born good.	People are born neutral.	People are born evil.
Clients control outcomes.	Therapists decide outcomes.	Responsibility is shared.
Feelings are most important.	Thinking is most important.	Behavior is most important.
Focus on the past.	Focus on the present.	Focus on the future.
Goals should be specific.	Broad themes are best.	Concentrate on the process.
Use structuring most often.	Use interpreting most often.	Reflect feelings most often.
Be active.	Be nondirective.	Let client decide what is best.
Function as a friend.	Function as a consultant.	Function as a teacher.
Use one primary theory.	Use several theories.	Combine theories into one.

their system was the best to achieve optimal outcomes. Of course, there is considerable research to suggest that the clinician's (espoused) theoretical orientation has little to do with client outcomes (Kottler & Balkin, 2017; Lambert, 2013; Okiishi et al., 2006). If there is one thing that the larger-than-life theorist has taught us, it is that personality, and specifically interpersonal skills, matters a lot. Schöttke, Flückiger, Goldberg, Eversmann, and Lange (2017) conducted a 5-year study on therapist traits and therapeutic outcomes. More than theoretical orientation, years of experience, client diagnosis, client severity, and alignment between client and therapist characteristics (e.g., sex, ethnicity), the primary indicator of client outcomes was the therapist's interpersonal skills. Overall, theories and techniques, therefore, represent a variety of models for achieving a similar outcome with our clients. The personality of the therapist can certainly be impactful, but ultimately the quality of the therapist's interpersonal skills is a key indicator of the ultimate results that are achieved.

The literature on common factors in psychotherapy is pretty conclusive on this point. Regardless of all of the theories, techniques, skills in psychotherapy, and experiences of therapists, it is the quality of the working alliance between the therapist and client that is the primary determining factor within our control. As mentioned previously, external factors such as client motivation, history, and external support account for a lot as well, but we do not have much control over those issues or circumstances. Nevertheless, as researchers seek answers to help clients, the content appears to focus overwhelmingly on the deficiencies of training or the benefits of a specific theory, technique, or strategy. Ironically, none of these elements appear to have much effect on the outcomes.

So, if there is one thing we can be certain about in psychotherapy, it is that we must live with a certain amount of uncertainty. Even with a solid understanding about the healing nature of the therapeutic relationship, no field remains stagnant. Psychotherapy as a profession and practice is constantly changing. We remain challenged by our clients to demonstrate greater accountability for our work together, as well as to challenge some of the myths that both stall their progress and our own effectiveness.

CONCLUDING THOUGHTS

If you recall, we began this journey together by presenting you with the question posed by a discerning, skeptical client who challenged one of the myths of our profession. The client listened carefully to the standard opening speech during a first session in which the therapist explained the nature of the process. But then you may remember that the client abruptly interrupted the introduction to question exactly how therapy really works.

> I know we talk and stuff. I've seen movies and television shows. You sit there and listen and say a few things and maybe even tell me some things I don't know. But all this stuff you told me about these different approaches, how some require me to think differently, and some want me to talk about feelings, and some require homework I'm supposed to do. I hope you realize how crazy this all sounds.

It *does* sound a little absurd when we try to describe this complex, mysterious business of a talking cure that is weighed down by so many myths and misunderstandings. And yet it is precisely these debates and discussions that lead to a deeper and more robust understanding of our work, one that shrugs off the shackles of ignorance and stubbornness that have remained tethered to practices that have so little supportive evidence.

James Randi, also known as the Amazing Randi, is a retired stage magician who built a career as a debunker of sorts. He would host televised programs and often visit late night talk shows where he would challenge individuals who claimed to have psychic abilities or healing powers. He also lectured at universities around the country committed to his mission to debunk faith healers, psychics, and frauds. During one such talk he showed a video demonstrating how he could perform noninvasive "psychic" surgery removing tumors from a patient, after which he showed how the trick has been performed. For his final act he bent a spoon, supposedly with his mind, after which he explained to the audience it was just a trick but one he refused to explain. He concluded with the declaration, "You too can be fooled."

We can be fooled indeed. We spend considerable resources attempting to perfect our craft out of a sincere desire to help our clients. We survive extremely long programs of study, obtain licensure and various certifications, and often pursue specialized training in theories or techniques, all of which we believe will provide a positive impact on the clients we serve. At the same time, we are hindered in our progress when we adopt techniques that lack empirical support, replication, or efficacy with our clients. Thus, we are reminded of four basic concepts that summarize our journey in understanding myths and misconceptions in therapy.

1. *Our research is not as good as we think.* About half of studies cannot be replicated. Findings in social science research are highly sample-specific—that is, who is in the study has more influence than the statistics that are supposed to indicate generalizability across a population.

2. *Complex problems are rarely, if ever, sufficiently addressed through simple solutions.* We get excited about the next technological breakthrough, whether in neuroscience, virtual reality devices, miracle drugs, or remote monitoring systems. We hope that tapping on a meridian or following an object with our eyes will create new neural pathways to less emotional distress. Yet, we tend to find that one technique does not create better outcomes than any other technique.

3. *We are good at what we do, and our clients do change and grow, but often not for the reasons we think they do.* A therapist might use candles to create a soothing ambience in the office, and some clients might respond in a positive way, noticing the aromas are relaxing; other clients might respond with finding such an environment hokey and overly stereotypical of new-age mental health settings. Ultimately, the progress of a client, or lack thereof, is unlikely to result from the aromas of the candles. The same can be said about our use of theories and techniques. These are rarely the reason why clients change.

4. *There is power in the relationship.* The curative factors of human connection cannot be easily measured or clearly understood. Our greatest gift is facilitating this connection with our clients, paving the way for progress, healing, and growth.

There is nothing wrong with carrying a healthy dose of skepticism toward therapy and what makes for a successful experience for our clients. As long as we remember that what we do is effective and not oversimplify the problems and processes of our clients' journeys, we can be comfortable with what we do not know and grow with our clients as we help them seek answers.

REFERENCES

Al Alwan, I. (2012). Is accreditation a true reflection of quality? *Medical Education, 46,* 542–544.

Alman, I. (2015, July 6). Ninety minute therapy sessions, *Psychology Today.* https://www.psychologytoday.com/us/blog/sex-sociability/201507/ninety-minute-therapy-sessions

American Association for Marriage and Family Therapy. (2015). *Code of ethics.* Alexandria, VA: Author.

American Counseling Association. (2014). *ACA code of ethics.* Alexandria, VA: Author.

American Psychological Association. (2017). *Ethical principles of psychologists and code of conduct.* Washington, DC: Author.

Amundson, G. (2015, November 1). Therapy views: Musings on the work and play of psychotherapy. *Therapy Views.* Retrieved from https://therapyviews.com/2015/11/01/do-psychiatric-drugs-offer-a-meaningful-resolution-of-human-suffering/

Amundson, J., Stewart, K., & Valentine, L. (1993). Temptations of power and certainty. *Journal of Marital & Family Therapy, 19*(2), 111–124.

Annenberg Public Policy Center. (2017). *Suicide rate is lower during holidays—but holiday-suicide myth persists.* Philadelphia, PA: Author.

Annenberg Public Policy Center. (2019). *Holiday-suicide myth fially debunked in most news stories.* Philadelphia, PA: Author.

Armbridge, B. (2013). 10 myths about psychology debunked. *TED.* https://www.ted.com/talks/ben_ambridge_10_myths_about_psychology_debunked/transcript

Armory, J., & Vuilleumier, P. (Eds., 2013). *The Cambridge Handbook of Human Affective Neuroscience* (pp. 55–168). Cambridge: Cambridge University Press.

Arnocky, S., Piche, T., Albert, G., Ouellette, D., & Barclay, P. (2017). Altruism predicts mating success in humans. *British Journal of Psychology, 108*(2), 416–435.

Arnstein, P., Vidal, M., Wells-Federman, C., Morgan, B., & Caudill, M. (2002). From chronic pain patient to peer: Benefits and risks of volunteering. *Pain Management Nursing, 3*(3), 94–103.

Arnow, K. D., King, A. C., & Wagner, T. H. (2019). Characteristics of mental health trials registered in ClinicalTrialsgov. *Psychiatry Research, 281.* https://doi-org.umiss.idm.oclc.org/10.1016/j.psychres.2019.112552

Arum, R., & Roksa, J. (2011). *Academically adrift: Limited learning on college campuses.* Chicago, IL: University of Chicago Press.

Bachman, F. (2012). *A man called Ove.* New York, NY: Simon and Schuster.

Balkin, R. S. (2006). A reexamination of trends in acute care psychiatric hospitalization for adolescents: Ethnicity, payment, and length of stay. *Journal of*

Professional Counseling: Practice, Theory & Research, 34(1–2), 49–59. doi:10.1080/ 15566382.2006.12033823

Balkin, R. S., Harris, N., Freeman, S. J., & Huntington, S. (2014). The forgiveness reconciliation inventory: An instrument to process through issues of forgiveness and conflict. *Measurement and Evaluation in Counseling and Development, 47*, 3–13. doi:10.1177/0748175613497037

Balkin, R. S., & Juhnke, G. A. (2018). *Assessment in counseling: Practice and applications.* New York, NY: Oxford University Press.

Balkin, R. S., & Kleist, D. M. (2017). *Counseling research: A practitioner-scholar approach.* Alexandria, VA: American Counseling Association.

Balkin, R. S., Perepiczka, M., Sowell, S. M., Cumi, K., & Gnilka, P. G. (2016). The forgiveness–reconciliation model: An empirically supported process for humanistic counseling. *Journal of Humanistic Counseling, 55*, 55–65, doi:10.1002/ johc.12024

Balkin, R. S., Richey Gosnell, K. M., Holmgren, A., & Osborne, J. W. (2017). Nonlinear analysis in counseling research. *Measurement and Evaluation in Counseling and Development, 50*, 109–155.

Balkin, R. S., Schlosser, L. Z., & Levitt, D. H. (2009). Religious identity and cultural diversity: Exploring the relationships between religious identity, sexism, homophobia, and multicultural competence. *Journal of Counseling & Development, 87*(4), 420–427. doi:10.1002/j.1556-6678.2009.tb00126.x

Balkin, R. S., & Schmit, E. L. (2018). A humanistic framework using nonlinear analysis to evaluate the working alliance and therapeutic goal attainment for adolescents in crisis. *Journal of Humanistic Counseling, 57*, 2–13. doi:10.1002/johc.12063

Balkin, R. S., & Sheperis, C. J. (2011). Evaluating and reporting statistical power in counseling research. *Journal of Counseling & Development, 89*, 268–272. doi:10.1002/j.1556-6678.2011.tb00088.x

Bandler, R., & Grinder, J. (1979). *Frogs into princes: Neuro-linguistic programming.* Moah, UT: Real People Press.

Barlow, D. H. (2010). Negative effects from psychological treatments. *American Psychologist, 65*, 13–19.

Barth, F. D. (2017, December 31). How confirmation bias affects you every single day. *Psychology Today.* Retrieved from https://www.psychologytoday.com/us/blog/ the-couch/201712/how-confirmation-bias-affects-you-every-single-day

Bartholomew, A. J., & Cirulli, E. T. (2014). Individual variation in contagious yawning susceptibility is highly stable and largely unexplained by empathy or other known factors, *PLoS One, 9*(3). doi:10.1371/journal.pone.0091773

Bartoskova, L. (2017). How do trauma therapists experience the effects of their trauma work, and are there common factors leading to post-traumatic growth? *Counselling Psychology Review, 32*(2), 30–45.

Bertrand, N., & Boulze-Launay, I. (2018). Maintenance of abstinence in self-help groups. *Alcohol and Alcoholism, 53*(1), 89–94.

Beutler, L. E., & Harwood, T. M. (2004). Virtual reality in psychotherapy training. *Journal of Clinical Psychology, 60*(3), 317–330.

Bien, T. H. (2004). Quantum change and psychotherapy. *Journal of Clinical Psychology, 60*(5), 493–501. doi:10.1002/jclp.20003

Bierenbaum, H., Nichols, M. P., & Schwartz, A. (1976). Effects of varying session length and frequency in brief emotive therapy. *Journal of Consulting and Clinical Psychology, 44*(5), 790–798.

Binder, P., Holgersen, H., & Nielsen, G. H. (2009). Why did I change when I went to therapy? A qualitative analysis of former patients' conceptions of successful psychotherapy, *Counselling and Psychotherapy, 9*(4), 250–256.

Blaise, C., & Kirsch, I. (2016). The placebo effect and psychotherapy: Implications for theory, research, and practice. *Psychology of Consciousness: Theory, Research, and Practice, 3*(2), 105–107.

Blanco, C. Rafful, C., & Olfson, M. (2013). The use of clinical trials in comparative effectiveness research in mental health. *Journal of Clinical Epidemiological Research, 66*, S29–S36. doi:10.1016/j.jclinepi.2013.02.013

Blum, N. S. (1994). Deceptive practices in managing a family member with Alzheimer's disease. *Symbolic Interaction, 17*(1), 21–36.

Bordin, E. S. (1979). The generalizability of the psychoanalytic concept of the working alliance. *Psychotherapy, 16*, 252–260.

Bowie, C., McLeod, J., & McLeod, J. (2016). "It was almost like the opposite of what I needed": A qualitative exploration of client experiences of unhelpful therapy. *Counselling & Psychotherapy Research, 16*(2), 79–87.

Brown, J., Scholle, S. H., & Azur, M. (2014). Strategies for measuring the quality of psychotherapy: A white paper to inform measure development and implementation. *U.S. Department of Health and Human Services.* https://aspe.hhs.gov/report/strategies-measuring-quality-psychotherapy-white-paper-inform-measure-development-and-implementation

Brunsma, D. (2004). *The school uniform movement and what it tells us about American education.* Lanham, MD: Scarecrow Education.

Brush, J. E., Sherbino, J., & Norman, G. R. (2017). How expert clinicians intuitively recognize a medical diagnosis. *American Journal of Medicine, 130*(6), 629–634.

Cahill, J., Paley, G., & Hardy, G. (2013). What do patients find helpful in psychotherapy? Implications for the therapeutic relationship in mental health nursing. *Journal of Psychiatric & Mental Health Nursing, 20*(9), 782–791. doi:10.1111/jpm.12015

Campbell, J. (1949). *The hero with a thousand faces.* New York, NY: Pantheon.

Carl, E., Stein, A. Z., Levihn-Coon, A., Pogue, J. R., Rothbaum, B., Emmelkamp, P., . . . Powers, M. B. (2018). Virtual reality exposure therapy for anxiety and related disorders: A meta-analysis of randomized controlled studies. *Journal of Anxiety Disorders, 61*, 27–36. doi:10.1016/j.janxdis.2018.08.003

Carroll, A. E. (2018, September 24). Congratulations! Your study went nowhere. *New York Times*, A23.

Castonguay, L. G., & Beutler, L. E. (Eds.). (2006). *Principles of therapeutic change at work.* New York, NY: Oxford University Press.

Centers for Disease Control. (2016). *Sexual identity, sex of sexual contacts, and health-risk behaviors among students in grades 9–12: Youth risk behavior surveillance.* Atlanta, GA: Author.

Chalmers, I., & Galsziou, P. (2009). Avoidable waste in the production and reporting of research evidence, *The Lancet, 374*(9683), 86–89.

Chapman, R., & Watson, M. (1999). Information processing and attribution errors in addictions counseling: Implications for clinical practice. *Alcoholism Treatment Quarterly, 17*(4), 67–78.

Chekroud, S. R., Gueorguieva, R., Zheutlin, A. B., Paulus, M., Krumholz, H. M., Krysta,l J. H., & Chekroud, A. M.(2018). Association between physical exercise and mental health in 1.2 million individuals in the USA between 2011 and 2015: A cross-sectional study. *The Lancet Psychiatry, 5*(9), 739–746.

Chentsov-Dutton, Y. E., Ryder, A. G., & Tsai, G. (2014). Understanding depression across cultural contexts. In I. H. Gotlib & C. L. Hammen (Eds.), *Handbook of depression* (3rd ed., pp. 337–354), New York, NY: Guilford Press.

Chessick, R. (1978). The sad soul of the psychiatrist. *Bulletin of the Menninger Clinic*, 42(1), 1–10.

Choudhary, E., Smith, M., & Bossarte, R. M. (2012). Depression, anxiety, and symptom profiles among female and male victims of sexual violence. *American Journal of Men's Health, 6*, 28–36.

Cipriano, M., & Gruca, T. S. (2014). The power of priors: How confirmation bias impacts market prices. *Journal of Prediction Markets, 8*(3). doi:10.5750/jpm.v8i3.974

Cohen, A. (1980). Modifications in psychoanalysis: The double session. *Psychoanalytic Review, 67*, 69–81.

Cohen, J. (1988). Statistical power analysis for the behavioral sciences (2nd ed.). New York, NY: Psychological Press.

Colloca, L. (2018). The fascinating mechanisms and implications of the placebo effect. *International Review of Neurobiology, 138*, 115–120.

Cooper, C. (2015, April 22). Scientific peer reviews are a "sacred cow" ready to be slaughtered, says former editor of BMJ. *The Independent*. Retrieved from https://www.independent.co.uk/news/science/scientific-peer-reviews-are-a-sacred-cow-ready-to-be-slaughtered-says-former-editor-of-bmj-10196077.html

Cuijpers, P., Reijnders, M., Karyotaki, E., de Wit, L., & Ebert, D. D. (2018). Negative effects of psychotherapies for adult depression: A meta-analysis of deterioration rates. *Journal of Affective Disorders, 239*, 138–145.

Cummings, N. A., & O'Donohue, W. T. (2008). *Eleven blunders that cripple psychotherapy in America*. New York, NY: Routledge.

Damasio, A. (2018). *The strange order of things: Life, feeling, and the making of cultures*. New York, NY: Pantheon.

David, D., Cristea, I., & Hofmann, S. G. (2018). Why cognitive behavioral therapy is the current gold standard of psychotherapy. *Frontiers in Psychiatry, 9*(4). doi:10.3389/fpsyt.2018.00004

Davis, R. J., Balkin, R. S., & Juhnke, G. A. (2014). Validation of the Juhnke–Balkin life balance inventory. *Measurement and Evaluation in Counseling & Development, 47*, 181–198. doi:10.1177/0748175614531796

Dawson, G. C. (2018). Years of clinical experience and therapist professional development: A literature review. *Journal of Contemporary Psychotherapy, 48*(2), 89–97. doi:10.1007/s10879-017-9373-8

de Shazer, S., Dolan, Y., Korman, H., McCollum, E., Trepper, T., & Berg, I. K. (2007). *More than miracles: The state of the art of solution-focused brief therapy*. New York, NY: Haworth Press.

Dewey, R. (2017). Psychology: An introduction. *Psych Web*. Retrieved from https://www.psywww.com/intropsych/

Diener, E., & Biswas-Diener, R. (2019). The replication crisis in psychology. In R. Biswas-Diener & E. Diener (Eds.), *Noba textbook series: Psychology*. Champaign, IL: DEF.

Dobmeier, R. A., & Reiner, S. M. (2012). Spirituality in the counselor education curriculum: A national survey of student perceptions. *Counseling & Values, 57*(1), 47–65. doi:10.1002/j.2161-007X.2012.00008.x

Dockett, L. (2019). Walk and talk. *Psychotherapy Networker*, November–December, 30–36.

Dormehl, L. (2014). *The formula*. New York, NY: TarcherPerigee.

Dreison, K. C., Luther, L., Bonfils, K. A., Sliter, M. T., McGrew, J. H., & Salyers, M. P. (2018). Job burnout in mental health providers: A meta-analysis of 35 years of intervention research. *Journal of Occupational Health Psychology, 23*(1), 18–30.

Duer, J. D. (2005). The impact of licensing laws on curricula in psychology master's programs. *Teaching of Psychology, 32*(2), 126–128.

Duhigg, C. (2016). *Smarter, faster, better: The transformative power of real productivity.* New York, NY: Random House.

Duke, N. K. (2016, June 3). What doesn't work: Literary practices we should abandon. *Edutopia.* Retrieved from https://www.edutopia.org/blog/literacy-practices-we-should-abandon-nell-k-duke

Dumont, F., & Lecomte, C. (1987). Inferential processes in clinical work: Inquiry into logical errors that affect diagnostic judgments. *Professional Psychology: Research and Practice, 18*(5), 433–438. doi:10.1037/0735-7028.18.5.433

Duncan, B. (2014). *On becoming a better therapist: Evidence-based practice one client at a time.* Washington, DC: American Psychological Association.

Ehrenreich, B. (2018). *Natural causes: An epidemic of wellness, the uncertainty of dying, and our illusion of control.* New York, NY: Twelve.

Ehrenreich-May, J., Rosenfield, D., Queen, A. H., Kennedy, S. M., Remmes, C. S., & Barlow, D. H. (2017). An initial waitlist-controlled trial of the unified protocol for the treatment of emotional disorders in adolescents. *Journal of Anxiety Disorders, 46*, 46–55. doi:10.1016/j.janxdis.2016.10.006

Ellis, A. (2001). *Feeling better, getting better, staying better.* San Luis Obispo, CA: Impact.

Ellis, A. (2006). Learning from a difficult customer. In J. A. Kottler & J. Carlson (Eds.), *The client who changed me: Stories of therapist personal transformation* (pp. 65–70). New York, NY: Routledge.

Elvish, R., James, I., & Milne, D. (2010). Lying in dementia care: An example of a culture that deceives in people's best interests. *Aging & Mental Health, 14*(3), 255–262. doi:10.1080/13607861003587610

Eysenck, H. (1952). The effects of psychotherapy: An evaluation. *Journal of Consulting and Clinical Psychology, 16*, 319–324.

Fine, H. J. (1980). Despair and depletion in the therapist. *Psychotherapy: Theory, Research, and Practice, 17*(4), 392–395.

Fish, J. (1973). *Placebo therapy.* San Francisco, CA: Jossey-Bass.

Fosha, D. (2006). Quantum transformation in trauma and treatment: Traversing the crisis of healing change. *Journal of Clinical Psychology, 62*(5), 569–583. doi:10.1002/jclp.20249

Frank, J. (1963). *Persuasion and healing.* Baltimore, MD: Johns Hopkins University Press.

Frankel, Z., & Levitt, H. M. (2009). Clients' experiences of disengaged moments in psychotherapy: A grounded theory analysis. *Journal of Contemporary Psychotherapy, 39*, 171–186.

Freud, S. (1922). *Beyond the pleasure principle* (C. J. M. Hubback, Trans.). London, England: International Psycho-Analytical.

Freud, S. (1953). The future prospects of psychoanalytic therapy. In J. Strachey (Ed. & Trans.), *The standard edition of the complete psychological works of Sigmund Freud* (Vol. 11, pp. 141–151). London, England: Hogarth Press. (Original work published 1910)

Freudenberger, H. J. (1974). *Burnout: The high cost of high achievement.* New York, NY: Anchor.

Frey, C. B., & Osborne, M. A. (2017). The future of employment: How susceptible are jobs to computerization? *Technological Forecasting and Social Change, 114,* 254–280.

Friedman, R. A. (2013, October 12). Shrinking hours. *New York Times.* Retrieved from https://www.nytimes.com/2013/10/13/opinion/sunday/shrinking-hours.html

Fruhauf, S. Figlioli, P., & Caspar, F. (2017). You won't get me: Therapist responses to patient impression management. *Journal of Nervous and Mental Diseases, 205,* 217–226.

Fruhauf, S., Figlioli, P., Oehler, D., & Caspar, F. (2015). What to expect in the intake interview? Impression management tactics of psychotherapy patients. *Journal of Social and Clinical Psychology, 34*(1), 28–49.

Gaab, J., Locher, C., & Blease, C. (2018). Placebo and psychotherapy: Differences, similarities, and implications. *International Review of Neurobiology, 38,* 241–255.

Gallo, M. M. (2015). *No one helped: Kitty Genovese, New York City, and the myth of urban apathy.* Ithaca, NY: Cornell University Press.

Gee, J., & Loewenthal, D. (2013). Working with despair: A phenomenological investigation. *Psychology and Psychotherapy: Research and Practice, 86*(2), 229–243.

Gemberling, T. M., & Cramer, R. J. (2014). Expert testimony on sensitive myth-ridden topics: Ethics and recommendations for psychological professionals. *Professional Psychology: Research and Practice, 45,* 120–127.

Gergen, K. J. (2000). *The saturated self.* New York, NY: Basic Books.

Gilovich, T., Griffin, D., & Kahneman, D. (2002). *Heuristics and biases: The psychology of intuitive judgment.* Cambridge, England: Cambridge University Press.

Glasser, W. (1965). *Reality therapy. A new approach to psychiatry.* New York, NY: Harper & Row.

Glasser, W. (1976). *Positive addiction.* New York, NY: Harper Collins.

Glasser, W. (1998). *Choice theory.* New York, NY: Harper Collins.

Goba, K. (2017, November 16). The empty throne of mental illness: Breaking psychiatry apart. *Medium.* Retrieved from https://medium.com/@kellygola/the-empty-throne-of-mental-illness-236e0377fb64

Gold, J., & Gold, I. (2012). The "Truman Show" delusion: Psychosis in the global village. *Cognitive Neuropsychiatry, 17*(6), 455–472.

Gold, J., & Gold, I. (2014). *Suspicious minds: How culture shapes madness.* New York, NY: Free Press.

Gorman, S. E., & Gorman, J. M. (2017). *Denying to the grave: Why we ignore the facts that will save us.* New York, NY: Oxford University Press.

Gorski, D. (2015, December 21). Is scientific peer review a "sacred cow" ready to be slaughtered? *Science-Based Medicine.* Retrieved from https://sciencebasedmedicine.org/is-scientific-peer-review-a-sacred-cow-ready-to-be-slaughtered/

Gottman, J. M., & Gottman, J. S. (2018). *The science of couples and family therapy: Behind the scenes at the love lab.* New York, NY: W. W. Norton.

Graber, M. (2013). The incidence of diagnostic error in medicine. *British Medical Journal Quarterly, 22,* 21–27.

Grad, G. I., & Zeligman, M. (2017). Predictors of post-traumatic growth: The role of social interest and meaning of life. *Journal of Individual Psychology, 73*(3), 190–207.

Green, J. D., Annunziata, A., Kleiman, S. E., Bovin, M. J., Harwell, A. M., Fox, A. M., . . . Marx, B. P. (2017). Examining the diagnostic utility of the DSM-5 PTSD symptoms among male and female returning veterans. *Depression And Anxiety, 34*(8), 752–760. doi:10.1002/da.22667

Grenyer, B. F. S., & Lewis, K. L. (2012). Prevalence, prediction, and prevention of psychologist misconduct. *Australian Psychologist, 47,* 68–76. doi:10.1111/j.1742-9544.2010.00019.

Grohol, J. M. (2008, April 15). Ding! Times up! *Psych Central.* Retrieved from https://psychcentral.com/blog/ding-times-up/

Guarnaccia, P. J., Canino, G., Rubio-Stipec, M., & Bravo, M. (1993). The prevalence of ataques de nervios in the Puerto Rico disaster study. The role of culture in psychiatric epidemiology. *Journal of Nervous and Mental Disease, 18,* 1157–1165.

Hagedorn, W. B. (2009). Preparing competent clinicians: Curricular applications based on the sexual addiction counseling competencies. *Sexual Addiction & Compulsivity, 16*(4), 341–360. doi:10.1080/10720160903399855

Halley, J. O. (2007). *Boundaries of touch: Parenting and adult–child intimacy.* Urbana, IL: University of Illinois Press.

Hanel, P. H., & Vione, K. C. (2016). Do student samples provide an accurate estimate of the general public? *PLoS One, 11*(12), e0168354. doi:10.1371/journal.pone.0168354

Harari, Y. N. (2015). *Sapiens: A brief history of humankind.* New York, NY: Harper.

Harcourt, A. H. (2015). *Humankind: How biology and geography shape human diversity.* New York: Pegasus.

Hardy, R. (2018). MDMA therapy achieves astounding 76% success rate for treating PTSD. *New Atlas.* Retrieved from: https://newatlas.com/mdma-ptsd-successful-trial-results/57074/

Harper-Jaques, S., & Foucault, D. (2014). Walk-in single-session therapy: Client satisfaction and clinical outcomes. *Journal of Systemic Therapies, 33*(3), 29–49. doi:10.1521/jsyt.2014.33.3.29

Haselton, M. G.; Nettle, D., & Andrews, P. W. (2005). The evolution of cognitive bias. In D. M. Buss (Ed.), *The handbook of evolutionary psychology* (pp. 724–746). Hoboken, NJ: Wiley.

Helstone, F. S., & van Zuuren, F. J. (1996). Clinical decision making in intake interviews for psychotherapy: A qualitative study. *British Journal of Medical Psychology, 69*(3), 191–206. doi:10.1111/j.2044-8341.1996.tb01864.x

Henrich, J., Heine, S. J., & Norenzayan, A. (2010). The weirdest people in the world. *Behavioral and Brain Sciences, 33,* 61–135.

Hill, C. E., Spiegel, S. B., Hoffman, M. A., Kivlighan, D. M., & Gelso, C. J. (2017). Therapist expertise in psychotherapy revisited. *Counseling Psychologist, 45*(1), 7–53.

Hodgetts, A., & Wright, J. (2007). Researching clients' experiences: A review of qualitative studies. *Clinical Psychology and Psychotherapy, 14,* 157–163.

Hollingsworth, D. K. (1985). The counselor and physical attractiveness: A response. *Journal of Counseling & Development, 63*(8), 488. doi:10.1002/j.1556-6676.1985.tb02741.x

Hoyt, M., Bobele, M., Slive, A., Young, J., & Talmon, M. (Eds.). (2018). *Single session therapy by walk-in or appointment.* New York, NY: Routledge.

Hoyt, M., & Talmon, M. (2014). *Capturing the moment: Single-session therapy and walk-in services.* London, England: Crown House.

Hoyt, W. T., & Del Re, A. C. (2018). Effect size calculation in meta-analyses of psychotherapy outcome research, *Psychotherapy Research, 28*(3), 379–388.

Hsu, L. K., & Folstein, M. F. (1997). Somatoform disorders in Caucasian and Chinese Americans. *Journal of Nervous and Mental Disease, 185,* 382–387.

Infrura, F. J., & Jayawickreme, E. (2019). Fixing the growth illusion: New directions for research in resilience and posttraumatic growth. *Current Directions in Psychological Science, 28*(2), 152–158.

James, I. A., Wood-Mitchell, A. J., Waterworth, A. M., Mackenzie, L. E., & Cunningham, J. (2006). Lying to people with dementia: Developing ethical guidelines for care settings. *International Journal of Geriatric Psychiatry, 21,* 800–801.

Janov, A. (1970). *Primal scream: Primal therapy: The cure for neurosis.* New York, NY: Delta.

Jarrett, C. (2016, July 29). 10 of the most widely believed myths in psychology. *Research Digest.* Retrieved from https://digest.bps.org.uk/2016/07/29/10-of-the-most-widely-believed-myths-in-psychology/

Jarrett, C. (2018, August 13). Interviews with 100 CBT-therapists reveal 43 percent of clients experience unwanted side effects from therapy. *Research Digest.* Retrieved from https://digest.bps.org.uk/2018/08/13/interviews-with-100-cbt-therapists-reveal-43-per-cent-of-clients-experience-unwanted-side-effects-from-therapy/

Johnson, J., Hall, L. H., Berzins, K., Baker, J., Melling, K., & Thompson, C. (2018). Mental healthcare staff well-being and burnout: A narrative review of trends, causes, implications, and recommendations for future intervention. *Australian and New Zealand Journal of Mental Health Nursing, 27*(1), 20–32.

Joseph, S. (2011). *What doesn't kill us: The new psychology of post-traumatic growth.* New York, NY: Basic Books.

Kächele, H., Erhardt, I., Seybert, C., & Buchholz, M. B. (2015). Countertransference as object of empirical research? *International Forum of Psychoanalysis, 24*(2), 96–108. doi:10.1080/0803706X.2012.737933

Kahneman, D. (2011). *Thinking fast and slow.* New York, NY: Farrar, Straus, and Giroux.

Karriker-Jaffe, K. J., Witbrodt, J., Subbaraman, M. S., & Kaskutas, L. A. (2018). What happens after treatment? Long-term effects of continued substance use, psychiatric problems and help-seeking on social status of alcohol-dependent individuals. *Alcohol and Alcoholism, 53*(4), 394–402. doi:10.1093/alcalc/agy025

Kaskutas, L. A. (2009). Alcoholics anonymous effectiveness: Faith meets science. *Journal of Addictive Diseases, 28*(2), 145–157.

Keeney, B. (2006). A family of pirates. In J. A. Kottler & J. Carlson (Eds.), *The client who changed me: Stories of therapist personal transformation* (pp. 71–84). New York, NY: Routledge.

Keeney, H., & Keeney, B. (2018). *Creative therapeutic technique: Skills for the art of bringing forth change.* Phoenix, AZ: Zeig, Tucker, Theisen.

Kelly, J. F., & Yeterian, J. D. (2011). The role of mutual-help groups in extending the framework of treatment. *National Institute of Alcohol Abuse and Alcoholism, 33*(4), 350–355.

Kennedy, P., Higginson, A. D., Radford, A. N., & Sumner, S. (2018). Altruism in a volatile world. *Nature, 555,* 359–362.

Khalsa, S. S., Portnoff, L. C., McCurdy-McKinnon, D., & Feusner, J. D. (2017). What happens after treatment? A systematic review of relapse, remission, and recovery in anorexia nervosa. *Journal of Eating Disorders, 5*(20). doi:10.1186/s40337-017-0145-3

Killingsworth, M. A., & Gilbert, D. T. (2010). A wandering mind is an unhappy mind. *Science, 330,* 932.

Kim, J. J., Brookman-Frazee, L., Gellatly, R., Stadnick, N., Barnett, M. L., & Lau, A. S. (2018). Predictors of burnout among community therapists in the sustainment phase of a system-driven implementation of multiple evidence-based practices in children's mental health. *Professional Psychology: Research & Practice*, 49(2), 132–141. doi:10.1037/pro0000182

Kinane, R. (2018, July 20). Comedy of my life: Jerry Seinfeld. *Entertainment Weekly*, p. 91.

King, S. (1990). *The stand*. New York, NY: Doubleday.

Kirsch, I. (2005). Placebo psychotherapy: Synonym or oxymoron? *Journal of Clinical Psychology, 61*, 791–803.

Knekt, P., Lindfors, O., Sares-Jäske, L., Virtala, E., & Härkänen, T. (2013). Randomized trial on the effectiveness of long- and short-term psychotherapy on psychiatric symptoms and working ability during a 5-year follow-up. *Nordic Journal of Psychiatry, 67*(1), 59–68. doi:10.3109/08039488.2012.680910

Kocet, M. M., & Herlihy, B. J. (2014). Addressing value-based conflicts within the counseling relationship: A decision-making model. *Journal of Counseling & Development, 92*, 180–186. doi:10.1002/j.1556-6676.2014.00146.x

Koren, M. (2013, June 28). Why do we yawn and why is it contagious? *The Smithsonian*, Retrieved from https://www.smithsonianmag.com/science-nature/why-do-we-yawn-and-why-is-it-contagious-3749674/

Korzybski, A. (1941). *Science and sanity: An introduction to non-Aristotelian systems and general semantics*. Fort Worth, TX: Institute of General Semantics.

Kottler, J. (1992). *Compassionate therapy: Working with difficult clients*. San Francisco, CA: Jossey-Bass.

Kottler, J. (1993). Facing failure as a counselor. *American Counselor, 2*(4), 14–19.

Kottler, J. A. (1996). *The language of tears*. San Francisco, CA: Jossey-Bass.

Kottler, J. A. (1997). *Travel that can change your life*. San Francisco, CA: Jossey-Bass.

Kottler, J. A. (2000). *Doing good: Passion and commitment for helping others*. New York, NY: Routledge.

Kottler, J. A. (2001). *Making changes last*. New York, NY: Routledge.

Kottler, J. A. (2010). *The Assassin and the Therapist: An Exploration of Truth in Psychotherapy and in Life*. New York: Routledge.

Kottler, J. A. (2012). *The therapist's workbook: Self-assessment, self-care, and self-improvement exercises for mental health professionals* (2nd ed.). New York, NY: Wiley.

Kottler, J. A. (2015a). *Stories we've heard, stories we've told: Life-changing narratives in therapy and everyday life*. New York, NY: Oxford University Press.

Kottler, J. A. (2015b). *The therapist in the real world: What you never learn in graduate school (But really need to know)*. New York, NY: W. W. Norton.

Kottler, J. A. (2017). *On being a therapist* (5th ed.). New York, NY: Oxford University Press.

Kottler, J. A. (2017). *Secrets of exceptional counselors*. Alexandria, VA: American Counseling Association.

Kottler, J. A. (2018a). *Living and being a therapist: A collection of readings*. San Diego, CA: Cognella.

Kottler, J. A. (2018b). *What you don't know about leadership but probably should: Applications to daily life*. New York, NY: Oxford University Press.

Kottler, J. A. (2019). *Fallen heroes: Tragedy, madness, resilience, and inspiration among famous athletes*. San Diego, CA: Cognella.

Kottler, J. A., & Balkin, R. (2017). *Relationships in counseling and the counselor's life*. Alexandria, VA: American Counseling Association.

Kottler, J., & Blau, D. (1989). *The imperfect therapist: Learning from failure in therapeutic practice*. San Francisco, CA: Jossey-Bass.

Kottler, J. A., & Carlson, J. (2002). *Bad therapy: Master therapists share their worst failures.* New York, NY: Brunner/Routledge.

Kottler, J. A., & Carlson, J. (2003). *The mummy at the dining room table: Eminent therapists reveal their most unusual cases and what they teach us about human behavior.* San Francisco, CA: Jossey-Bass.

Kottler, J. A., & Carlson, J. (2006). *The client who changed me: Stories of therapist personal transformation.* New York, NY: Routledge.

Kottler, J. A., & Carlson, J. (2007). *Moved by the spirit: Discovery and transformation in the lives of leaders.* Atascadero, CA: Impact.

Kottler, J. A., & Carlson, J. (2008). *Their finest hour: Master therapists share their greatest success stories* (2nd ed.). Bethel, CT: Crown.

Kottler, J. A., & Carlson, J. (2009). *Creative breakthroughs in therapy: Tales of transformation and astonishment.* New York, NY: Wiley.

Kottler, J. A., & Carlson, J. (2011). *Duped: Lies and deception in psychotherapy.* New York, NY: Routledge.

Kottler, J. A., & Carlson, J. (2014). *Master therapists: Practicing what you preach.* New York: Wiley.

Kottler, J. A., & Carlson, J. (2015). *On being a master therapist: Practicing what we preach.* New York, NY: Wiley.

Kottler, J. A., & Carlson, J. (2016). *Therapy over 50: Aging issues in psychotherapy and the therapist's life.* New York, NY: Oxford University Press.

Kottler, J. A., Carlson, J., & Keeney, B. (2004). *American shaman: An odyssey of global healing traditions.* New York, NY: Routledge.

Kottler, J. A., & Marriner, M. (2009). *Changing people's lives while transforming your own: Paths to social justice and global human rights.* New York, NY: Wiley.

Kottler, J. A., & Montgomery, M. (2019). Theories of counseling and therapy: An experiential approach (3rd ed.). San Diego, CA: Cognella.

Kottler, J. A., & Safari, S. (2019). *Making a difference: A journey of adventure, disaster, and redemption inspired by the plight of at-risk girls.* San Diego, CA: Cognella.

Lambert, M. J. (Ed.). (2013). *Bergin and Garfield's handbook of psychotherapy and behavior change* (6th ed.). New York, NY: Wiley.

Lambert, M. J., & Shimokawa, K. (2011). Collecting client feedback. *Psychotherapy, 48*(1), 72–79.

Landrum, J., Jr. (2016, December 15). Q&A: The Dream on new EP, Kanye–Trump meeting, and Grammys. Seattle Times. Retrieved from https://www.seattletimes.com/entertainment/qa-the-dream-on-new-ep-kanye-trump-meeting-and-grammys/

Larrick, R. P., Burson, K. A., & Soll, J. B. (2007). Social comparison and confidence: When thinking you're better than average predicts overconfidence (and when it does not). *Organizational Behavior and Human Decision Processes, 102*(1), 76–94. doi:10.1016/j.obhdp.2006.10.002

Lehrer, J. (2008, October 9). The certainty bias: A potentially dangerous mental flaw. *Scientific American.* Retrieved from https://www.scientificamerican.com/article/the-certainty-bias/

Lenz, A. S., Dell'Aquila, J., & Balkin, R. S. (2018). Effectiveness of integrated primary and behavioral healthcare. *Journal of Mental Health Counseling, 40,* 249–265. doi:10.17744/mehc.40.3.06

Lenz, A. S., Haktanir, A., & Callender, K. (2017), Meta-analysis of trauma-focused therapies for treating the symptoms of posttraumatic stress disorder. *Journal of Counseling & Development, 95,* 339–353. doi:10.1002/jcad.12148

Leucht, S., Heifer, B., Gartlehner, G., & Davis, J. M. (2015). How effective are common medications: A perspective based on meta-analyses of major drugs. *BMC Medicine, 13*, 253. doi:10.1186/s12916-015-0494-1

Liang, J., Matheson, B. E., & Douglas, J. M. (2016). Mental Health Diagnostic Considerations in Racial/Ethnic Minority Youth. *Journal of child and family studies, 25*(6), 1926–1940. doi:10.1007/s10826-015-0351-z

Liebherz, S., Schmidt, N., & Rabung, S. (2016). How to assess the quality of psychotherapy outcome studies. *Psychotherapy Research, 26*(5), 573–589.

Lilienfeld, S. O. (2007). Psychological treatments that cause harm. *Perspectives on Psychological Science, 2*, 53–70.

Liston, C., McEwen, B. S., & Casey, B. J. (2009). Psychosocial stress reversibly disrupts prefrontal processing and attentional control. *Proceedings of the National Academy of Sciences, 106*, 912–917.

Lizzio, A., Wilson, K., & Que, J. (2009). Relationship dimensions in the professional supervision of psychology graduates: Supervisee perceptions of processes and outcome. *Studies in Continuing Education, 31*(2), 127–140. doi:10.1080/01580370902927451

Lovett, S., & Robertson, J. (2017). Coaching using a leadership self-assessment tool. *Leading and Managing, 23*(1), 42–53.

Lyford, C. (2019). Ketamine: The latest wonder drug? *Psychotherapy Networker*, March–April, 11–13.

MacKay, L. M. (2017). Differentiation of Self: Enhancing Therapist Resilience When Working with Relational Trauma. *Australian & New Zealand Journal of Family Therapy, 38*(4), 637–656. doi:10.1002/anzf.1276

Madrick, J. (2015, March 9). Why economists cling to discredited ideas. *American Prospect*. Retrieved from http://prospect.org/article/why-economists-cling-discredited-ideas

Mallory, C., Brown, T., & Conron, K. J. (2018, January). Conversion therapy and LGBT youth. *The Williams Institute*. Retrieved from https://williamsinstitute.law.ucla.edu/wp-content/uploads/Conversion-Therapy-LGBT-Youth-Jan-2018.pdf

Marantz, A. (2013, September 16). Unreality star: The paranoid used to fear the CIA. Now their delusions mirror "The Truman Show." *The New Yorker*. Retrieved from https://www.newyorker.com/magazine/2013/09/16/unreality-star

Marlatt, A. (2006). A new name. In J. A. Kottler & J. Carlson (Eds.), *The client who changed me: Stories of therapist personal transformation* (pp. 55–64). New York, NY: Routledge.

Marsh, A. A. (2016). Neural, cognitive, and evolutionary foundations of human altruism. *Personality Traits and Processes, 7*(1), 59–71.

Marshall, C., & Rossman, G. B. (2011). *Designing qualitative research* (5th ed.). Los Angeles, CA: SAGE.

Martin, P. (2011). Celebrating the wounded healer. *Counselling Psychology Review, 26*(1), 10–19.

Maslach, C. (2015). *Burnout: The cost of caring.* Los Altos, CA: Malor.

Maslach, C., & Leiter, M. P. (2015). It's time to take action on burnout. *Burnout Research, 2*(1), 4–5.

Mathai, D. S., Meyer, M. J., Storch, E. A., & Kosten, T. R. (2020). The relationship between subjective effects induced by a single dose of ketamine and treatment response in patients with major depression: A systematic review. *Journal of Affective Disorders, 264*, 123–129.

Matuska, K., & Christiansen, C. (2008). A proposed model of lifestyle balance. *Journal of Occupational Science, 15*, 9–19.

Mauss, I. B., & Robinson, M. D. (2009). Measures of emotion: A review. *Cognitive Emotion, 23*, 209–237. doi:10.1080/02699930802204677

McGuire, T. G., & Miranda, J. (2008). New evidence regarding racial and ethnic disparities in mental health: Policy implications. *Health Affairs, 27*, 393–403. doi:10.1377/hlthaff.27.2.393

McLeod, S. A. (2018). What are the most interesting ideas of Sigmund Freud? *Simply Psychology*. Retrieved from https://www.simplypsychology.org/Sigmund-Freud.html

McManus, F., Rakovshik, S., Kennerley, H., Fennell, M., & Westbrook, D. (2012). An investigation of the accuracy of therapists' self-assessment of cognitive-behaviour therapy skills. *British Journal of Clinical Psychology, 51*(3), 292–306.

McSpadden, K. (2015, May 14). You now have a shorter attention span than a goldfish. *Time*. Retrieved from http://time.com/3858309/attention-spans-goldfish/

Mears, G. (2016). Conducting an intake interview. In I. Marini & M. A. Stebnicki (Eds.), *The professional counselor's desk reference* (pp. 83–86). New York, NY: Springer.

Mercier, H., & Sperber, D. (2017). *The enigma of reason*. Cambridge, MA: Harvard University Press.

Michel, A. (2016, February). Burnout and the brain. *Association for Psychological Science*. Retrieved from https://www.psychologicalscience.org/observer/burnout-and-the-brain

Miller, D. (2012, December 2). The end of the 50 minute hour? *Psychology Today*. Retrieved from https://www.psychologytoday.com/us/blog/shrink-rap-today/201212/the-end-the-50-minute-hour

Miller, S. D. (2015). Do psychotherapists improve with time and experience? Retrieved from https://www.scottdmiller.com/do-psychotherapists-improve-with-time-and-experience/

Miller, S. D., & Hubble, M. (2011, March/April). The road to mastery. *Psychotherapy Networker*, 22–31.

Miller, S. D., Hubble, M. A., Chow, D., & Seidel, J. (2015). Beyond measures and monitoring: Realizing the potential of feedback-informed treatment. *Psychotherapy, 52*(4), 449–457.

Miller, W. R. (2004). The phenomenon of quantum change. *Journal of Clinical Psychology, 60*(5), 453–460.

Miller, W. R., & Rollnick, S. (1991). *Motivational interviewing: Preparing people to change addictive behavior*. New York, NY: Guilford Press.

Mitchell, A. J., McGlinchey, J. B., Young, D., Chelminski, I., & Zimmerman, M. (2009). Accuracy of specific symptoms in the diagnosis of major depressive disorder in psychiatric out-patients: Data from the MIDAS project. *Psychological Medicine, 39*(7), 1107–1116. doi:10.1017/S0033291708004674

Morris, Z. S., Wooding, S., & Grant, J. (2011). The answer is 17 years, what is the question: Understanding time lags in translational research. *Journal of the Royal Society of Medicine, 104*(12), 510–520.

Mountford, C. P. (2005). One size does not fit all. *Counselling and Psychotherapy Journal, 16*(5), 43–45.

Muhlheim, L. (2013, March). Who killed the 50 minute session? What consumers should know about changes to psychotherapy sessions in 2013 [blog post]. Retrieved on from https://www.kantorlaw.net/blog/2013/march/who-killed-the-50-minute-session-what-consumers/

Mullen, P. R., Morris, C., & Lord, M. (2017). The experience of ethical dilemmas, burnout, and stress among practicing counselors. *Counseling & Values, 62*(1), 37–56. doi:10.1002/cvj.12048

Murphy, S. C., Barlow, F. K., & Von Hippel, W. (2018). A longitudinal test of three theories of overconfidence. *Social Psychological and Personality Science, 9*(3), 353–363.

Nafisi, N., & Stanley, B. (2007). Developing and maintaining the therapeutic alliance with self-injuring patients. *Journal of Clinical Psychology, 63*(11), 1069–1079. doi:10.1002/jclp.20414

Nakash, O., & Alegría, M. (2013). Examination of the role of implicit clinical judgments during the mental health intake. *Qualitative Health Research, 23*(5), 645–654. doi:10.1177/1049732312471732

National Association of Social Workers. (2017). *Code of ethics.* Washington, DC: Author.

National Institute of Drug Abuse. (2018). Drugs, brains, and behavior: The science of addiction. Retrieved from https://www.drugabuse.gov/publications/drugs-brains-behavior-science-addiction/treatment-recovery

Neckel, S., Schaffner, A. K., & Wagner, G. (2017). Burnout, fatigue, exhaustion. New York, NY: Springer.

Neimeyer, R. (2006). Using metaphors to thaw a frozen woman. In J. A. Kottler & J. Carlson (Eds.), *The client who changed me: Stories of therapist personal transformation* (pp. 49–54). New York, NY: Routledge.

Nemko, M. (2019). The psychotherapist of 2040? *Psychology Today,* June 24. Retrieved from: https://www.psychologytoday.com/us/blog/how-do-life/201906/the-psychotherapist-2040

Nissen-Lie. H. A., Havik, O. E., Høglend, P. A., Rønnestad, M. H., & Monsen, J. T. (2015). Patient and therapist perspectives on alliance development: Therapists' practice experiences as predictors. *Clinical Psychology & Psychotherapy, 22*(4), 317–327. doi:10.1002/cpp.1891

Nissen-Lie, H. A., Monsen, J. T., & Rønnestad, M. H. (2010). Therapist predictors of early patient-rated working alliance: A multilevel approach. *Psychotherapy Research, 20*(6), 627–646. doi:10.1080/10503307.2010.497633

Nissen-Lie, H. A., Monsen, J. T., Ulleberg, P., & Rønnestad, M. H. (2013). Psychotherapists' self-reports of their interpersonal functioning and difficulties in practice as predictors of patient outcome. *Psychotherapy Research, 23*(1), 86–104. doi:10.1080/10503307.2012.735775

Nissen-Lie, H. A., Rønnestad, M. H., Høglend, P. A., Havik, O. E., Solbakken, O. A., Stiles, T. C., & Monsen, J. T. (2017). Love yourself as a person, doubt yourself as a therapist? *Clinical Psychology & Psychotherapy, 24*(1), 48–60. doi:10.1002/cpp.1977

Noble, J. (2015). Exploring the effective length of therapy in a healthcare organization. *Counselling Psychology Review, 30*(4), 57–68.

Norcross J. C. (Ed.). (2011). *Psychotherapy relationships that work: Evidence-based responsiveness.* New York, NY: Oxford University Press.

Norcross, J. C., Koocher, G., & Garofalo, A. (2006). Discredited psychological treatments and tests: A Delphi poll. *Professional Psychology, 37*(5), 515–522.

Norcross, J. C., & Lambert, M. J. (2011). Psychotherapy relationships that work II. *Psychotherapy, 48*(1), 4–8. doi:10.1037/a0022180

Norcross, J. C., & Lambert, M. J. (2014). Relationship science and practice in psychotherapy: Closing commentary. *Psychotherapy*, *51*(3), 398–403. doi:10.1037/a0037418

Norcross, J. C., & VandenBos, G. R. (2018). *Leaving it at the office: A guide to psychotherapist self-care.* New York, NY: Guilford.

North, A. (2016). A millennial mistake: Three arguments against radical social constructivism. *Journal of Counseling & Development*, *94*(1), 114–122. doi:10.1002/jcad.12067

O'Connor, D. B., Connor, M., Jones, F., McMillan, B., & Ferguson, E. (2009). Exploring the benefits of conscientiousness: An investigation of the role of daily stressors and health behaviors. *Annals of Behavioral Medicine, 37*(2), 184–197.

O'Donohue, W., Cummings, C., & Willis, B. (2018). The frequency of false allegations of child sexual abuse: A critical review. *Journal of Child Sexual Abuse*, *27*(5), 459–475. doi:10.1080/10538712.2018.1477224

Okiishi, J. C., Lambert, M. J., Eggett, D., Nielsen, L., Dayton, D. D., & Vermeersch, D. A. (2006). An analysis of therapist treatment effects: Toward providing feedback to individual therapists on their clients' psychotherapy outcome. *Journal of Clinical Psychology*, *62*(9), 1157–1172. doi:10.1002/jclp.20272

Open Science Collaboration. (2015). Estimating the reproducibility of psychological science. *Science*, *349*(6251), aac4716.

Oppenheimer, M. (2012, February 3). A counselor's convictions puts her profession on trial. *The New York Times*. Retrieved from https://www.nytimes.com/2012/02/04/us/when-counseling-and-conviction-collide-beliefs.html

Orlinsky, D. E., & Ronnestad, M. H. (2005). (Eds.). *How psychotherapists develop: A study of therapeutic work and professional growth.* Washington, DC: American Psychological Association.

Paik, A., Sanchagrin, K. J., & Heimer, K. (2016). Broken promises: Abstinence pledging and sexual and reproductive health. *Journal of Marriage and Family*, *78*(2), 546–571.

Peterson, R. L. (2004). Evaluations and the culture of professional psychology education programs. *Professional Psychology: Research and Practice*, *35*(4), 420–426.

Pinker, S. (2018). *Enlightenment now: The case for reason, science, humanism, and progress.* New York, NY: Viking.

Pohl, R. F. (2017). Cognitive illusions: Intriguing phenomena in thinking, judgment and memory (2nd ed.). New York, NY: Routledge.

Pomerantz, A. S., Corson, J. A., & Detzer, M. J. (2009). The challenge of integrated care for mental health: Leaving the 50 minute hour and other sacred things. *Journal of Clinical Psychology in Medical Settings*, *16*(1), 40–46.

Pomeroy, R. (2018, January 8). The six stages of failed psychological theory. *Real Clear Science*. Retrieved from https://www.realclearscience.com/blog/2018/01/08/the_six_stages_of_a_failed_psychological_theory.html

Poole, R., & Higgo, R. (2017). Psychiatric interviewing and assessment (2nd ed.). New York, NY: Cambridge University Press.

Post, S. G. (Ed.). (2007). *Altruism and health: Perspectives from empirical research.* New York: Oxford University Press.

Post, S. G. (2011). *The hidden gifts of helping: How the power of giving, compassion, and hope can get us through hard times.* San Francisco: Jossey-Bass.

Preston, P. (2005). The power image: Strategies for acting and being powerful. *Journal of Healthcare Management*, *50*(4), 222–225. doi:10.1097/00115514-200507000-00004

Prochaska, J. O., & DiClemente, C. C. (2005). The transtheoretical approach. In J. C. Norcross & M. R. Goldfried (Eds.), *Handbook of psychotherapy integration.* (2nd ed., pp. 147–171). New York, NY: Oxford University Press.

Prochaska, J. O., & Norcross, J. C. (2014). *Systems of psychotherapy: A transtheoretical analysis* (8th ed.). Pacific Grove, CA: Brooks/Cole.

Proctor, G., & Hargate, R. (2013). Quantitative and qualitative analysis of a set of goal attainment forms in primary care mental health services. *Counselling & Psychotherapy Research, 13*(3), 235–241. doi:10.1080/14733145.2012.742918

Puniewska, M. (2016, August 17). The myth of modern burnout. *The Week.* Retrieved from https://theweek.com/articles/641796/myth-modern-burnout

Rabu, M., Moltu, C., Binder, P. E., & McLeod, J. (2016). How does practicing psychotherapy affect the personal life of the therapist? A qualitative inquiry of senior therapists' experiences. *Psychotherapy Research, 26*(6), 737–749.

Rao, V. R., Sellers, K. K., Wallace, D. L., Lee, M. B., Bijanzadeh, M., Sani, O. G., . . . Chang, E. F.(2018). Direct electrical stimulation of lateral orbitofrontal cortex acutely improves mood in individuals with symptoms of depression. *Current Biology, 28*(24), 3893–3902.

Renden, J. (2015). *Upside: The new science of post-traumatic growth.* New York, NY: Touchstone.

Retsas, A. (2000). Barriers to using research evidence in nursing practice. *Journal of Advanced Nursing, 31,* 599–606. doi:10.1046/j.1365-2648.2000.01315.x

Rogers, C. (1957). The necessary and sufficient conditions of therapeutic personality change. *Journal of Consulting Psychology, 21,* 95–103.

Rosenthal, D., & Frank, J. (1956). Psychotherapy and the placebo effect. *Psychological Bulletin, 53*(4), 294–302).

Rosnow, R. L., & Rosenthal, R. (1989). Statistical procedures and the justification of knowledge in psychological science. *American Psychologist, 44,* 1276–1284. doi:10.1037-0003-066x.44.10.1276

Rozenblit, L., & Keil, F. (2010). The misunderstood limits of folk science: An illusion of explanatory depth. *Cognitive Science, 26*(5), 521–562.

Rubin, A., & Bellamy, J. (2012). *Practitioner's guide to using research for evidence-based practice* (2nd ed.). Hoboken, NJ: Wiley.

Rush, B., Castel, S., Brands, B., Toneatto, T., & Veldhuizen, S. (2013). Validation and comparison of diagnostic accuracy of four screening tools for mental disorders in people seeking treatment for substance use disorders. *Journal of Substance Abuse Treatment, 44*(4), 375–383. doi:10.1016/j.jsat.2012.08.221

Saeed, S. A., & Pastis, I. (2018). Using telehealth to enhance access to evidence-based care. *Psychiatric Times, 35*(6), 9–22.

Santarsieri, D., & Schwartz, T. L. (2015). Antidepressant efficacy and side-effect burden: a quick guide for clinicians. *Drugs in context, 4,* 212290. doi:10.7573/dic.212290

Santelli, J. S., Kantor, L. M., Grilo, S. A., Speizer, I. S., Lindberg, L. D., Heitel, J., & Ott, M. A. (2017). Abstinence-only-until-marriage: An updated review of US policies and programs and their impact. *Journal of Adolescent Health, 61*(3), 273–280. doi:10.1016/j.jadohealth.2017.05.031

Sapyta, J., Reimer, M., & Bickman, L. (2005). Feedback to clinicians: Theory, research, and practice. *Journal of Clinical Psychology, 61*(2), 145–153.

Sargent, W. C., Shaffer, H. J., & Lawford, C. (1986). Two cases of misdiagnosis: Some essentials of intake. *Journal of Substance Abuse Treatment, 3*(2), 69–75. doi:10.1016/0740-5472(86)90055-3

Schermuly-Haupt, M. L., Linden, M., & Rush, A. J. (2018). Unwanted events and side effects in cognitive behavior therapy. *Cognitive Therapy and Research, 42*(3), 219–229.

Schmit, E. L., Balkin, R. S., Hunnicutt Hollenbaugh, K. M., & Oliver, M. (2018). Examining the relationship between working alliance and therapeutic goal attainment with adolescents in crisis. *Journal of Child and Adolescent Counseling, 4*, 20–33. doi:10.1080/23727810.2017.1351773

Schneiderman, S. (1984). *Jacques Lacan: The death of an intellectual hero*. Cambridge, MA: Harvard University Press.

Schöttke, H., Flückiger, C., Goldberg, S. B., Eversmann, J., & Lange, J. (2017). Predicting psychotherapy outcome based on therapist interpersonal skills: A five-year longitudinal study of a therapist assessment protocol. *Psychotherapy Research, 27*(6), 642–652. doi:10.1080/10503307.2015.1125546

Schuckard, E., Miller, S. D., & Hubble, M. A. (2017). Feedback-informed treatment: Historical and empirical foundations. In D. S. Prescott, C. L. Maeschalck, & S. D. Miller (Eds.), *Feedback-informed treatment in clinical practice: Reaching for excellence* (pp. 13–35). Washington, DC: American Psychological Association.

Schumann, S., & Klein, O. (2015). Substitute or stepping stone? Assessing the impact of low-threshold online collective actions on offline participation. *European Journal of Social Psychology, 45*, 308–322.

Sedlacek, W. E. (2004). *Beyond the big test*. San Francisco, CA: Wiley.

Sessa, B., Higbed, L., & Nutt, D. (2019). A review of 3,4 MDMA assisted psychotherapy. *Frontiers of Psychiatry, 20*. https://doi.org/10.3389/fpsyt.2019.00138

Shapiro, E. L. (2000). The double session in psychoanalytic therapy. *Journal of Psychotherapy Research and Practice, 9*(1), 18–24.

Shedler, J. (2017). Selling bad therapy to trauma victims. *Psychology Today*, Nov. 19. Retrieved from: https://www.psychologytoday.com/us/blog/psychologically-minded/201711/selling-bad-therapy-trauma-victims

Shi, Q., & Doud, S. (2017). An examination of school counselors' competency working with lesbian, gay and bisexual and transgender (LGBT) students. *Journal of LGBT Issues in Counseling, 11*(1), 2–17. doi:10.1080/15538605.2017.1273165

Siegel, E. (2018, November 21). This is the one key difference separating good science from junk science. *Forbes*. Retrieved from https://www.forbes.com/sites/startswithabang/2018/11/21/this-is-the-one-key-difference-separating-good-science-from-junk-science/#4dd11003615e

Simionato, G. K., & Simpson, S. (2018). Personal risk factors associated with burnout among psychotherapists: A systematic review of the literature. *Journal of Clinical Psychology, 74*(9), 1431–1456.

Skalski, J. E., & Hardy, S. A. (2013). Disintegration, new consciousness, and discontinuous transformation: A qualitative investigation of quantum change. *The Humanistic Psychologist, 41*(2), 159–177.

Skovholt, T. M., & Trotter-Mathison, M. (2010). *The resilient practitioner: Burnout prevention and self-care strategies for counselors, therapists, teachers, and health professionals* (2nd ed.). New York, NY: Routledge.

Sleek, S. (2018, November 19). Replications of psychological findings don't appear to hinge on study-population differences, global multilab project shows. *Association for Psychological Science*. Retrieved on December 6, 2018 from https://www.psychologicalscience.org/news/releases/replications-of-psychological-findings-dont-appear-to-hinge-on-study-population-differences-global-multilab-project-shows.html

Sloman, S., & Fernbach, P. (2017). *The knowledge illusion: Why we never think alone.* New York, NY: Riverhead.

Slovic, P., Finucane, M. L., Peters, E., & MacGregor, D. G. (2007). The affect heuristic. *European Journal of Operational Research, 3,* 1333–1352.

Smith, B. L. (2012). Inappropriate prescribing. *Monitor on Psychology, 43*(6), 36.

Smith, L. C., & Okech, J. E. (2016). Ethical issues raised by CACREP accreditation of programs within institutions that disaffirm or disallow diverse sexual orientations. *Journal of Counseling & Development, 94,* 252–264. doi:10.1002/jcad.12082

Smith, M. K., Trivers, R., & von Hippel, W. (2017). Self-deception facilitates interpersonal persuasion. *Journal of Economic Psychology, 63,* 93–101.

Smith, S., & Macduff, C. (2017). A thematic analysis of the experience of UK mental health nurses who have trained in solution focused brief therapy. *Journal of Psychiatric & Mental Health Nursing, 24*(2–3), 105–113. doi:10.1111/jpm.12365

Soliman, I. W., Cremer, O. L., de Lange, D. W., Slooter, A. J. C., van Delden, J. H. J. M., van Dijk, D., & Peelen, L. M. (2018). The ability of intensive care unit physicians to estimate long-term prognosis in survivors of critical illness. *Journal of Critical Care, 43,* 148–155.

Solovey, A. D., & Duncan, B. L. (1982). Ethics and strategic therapy: A proposed ethical direction. *Journal of Marital and Family Therapy, 18*(1), 53–61.

Sommers-Flanagan, J., & Sommers-Flanagan, R. (2017). *Clinical interviewing* (6th ed.). New York, NY: Wiley.

Sommers-Flanagan, J., & Sommers-Flanagan, R. (2018). Recursive and emerging themes in psychotherapy: Past, present, and future. *Psychotherapy Bulletin, 53*(4), 7–12.

South-Paul, J. E. (2015). Disparities in health care for minorities: An ecological perspective. In R. Bangs & L. E. Davis (Eds.), *Race and social problems: Restructuring inequality.* (pp. 209–225). New York, NY: Springer Science + Business Media.

Spense, D. P. (1982). *Narrative and historical truth.* New York, NY: W. W. Norton.

Spillane, R., & Martin, J. (2018). *What went wrong with psychology? Myths, metaphors, and madness.* Newcastle, UK: Cambridge Scholars.

Statista Inc. (2018, August 9). Amount of time U.S. primary care physicians spent with each physician as of 2018. *Statista.* Retrieved from:https://www.statista.com/statistics/250219/us-physicians-opinion-about-their-compensation/

Steel, C., Macdonald, J., Schröder, T., & Mellor-Clark, J. (2015). Exhausted but not cynical: Burnout in therapists working within improving access to psychological therapy services. *Journal of Mental Health, 24*(1), 33–37. doi:10.3109/09638237.2014.971145

Steinert, C., Hofmann, M., Kruse, J., & Leichsenring, F. (2014). Relapse rates after psychotherapy for depression—stable long-term effects? A meta-analysis. *Journal of Affective Disorders, 168,* 107–118. doi:10.1016/j.jad.2014.06.043

Stevens, P., & Smith, R. L. (2018). *Substance use counseling: Theory and practice* (6th ed.). Columbus, OH: Pearson.

Stewart, R. W., Orengo-Aguayo, R. E., Cohen, J. A., Mannarino, A. P., & de Arellano, M. A. (2017). A pilot study of trauma-focused cognitive–behavioral therapy delivered via telehealth technology. *Child Maltreatment, 22*(4), 324–333. doi:10.1177/1077559517725403

Sussman, M. B. (1995). *A perilous calling: The hazards of psychotherapy practice.* New York, NY: Wiley.

Swift, A. (2017, May 22). In U.S., belief in creationist view of humans at new low. Gallup. Retrieved from https://news.gallup.com/poll/210956/belief-creationist-view-humans-new-low.aspx

Talmon, M. (1990). *Single session therapy.* San Francisco, CA: Jossey-Bass.

Tasca, G. A., Sylvestre, J., Balfour, L., Chyurlia, L., Evans, J., Fortin-Langelier, B., . . . Wilson, B. (2015). What clinicians want: Findings from a psychotherapy practice research network survey. *Psychotherapy, 52*(1), 1–11. doi:10.1037/a0038252

Tauber, A. I. (2009). Freud's philosophical path: From science of mind to philosophy of human being. *Scandinavian Psychoanalytic Review, 32*, 32–43.

Thal, S. B., & Lommen, M. J. (2018). Current perspective on MDMA-assisted psycho-therapy for posttraumatic stress disorder. *Journal of Contemporary Psychotherapy, 48*(2), 99–108.

Thomas, M. L. (2006). The contributing factors of change in a therapeutic process. *Contemporary Family Therapy, 28*(2), 201–210. doi:10.1007/s10591-006-9000-4

Thomason, T. C. (2010). Psychological treatments to avoid. *Alabama Counseling Association Journal, 36*(1), 39–48.

Thompson, B. (2002). "Statistical," "practical," and "clinical," how many kinds of sig-nificance do counselors need to consider? *Journal of Counseling & Development, 80*(1), 64–71.

Thompson, I. A., Amatea, E. S., & Thompson, E. S. (2014). Personal and Contextual Predictors of Mental Health Counselors' Compassion Fatigue and Burnout. *Journal of Mental Health Counseling, 36*(1), 58–77. doi:10.17744/mehc.36.1.p61m73373m4617r3

Thyer, B. A., & Pignotti, M. G. (2015). *Science and pseudoscience in social work practice.* New York, NY: Springer.

Timm, M. (2015). Deconstructing pathology: A narrative view of the intake process. *Journal of Constructivist Psychology, 28*(4), 316–328.

Timulak, L., & Keogh, D. (2017). The client's perspective on (experiences of) psycho-therapy: A practice friendly review. *Journal of Clinical Psychology, 73*(11), 1556–1567. doi:10.1002/jclp.22532

Toporek, R. L. (2002). *The relationship between counseling graduate students' attributions about the problems of poor people, racial attitudes, and multicultural counseling training.* (Dissertation Abstracts International Section A: Humanities and Social Sciences).

Trivers, R. (2011). *The folly of fools: The logic of deceit and self-deception in human life.* New York, NY: Basic Books.

Turner, J., Brown, J. C., & Carpenter, D. T. (2018). Telephone-based CBT and the thera-peutic relationship: The views and experiences of IAPT practitioners in a low-in-tensity service. *Journal of Psychiatric & Mental Health Nursing, 25*(5/6), 285–296. doi:10.1111/jpm.12440

Turner, P. R., Valtierra, M., Talken, T. R., Miller, V. I., & DeAnda, J. R. (1996). Effect of session length on treatment outcome for college students in brief therapy. *Journal of Counseling Psychology, 43*, 228–232.

Utley, T. (2016, January 25). 4 technologies innovating mental health in 2016. *Forbes.* Retrieved from https://www.forbes.com/sites/toriutley/2016/01/25/4-technologies-innovating-mental-health-in-2016/#5f0812d06bb3

Valentine, J. C., Aloe, A. M., & Lau, T. S. (2015). Life after NHST: How to describe your data without "p-ing" everywhere. *Basic and Applied Social Psychology, 37*(5), 260–273. doi:10.1080/01973533.2015.1060240

Vanheule, S., Desmet, M., Meganck, R., Inslegers, R., Willemsen, J., De Schryver, M., & Devisch, I. (2014). Reliability in psychiatric diagnosis with the DSM: Old wine in new barrels. *Psychotherapy and Psychosomatics, 83,* 313–314. doi:10.1159/ 000358809

Villacieros, M., Olmos, R., & Bermejo, J. C. (2017). The empathic process and misconceptions that lead to burnout in healthcare professionals. *Journal of Spanish Psychology, 20,* 1–12.

Walsh, R. (2011). Lifestyle and mental health. *American Psychologist, 66*(7), 579–592.

Wampold, B. E. (n.d.). Qualities and actions of effective therapists. *American Psychological Association.* Retrieved from https://www.apa.org/education/ce/ effective-therapists.pdf

Wampold, B. E. (2001). *The great psychotherapy debate: Models, methods, and findings.* Mahwah, NJ: Lawrence Erlbaum.

Wampold, B. E. (2018). *The basics of psychotherapy: An introduction to theory and practice* (2nd ed.). Washington DC: American Psychological Association.

Wampold, B. E., & Imel, Z. E. (2015). *The great psychotherapy debate: The evidence of what makes psychotherapy work.* New York, NY: Routledge.

Whitehead, C., Kuper, A., Freeman, R., Grundland, B., & Webster, F. (2014). Compassionate care? A critical discourse analysis of accreditation standards, *British Journal of Medical Education, 48,* 632–643.

Whiten, A. (2018). Social, Machiavellian, and cultural cognition: A golden age of discovery in comparative and evolutionary psychology. *Journal of Comparative Psychology, 132,* 437–441. doi:10.1037/com0000135

Will, H. (2018). The concept of the 50-minute hour: Time forming a frame for the Unconscious. *International Forum of Psychoanalysis, 27,* 14–23. doi:10.1080/ 0803706X.2017.1372627

Willett, B. (2015, January 2). The facts and numbers about new year's resolutions. *Self-Development Addict.* Retrieved from https://selfdevelopmentaddict.com/2015/ 01/02/the-facts-and-numbers-about-new-years-resolutions/

Wood, D. (2006). Review of quantum change: When epiphanies and sudden insights transform ordinary lives. *Journal of Transpersonal Psychology, 38*(2), 256–258.

Wu, G., Feder, A., Cohen, H., Kim, J. J., Calderon, S., Charney, D. S., & Mathé, A. A. (2013). Understanding resilience. *Frontiers in Behavioral Neuroscience, 7,* 10. doi:10.3389/fnbeh.2013.00010

Yapko, M. (2006). Caught in a controversy. In J. A. Kottler & J. Carlson (Eds.), *The client who changed me: Stories of therapist personal transformation.* New York, NY: Routledge.

Yong, E. (2018, November). Psychology's replication crisis is running out of excuses. *The Atlantic.* Retrieved from https://www.theatlantic.com/science/archive/ 2018/11/psychologys-replication-crisis-real/576223/

Zarate C. A., Jr., Singh J. B., Carlson P. J., Brutsche, N. E., Ameli, R., Luckenbaugh, D. A., . . . Manji, H. K.(2006). A randomized trial of an N-methyl-D-aspartate antagonist in treatment-resistant major depression. *Archives of General Psychiatry, 63*(8), 856–864.

INDEX

References to tables and figures are denoted by an italic *t* or *f* following the page number.
For the benefit of digital users, indexed terms that span two pages (e.g., 52–53) may, on occasion, appear on only one of those pages.

selflessness, 193, 194*t*
self-medication, 116
self-mythology, dispelling, 236
self-promotion, in impression
    management, 140–41
self-serving bias, 37*t*
self-supervision strategies
    overview, 113
    personal struggles, questions
        about, 114–18
    reviewing and critically examining
        clinical behavior, 118
Semmelweis, Ignaz, 24–25
service
    involvement in social justice
        projects, 196
    reciprocal gifts of altruism, advocacy,
        and, 193
    transformative experiences in, 198
session length. *See* 50-minute hour
sessions, attribution error related
    to, 54, 56
sexism, relationship to religious
    identity, 204–5
sexual assault, myths about, 234–35
sexual risk-avoidance, 60–61
Seybert, C., 206
side effects of therapy, 78–84
Siegel, Ethan, 62
significance, of
    research, 71, 72*f*, 100
significant others, treatment
    sabotaging by, 94
simple solutions for complex problems,
    61, 241
skull shape, study of, 30
slacktivism, 192–93
Smith, Adam, 25
Smith, L. C., 206
Smith, Richard, 29
social justice
    complicated nature of advocacy
        efforts, 191
    involvement in projects, 196
    practicing leadership in everyday
        life, 200
    realities often ignored about advocacy
        efforts, 190
    reciprocal gifts of altruism, advocacy,
        and service, 193

scolding therapists about, 189
    transformative experiences, 198
socioeconomic status, and context for
    diagnostic impressions, 136
solitude, role in lasting change, 186
Solovey, A. D., 209–10
somatic symptoms, 136–37
specializations, 105
Spense, D. P., 50–51
spiritual conversions, 179–80
standardization
    effect on unique programs, 107
    linked to accreditation, 102
    professional standards, 106
    and specialization, 105
    usefulness of, 109
statistical significance, 71, 72*f*, 100
Steinert, C., 175–76
stigma of diagnostic labels, 133
stories
    client, identifying, 112
    empowering, role in lasting
        change, 185
student uniforms, 61
subjective reality, 23–24
substance use, 13, 56, 175–76
success of therapy, 66, 76. *See also* failure
    in therapy
suicide, 28, 73, 126–27
sunk cost fallacy, 37*t*
supervision. *See* learning to do therapy;
    self-supervision strategies
supplication, in impression
    management, 140
support groups, role in lasting
    change, 186
surrendering, in impression
    management, 140
symptoms, assessing in intake
    interview, 124–25
systemic inequities, addressing, 197–98

Talmon, M., 144
teachers, clients as best, 110
teaching practices, effectiveness
    of, 11–12
technology
    and future of psychotherapy,
        229, 230–32
    and understanding of clients, 98–99